SINS

OF MY

FATHER

GROWING UP WITH AMERICA'S MOST
DANGEROUS WHITE SUPREMACIST

SINS

OF MY

FATHER

GROWING UP WITH AMERICA'S MOST
DANGEROUS WHITE SUPREMACIST

BY

KELVIN PIERCE

WITH

CAROLE DONOGHUE

Kelvin Pierce

208-A Dominion Road NE

Vienna, VA 22180

me2cloudbase@yahoo.com

Book Layout: TheBookMakers.com

Sins of my Father - GROWING UP WITH AMERICA'S MOST DANGEROUS WHITE SUPREMACIST / Kelvin Pierce. —1st ed.

Print ISBN: 9798609361912

CONTENTS

PREFACE

This book is about my father, William Luther Pierce III. Those who know the history of white nationalism in our country will recognize his name and know his infamous book, The Turner Diaries, which he wrote in 1978. It was the blueprint for the 1995 bombing of the Murrah Federal Building in Oklahoma City by Timothy McVeigh that stole the lives of 168 men, women and children and injured 684 others, and it is still mandatory reading for many right-wing extremist groups in the U.S., Europe and elsewhere.

On April 19, 2020 it will be 25 years since McVeigh's atrocity, for which he was executed in 2001. My father, who claimed to have helped prepare McVeigh's defense, died of cancer a year later, but even now he remains an icon of the white supremacy movement. I have spent the last few years trying to understand what made him what he was, a task that to me has become more urgent as the carnage of mass-shootings by white nationalists spreads from city to city. For most of my life I loathed him as much as I longed for him to love me, but he was just not capable of doing so. His private side was every bit as twisted as the public side people saw on TV or read about in the papers when he ranted about "swarthy hooked-nosed Jews" and sold guns as "Negro control equipment, " but only my mother knew the extent of the abuse that my twin brother Erik and I endured at his hands.

Dad was all about hate. He lived it, breathed it, 24/7. He tried hard to teach us to do the same, and for a while succeeded, at least with me. He got so good at hate that he assumed the mantle of George Lincoln Rockwell, the founder of the American Nazi Party assassinated in 1967. Today, my father would be on a domestic terror watch list, if not in prison for child abuse and endangerment, and other crimes. He most certainly was on the radar of the FBI, U.S. Secret Service, and other major law enforcement agencies for years but they never managed to nail him.

1

I lived much of my early life fearing that people would find out that I was his son. Dad had dedicated his life to saving the whole white race from Jews, "niggers," Communists, feminists and gays, and all others whom he believed were contaminating his country and culture. And the more press he got, the more I was terrorized at home, beaten up in school and out, and ostracized as "that Nazi kid." I shrunk inward and hid in my own world, the only place it was safe, but my imagination got me into all kinds of trouble with my father as a result.

The Southern Poverty Law Center branded my father as "one of the most influential and dangerous ideologues of the white nationalist movement" for the 30 years before his death. He was all that, and more. He would fly into sudden violent, volcanic rages, to the point that he even killed the only two living things he truly loved, our sweet Siamese cats. The only time he was truly happy was when he could lock himself in his study with his books and Nazi paraphernalia, to write about the race wars to come that he hoped to organize and orchestrate.

When he wasn't writing or addressing fund-raising rallies for his neo-Nazi organization, the National Alliance, he liked to experiment with chemicals and explosives in the basement of our home or in the woods behind it. He had me help him produce nitroglycerine and showed me how to make bombs. To my mother's terror, he hid weapons and other dangerous stuff in the crawl space of our house until a few days before the FBI came sniffing around. Sometimes he used me as a guinea-pig, once knocking me flat on my rear from a powerful electric shock. While I was frightened I was happy, too, because I was spending time with him. I thought that I'd earn his love and respect, if only I could play my part well, but I was wrong.

I would have done anything for a word of praise, a hug, or a kiss from him, but in the end, I always failed him. No matter how hard I tried, I couldn't become the little Aryan he wanted and so he abandoned his attempt to mold me. As for my brother, Erik, he didn't even try with him. The only time I saw him display any affection toward either of us was after his death, when I found among his belongings a photograph of us as babies, sitting on his lap. He was smiling.

It wasn't until I left for college and met the outside world that I realized what a monster he was. When he left my mother, he wrote her a letter saying he was going because he loved his political party more. He went on to marry four other women, mostly mail-order brides. He died at his secluded compound on a West Virginia mountaintop before he had the chance to wed a sixth woman that he had squirreled away out of sight of his fifth wife. He spent his last days restructuring the National Alliance to make sure it survived him and gave no thought to us at all - his Nazi acolytes didn't even know our names or that we existed, although they did try to recruit me a few days after his death, like some sort of prized trophy to hang on the wall.

I never fully discovered what turned him from being a physics professor at a small Oregon college into a hate-spewing bigoted man who could beat his kids until they bled, or why he feared minorities and fantasized about killing them in the most bloody way he could.

It wasn't until my 30's that I felt safe enough to confide in a few friends about my father and how he affected my life. What finally forced me from the silence of the sidelines was the 2016 presidential election campaign and the hate in the streets of Charlottesville, Va., that killed a young protester, Heather Heyer, during "Unite the Right" rally. The swastikas and the flaming torches brought back so many memories, such visceral feelings, that I knew I had to speak out about the racism still so deeply rooted in our society.

As my wife and daughters pointed out, it was time I stopped hiding. I have now started to share my story in public in talks to anti-hate groups and other organizations and at first I was taken aback when I saw some people in the audience cry. They told me later how healing it was for them to hear my story, given current events in our country.

About the same time I started writing this book, hoping to exorcise my father's ghost and to set down on paper some of the events of my childhood growing up with America's leading neo-Nazi. It is based on my memories, conversations with my mother and others who knew him, and private family papers. I have tried to add some historical context to my story. It is not meant to be a full historical record, but it has played a vital part in my healing process, which continues to this day.

When I see how our president, Donald Trump, uses immigration, national security and his "Deep State" conspiracies to stoke the fires of the same fascist forces that my father used to incite and exploit people, I feel more compelled than ever to tell my own story and paint a picture of the real Bill Pierce, not the man that his followers have idolized to this day.

Most of all, I'd like this book to be read by young people in hopes that they may stop the hatred and start the healing. I know now that hatred is a mental disease, but there is help for it, if you're willing to do the work to get there. I want people to know that they can choose which thoughts in their heads they listen to, and that their hatred of others is just a temporary adrenaline fix, like a drug that makes you feel better about yourself and your lack of self-worth but only for a short time.

I have tried to figure out my father but still haven't. Now, 17 years after his death, I am trying to forgive him as a way to repair my own life, but it's hard. Perhaps C.S Lewis said it best: "You can't go back and change the beginning, but you can start where you are and change the ending.

CHAPTER 1

MEMENTO MORI

I'd fumbled my keys at the front door and the phone was on its fifth ring by the time I got across the room to snatch up the receiver. It was my Uncle Sandy, my father's brother. I hadn't heard from him in years and knew instantly that something was very wrong. But still, his words threw me. He said Dad was dead. We hadn't even known that he was sick — not one person in his racist retinue had bothered to tell us that he was terminally ill. Memories flashed by of his cruelty that scarred our backs, his obsession with race and eugenics, his nifty basement experiments with explosives and other stuff that terrified me as a kid but made me laugh at the same time. When I focused on the phone call again, Uncle Sandy was suggesting that I might want to attend a memorial service that Dad's "people" were holding up at the mountaintop compound Dad had hewn out of raw rock in West Virginia. Uncle Sandy asked if I wanted to go. I said I would.

After I hung up, I started to cry. Quite why, I didn't know. After all, I had spent most of my life hating Dad, and he surely hated me. He hadn't spoken to me in seven years and never acknowledged the adoption of my two baby girls from Eastern Europe six years earlier. I had sent him pictures and letters about them, but he never bothered to reply. I strongly suspected that he didn't approve of them because they weren't white enough for his tastes.

When I finally stopped blubbing, I realized why I was so upset. I had wanted him to love me and be proud of me, and for us to be able to talk and enjoy each other and have a normal relationship. Now I knew

5

beyond doubt that was never going to happen. He was gone and any remote chance of us coming together as father and son was gone for good, too.

After I got myself together I called my twin brother, Erik, and told him the news. "He evidently died from cancer but I don't know much more than that," I said. Erik said he didn't really care — Dad was a complete jerk and he didn't give a damn about any memorial service. I suggested that it might give us closure to attend and we'd be able to see Uncle Sandy, too, but he was adamant. "That bastard didn't give a damn about me or my kids, and there is no damn way I'm going to his service," Erik said. "He was a horrible father and nothing will change that!"

To be honest, I couldn't disagree.

I decided to go because I was looking for answers, I suppose. I also wanted to see Uncle Sandy. I absolutely adored him and hadn't seen him in forever, reason enough to go. After several hours of driving through the mountains of West Virginia with my wife and our 6-yearold daughters, we arrived at Dad's compound near Hillsboro, W. Va.

We went up the long, twisting, gravel driveway riddled with potholes and parked in front of the main building. It was a large two-story commercial-looking affair that served as Dad's offices, bookstore and the church that he formed in hopes of getting a federal tax exemption. The building seemed to be made of steel and was about 60 feet wide and 25 feet tall, with a few windows and a set of double doors that served as the main entrance. There was a huge ancient rune symbol, at least 12 feet tall, mounted above the doors. The symbol is evidently called a life rune and symbolizes upward progress or oneness with nature, or something like that. It was the symbol Dad adopted for his hate group when he formed it 30 years earlier.

We were walking slowly toward the front door when two young white men in their early 20's came out. They stared at me for a few seconds and then turned, had a whispered conversation, and hustled back into the building. Then another man emerged and began striding toward us as the two younger men peeked out from behind the door.

"Hi, my name is Erich," he said, his arm outstretched in greeting. "You must be Dr. Pierce's son. I took over for your father after he passed away. Please come in." He led us inside, past the two guys who were gawking at me as if they'd seen a ghost. "Don't mind them. They didn't know Dr. Pierce had a son and I'm not sure if you realize just how much you look like your father. You gave them quite a shock when they saw you," he said with a smile.

We went into an office, the centerpiece of which was a large desk with piles of magazines stacked upon it. Most of the walls were hidden behind well-stocked bookshelves. I immediately recognized a few of the items on the desk and knew it was Dad's lair.

I stood for a few minutes, taking everything in, then moved toward Dad's chair and sat down at his desk. I opened the desk drawer and saw more familiar items. I picked up the swastika pin I recognized from childhood days of sneaking into his office when he wasn't home. The two young men were still watching me, peering around the doorframe. Eventually I asked why they kept staring at me. "You have to forgive us," one of them said. "We feel like we just lost our father and we don't know what to do." Well, don't look to me, I thought to myself.

Then Erich handed me a piece of paper. "This is your father's will," he said. It was a one page typed document that said everything Dad owned was being left to the National Alliance, the latest iteration of his hate group. I looked at the signature and asked Erich who it belonged to. I didn't recognize it, it wasn't even legible. "That's your father's," Erich replied, firmly. "He was quite sick when he signed it but I assure you he signed it." When I asked when exactly he had signed it, Erich said it was the day before he died.

I handed the paper back to Erich, somewhat skeptically. "OK, whatever," I said, looking at him intently in the eye. He then leaned over the desk, moving very close to me. "You know, before I started working with your father I was a professional boxer. You ever do any boxing?"

I read that as an attempt at intimidation. I turned away and continued to look through Dad's things and the books on the shelves. I recognized several from my childhood, when I used to spend hours looking at pictures from World War Two, all the Navy ships and the Air Force planes. I turned back toward Erich and assured him that I hadn't come to make a claim on anything. "I just wanted some closure over Dad's death because it's been so long since I've seen him or talked with him." At that, he seemed to relax. "I understand, and if there are any small items that you would like to have, that should be OK." He said the service for Dad was scheduled for 6 p.m. and quite a crowd of supporters was expected.

"Your father was a true American icon and we will be reviewing all of his accomplishments over the years," he said, or something to that effect. I thought about what that was going to look like for a few seconds and shuddered at the thought that the only memories of my Dad for these people would all be about his hatred.

I sat quietly for a few minutes, and then asked Erich if I might say a few words at the service. The thought of speaking in front of all those people really scared me — I was shy and greatly afraid of public speaking, but I felt compelled to try to portray him as a human being, too. I really wasn't sure what I would say, since most of my memories of him were downright awful, but still I wanted to try. Erich wasn't at all sure that would be possible. "I'll have to confer with a few others and let you know," he said. He didn't seem at all comfortable with the idea.

After my conversation with Erich, I decided I needed some air. I walked outside just in time to see Uncle Sandy and his wife arriving. I was very happy to see him and we immediately started catching up on our lives. A few minutes later, Erich came out of the main building and said his guys had decided it was alright for me to speak at my father's service. That was big of them, I thought. Problem was I had no idea what I was going to say.

By now, several dozen men and women had arrived and were milling about and talking in small groups. One of the men approached me and introduced himself as Charles.

"I knew your father well and was here with him at the end," he said. "I'm a doctor and he asked me to come here because he didn't trust the doctors at the hospital. "You know, he worried because he said so many of them were Jews, and he thought they might try to kill him," he said. I asked him what exactly had happened, given that he seemed more thoughtful and intelligent than many of the others associated with Dad.

"Well, your father had cancer," said Charles. "It was adenocarcinoma, a cancer of the adrenal glands. Several months ago he began losing weight and had lost quite a bit before his secretary finally insisted he go see a doctor. He resisted because he didn't trust the doctors, but eventually made an appointment. He said he didn't feel particularly sick but had lost about 30 pounds and wasn't sure why."

After a series of tests, Dad was diagnosed with Stage 4 cancer. He was admitted to the hospital and started treatments. After about two weeks, he was told that the treatments were helping and his progress was so promising that he could go home and continue on an outpatient basis. But he quickly got worse and within a few weeks was back in the hospital. This time they told him the prognosis was dire and that he needed to stay in the hospital.

"That's when I went to see him," Charles said. "He phoned and said he didn't trust the doctors. I spoke to them and decided that he did, indeed, have Stage 4 cancer. After discussing his options with me he decided to go home and discontinue further treatment."

Once home, Dad declined rapidly, to the point where he couldn't get out of bed any more. Soon, he refused to eat or drink anything at all. "I suspected he knew the end was near and did not want to prolong it any longer than necessary," said Charles. "Without taking in any fluids he became very weak and for his last few days he was so weak that he couldn't speak. He passed a few days later. Your father was a very strong man and he went out on his own terms."

By now, I had tears running down my cheeks as I thought about Dad dying this way and that I would never have the chance to make things right between us. "You know, I had no idea that he was even sick. Why didn't he tell me?" I wondered aloud. I was feeling sad about how he must have suffered, but also angry. Even at the end, he didn't think about us. He didn't take the opportunity to talk to us one last time. "This just confirms to me that he really just didn't give a damn about me or my brother," I said, wiping tears from my face.

Charles put his hand on my shoulder. "Your father and I spoke several times before his death and he told me near the end that one of his only regrets in life was in regards to you and your brother. He said he sincerely regretted not having a better relationship with you two," Charles said. My immediate thought was that was all bullshit, and Charles was just trying to make me feel better. I didn't believe him, but appreciated him saying it anyway.

About 20 minutes later, Erich came outside and announced that the service was about to start. By now, there were 45 or 50 people there and we all went inside and sat down in the big open area that served as the church and meeting room. Hanging on the wall at the end of the room was a large painting of Dad with his cat perched on his shoulders. There was also a brass urn on a wooden pedestal next to a podium that I assumed that contained his ashes. The same rune symbol that was on the outside of the building adorned the front of the podium and there were several vases of flowers. Erich eulogized Dad but I don't remember much of what he said because I was so anxious about having to speak myself. Before I knew it, Erich had introduced me as Dr. Pierce's son and invited me to come up and say a few words about my father.

The room was silent as I stood gazing at the faces before me, trying to gather the nerve to speak. My head felt hot and my face was flushed red. "I just wanted to share with you all a side of my Dad that I am not sure any of you knew about," I began. "Before he decided to devote his entire life to saving the white race he was a husband and father and a physicist. He had a PhD in physics and was extremely smart and talented in his field." I told them about his work as a research professor at Oregon State University, how his projects were written up in Scientific American and how physicists from all over the world wrote to ask about his work.

I also told them that Dad was quite a troublemaker growing up, and how he liked to play practical jokes on his classmates, using his knowledge of chemistry. He would mix up a substance that was inert when wet but which became highly unstable once dry. He would put this substance on his classmates' books and desks and then wait for the fun to start with sudden explosions in class. He tried to pass his knowledge onto me, too, teaching me how to mix chemicals and the like, but the only time I was interested was when the results of his tinkering ended with a bang.

Once he began his work with the National Alliance, he pretty much devoted his entire life to his cause. I know he felt that the work he was doing was extremely important and he made huge sacrifices in order to do it. "I only wish I had the chance to say goodbye to him," I said.

By now, tears were streaming down my face and I couldn't speak anymore, so I simply walked back toward my seat. Before I could reach it, several people approached me, thanked me for my words and expressed how they felt about Dad. He was very much admired by his followers and they all seemed in awe of him. One man told me how moved he was by how much I must have loved my Dad. I can only assume he came to that conclusion because I was crying. I did love Dad in a way, but this man had no idea how complicated our relationship really was.

After greeting everyone who wanted to speak to me, I went outside to clear my head. I had really mixed feelings about the service and the words I'd spoken. I felt good about letting people get a glimpse of Dad's more personal side but I also felt I'd misled them. I got the strong impression that they thought that I agreed with what Dad did and supported his racist beliefs, but that was nowhere near the truth. But this was a memorial service, so I let those feelings go.

As the crowds thinned out I decided to go to Dad's trailer where he had lived and died to see if there was anything I wanted to take with me. I walked up the hill to the trailer, which was about a half mile away. I went inside and was immediately greeted by Hadley, Dad's beautiful blue point Siamese, the same cat that was pictured on Dad's shoulder in the painting at the memorial service. Hadley came right up to me and started purring and rubbing against my leg, so I started petting and talking to him. There was a woman inside the trailer who had been Dad's secretary. "Oh my, you look so much like your father," she said. Hadley and Dad had been inseparable. "Hadley would ride on your Dad's shoulder when he walked to and from his office and had seemed very depressed since your Dad died," she said. I asked her if she had found a home for Hadley yet, thinking I'd take him home with us, but she said she was planning to keep him and take care of him herself. I was disappointed but said nothing.

It was strange to be sitting at Dad's desk so brazenly, going through his things. I remember sneaking into his office at home when I was a kid, looking at his bust of Adolf Hitler and all his Nazi pins and his clear glass swastika paperweight. There were hundreds of books about Hitler and the origins of race but one of the items I liked most was a pair of gold-colored U.S. Navy pilot wings. I found out later that they had belonged to George Lincoln Rockwell, the founder of the American Nazi Party. Dad acquired them after Rockwell was assassinated.

As a kid, I would sit in Dad's chair and study these things and imagine what it was like to be smart like him and understand all these books and gadgets. And I always looked for his latest edition of "Der Spiegel" magazine. The first time I saw the magazine there was a picture of a woman with her breasts exposed. I stared at it for ages and eagerly looked for more but never saw similar photos in subsequent issues. I also found a "White Power" button on his desk and proudly pinned it to my jacket. It wasn't too long before I was surrounded by several unimpressed black kids at school and given a good beating. I understood by then that Dad hated Negroes, but I had no real idea what "White Power" stood for.

Among Dad's things I found a box of pictures. I was really taken aback when I saw some of my brother and me, with Mom and Dad, when we were very young. In one, I was sitting on Dad's leg. I was about a year old and he was smiling. There were also photos of us playing in a kiddie pool when we were babies, with Mom and Dad looking happy. I was astonished. I had no idea that Dad ever held us before. There were pictures of us all the way up to high school but those where Dad seemed content only went up to the time we were about 2 years old. I sat for several minutes trying to imagine Dad being happy and playing with us but I just couldn't conjure up the image. What happened to him? He certainly didn't look like the man I knew.

I spent a few more hours going through Dad's personal things in his trailer and decided to take home with me a medium-sized box of pictures and letters. I had no idea when he left Mom that he had taken so many family pictures with him. Was it to spite Mom, or because he cared? There were dozens of pictures of them together before they had us, and of all of us as a family. I wondered if I had been wrong and perhaps he did actually care about us. I really wanted to believe it was the latter but every fiber of my being said it wasn't. The letters in the box were between him and his mother and my Mom. Some were very personal, which gave me further insight into the feelings he had hidden from us so effectively. There was even a copy of the letter he wrote Mom explaining in detail why he had decided to leave her.

I took a few other personal items, like some of his books that I remembered about the Second World War and aircraft, and a few other personal items. I loaded them into my car and we piled in for the long drive home. I was mostly silent for the six-hour drive, wrestling with so many conflicting feelings. I slowly realized that maybe I didn't have a clue about what Dad really thought of us. Then I noticed a feeling of empathy creeping in. I didn't share his political beliefs except for a brief time in my teens, when I knew no better. It was just an overwhelming feeling of sadness for Dad, on a deep and personal level. I kept wondering what compelled him to take the course he did, whether he was driven by internal demons to rage and hate, or whether he was simply mentally ill. Were there reasons for the way he felt about Jews and minorities, or had the hatred always existed? Did he merely craft a calculated facade to fund his lifestyle and appeal to other mistaken bigots, surrounded by societal misfits on that windy mountain top?

CHAPTER 2

PIERCE ON THE PEAK

I didn't realize who the rather aggressive Erich was, or the role he played in my father's world, until I received a couple of letters from him shortly after the memorial service. Then it sank in. He was Erich Josef Gliebe, a former professional boxer once known as "The Aryan Barbarian," the son of a World War Two German soldier whom he adored beyond words. He had given up his boxing career to become a tool-and-die maker so that he could devote more time to the white supremacist cause. I had no idea when I met him that it was Dad's dying wish that Erich succeed him as head of his neo-Nazi hate group, the National Alliance.

Erich's first letter read more like a marketing missive than anything else. He invited me to a 2002 leadership conference at Dad's West Virginia compound, proclaiming the "very tangible benefits" for the Alliance that the meetings delivered. At each conference, he said, the Alliance teamed up promising new members with some of the older ones, "who we believe could be developed into more useful members," to explore how those with "leadership potential" could work effectively for the Alliance. Before arriving, attendees should "think very carefully about their role in the Alliance" and how they could "better use their skills or opportunities to be more effective."

The letter made me smile because I knew how much Dad hated those conferences — he would have to shed the old jeans, jacket and sweater he favored and don a suit and tie, make a speech and glad-hand members, when he'd much rather have been alone, reading or writing his essays.

It was an invitation-only meeting and those attending had to keep it hush-hush. About 50 people would be present, and the formal part of the meeting would run eight hours, he said. People could stay overnight for further discussions but since the residential facilities at the compound were full, they would have to stay at a motel five miles away and might have to double up as the number of rooms was limited. (1)

I pleaded a conflicting appointment, while thanking him for the CDs, newsletters and a book about Dad he had given me. "For various reasons, I have never read any of his writings before and he never felt compelled to discuss his work with me," I said, adding that I still had "tons of unanswered questions" about my father. (2)

Erich's second communication was far less formal. "Your father and I were best friends and I admired him tremendously. I am happy to hear that you have begun to read his writings, which have had a positive influence on thousands (millions?) of people around the world," he said, offering his personal phone number in case I wanted to talk to him. (3) Erich was later drummed out of the Alliance — apparently his fondness for strippers and some of his spending habits, like ordering $50,000 of Chinese-made boots with swastikas etched into their soles didn't impress some members.

I started receiving regular mailings from the Alliance, which listed me as an honorary member, and I realized that by attending and speaking at Dad's service I may have given them the impression that I was sympathetic to their cause. I ignored the mailings and after a few years, they slowed and then stopped completely as the National Alliance fell apart. I'm ashamed to admit in retrospect that my immediate reaction to being considered for possible leadership within Dad's group was to feel flattered. I'd never been held in such esteem before, quite the opposite, actually. Once, in a flight of fancy, I pictured myself taking over from Dad and doing what he did, except that there was a major problem: I didn't agree with his beliefs and I knew, beyond doubt, that I could never live the life of hate that he had done.

I remember as a kid Dad devouring history books, particularly tomes on European history, culture and morals, and he knew that a movement built around a single person would not survive once that person died.

The clearest example of that was his former boss George Lincoln Rockwell and his American Nazi Party, which tore itself to shreds within three years of his assassination in 1967. Dad witnessed it all, yet when it came to his own demise 35 years later he totally ignored the principle that he had believed in for so long.

When he learned that he was dying, he gave no thought to Mom, my brother or me, or our future, which makes me angry to this day. Instead, he set about trying to organize the Alliance's affairs to ensure a smooth transfer of power. He had refused further treatment at the hospital and returned home to meet with each staff member to discuss their work and outline a plan for when he would no longer be there. Six days after his death, the Alliance's 17-strong professional staff announced they had chosen Erich to be their new leader, in accordance with his wishes.

I suppose about now that I should talk about my father's "achievements," if you can call them that, so that you understand some of what follows in this book.

It's said that the guy who has the most marbles at the end of the game wins. For a man who had essentially taken a vow of poverty when I was just a kid, he amassed a fair number of marbles before he died in the same trailer he'd lived in for more than 20 years.

I can only hope to God that doesn't mean he won.

At the time of his death, Dad presided over a racist empire that produced revenue of about $1 million a year, which I suppose should be considered quite a success for a man who lived almost entirely off my mother's earnings for 20 years. He ruled his empire from his roost on a 346-acre hilltop compound near Hillsboro, W. Va. He is said to have purchased the land with money donated by "The Order," a gang of mostly Alliance members and supporters who stole $4 million by robbing armored cars, and shot dead Alan Berg, a liberal Jewish talk-show host, on the streets of Denver. The Order was led by Robert Mathews, a young West Coast Alliance member who Dad had been grooming for great things. Mathews died, aged 31, in an explosion at a house on Whidbey Island, Wash., in 1984 after a three-day standoff with the FBI.

Dad liked to portray the Alliance as a group dedicated to the welfare and salvation of the white race, and not the lucrative hate business that it became. He had various streams of income, apart from membership fees and donations from deluded donors. There was a high-brow glossy magazine called National Vanguard, which was meant to rouse intellectuals and professionals to join his cause. In addition, he had a crude monthly publication, the members-only National Alliance Bulletin, filled with venom and calls for action against the Jews and others whom he believed were undermining the white race and secretly controlling the government. He also operated National Vanguard Books, a mail-order firm offering racist and anti-Semitic literature, along with tapes of his weekly half-hour radio show, "American Dissident Voices," which broadcast over shortwave stations that could be heard in New England, Florida, California and several states in the South. Later, it could also reach some places in Europe.

He also sold a comic book for 15- to-18-year-olds, called "The Saga of...White Will!!" It featured the adventures of a blond-haired, blue-eyed boy-hero who fights administrators at a "multicultural" school where kids are taught that historical figures, such as Beethoven were black, and that whites who sympathize with blacks are called "wiggers," and where "groids" steal lunch money and assault girls. The first-run printing of the comic ran to 35,000 copies. (4)

Then, there were the sales of his book "The Turner Diaries," which inspired Timothy McVeigh to bomb the Alfred P. Murrah federal building in Oklahoma City in 1995. The Turner Diaries, and his subsequent offering, "Hunter," were designed to appeal to poor, grievance-nursing whites and became the how-to manual for The Order and subsequent rightwing spin-offs.

Both books featured protagonists who work to halt what Dad called the "degeneration" of the white race and allowed him to 'kill' all the people he hated —in no particular order, Jews and rabbis, blacks and interracial couples, Communists, intellectuals and academics, gays, reporters and feminists, of course, Hollywood actors, talk-show hosts, state governors, congressmen, a cardinal and a couple of bishops. They all died in gory attacks: there were exploding skulls, flying brain tissue, slit throats, knifings, shotgun blasts, hangings and bombings. Dad wrote other books, non-fiction treatises, but it was his crude fiction that earned him the big bucks and the infamy he so richly deserved. I don't know how many copies have been sold, but in 2000, Britain's The

Guardian newspaper put the number at more than 500,000 just for The Turner Diaries. Both books are still for sale and available on the Internet. (5).

The Turner Diaries was at one point banned in Germany, France, Canada and Britain as hate literature. I don't know if it still is proscribed since the advent of the Internet makes it almost impossible to stop it being brought into the country. Sales of the book by Amazon and other retail websites were investigated by the German Ministry of Justice at the request of the Simon Wiesenthal Center in Los Angeles. In Germany, offering material that incites racial hatred is illegal but Amazon declined to stop selling it until officially notified by the German government that it was contravening the law. An Amazon spokeswoman at the time said that none of the books the firm sells in Germany is illegal. Many books might be deemed to be offensive, she said, "but Amazon can't be the judge of what people can and can't read." Britain also regards the novels as hate literature, but again, it's hard to enforce such laws when hate arrives courtesy of e-commerce at the front door. (6).

Dad was a college professor and a physicist, and perhaps that's why he was quick to latch onto the potential of the Internet as a recruitment tool — it was a cheap and efficient way to spread his demand that Europe and the Americas be turned into a whites-only homeland. The Internet is a medium "where we are on an equal footing with CBS, NBC and all the rest of them," he proclaimed.

One of his first moves was to set up an interactive National Vanguard website, which the Anti-Defamation League later called "one of the most technically sophisticated hate sites" on the Web. Through the site, his followers could listen to his broadcasts, read his essays, buy tapes of his speeches, and shop from a large library of books on race, Jews, National Socialism, Zionism, Communism and all the other 'isms' he hated so much. They could even apply for Alliance membership online, a fairly new phenomenon in those days. Today, people of his political persuasion can still download his broadcasts, print copies of his screeds, and read neo-Nazi diatribes on the site's searchable index of topics. (7).

Dad claimed in a 1998 American Dissident Voices broadcast that about 12,000 people visited his website daily, a small number by today's standards. Now, white supremacists use social media platforms to weaponize the web. Sadly, some of their sites are more popular than mainstream media news outlets in major cities. One of the most visited neo-Nazi sites is The Daily Stormer. After the massacre of 50 Muslim worshippers in New Zealand in March, 2019, a Daily Stormer headline read, "If You Were Unfazed Watching Brenton Tarrant Take Revenge, You're Not Evil — You're Normal."

You might think that sort of material would turn off most people but as of February 2019, there were 2.83 million total visits to the Daily Stormer site. The average visit lasted 6.37 minutes and 3.51 pages were viewed (8). The Stormer was founded and is edited by Andrew Anglin, believed to be about 35 years-old, who has fled the U.S. in the wake of multi-million-dollar awards against him for his online hate and harassment of black and Jewish individuals. By comparison, the mainstream media Des Moines Register website saw only 2.16 million visits of an average 4.50 minutes duration, with 2.48 pages visited. (8). Today, the reconstituted National Alliance, now based in Tennessee, operates three websites — natall.com, nationalvanguard.org and whitebiocentrism.com.

There has been reluctance until recently among major social media platforms and hosting companies to take action against sites promoting racial hatred, but belated progress has been made in the wake of mass shootings. Facebook agreed to change its policy on white nationalists in March, 2019. The company had previously banned posts, photos and other content promoting white supremacist content but allowed users to share similar content from white nationalists and white separatists. Civil rights advocates argued that the philosophies behind the posts were indistinguishable and undermined Facebook's efforts to combat hate speech. Unfortunately, as soon as a hate site is knocked offline, it pops up on another server a day or so later.

Under Dad's leadership, the Alliance also launched what was to become the first of several violent video games marketed by Nazi groups. His game, "Ethnic Cleansing," was a first-person shooter game for Microsoft Windows produced, by the Resistance Records Label. "Enjoy shooting it out with the muds in this exciting 3-D environment," the Alliance invited. "In this game, the Race War has already begun. Your character, Will, runs through a ghetto blasting away at various blacks and spics to attempt to gain access to the subway system...where the Jews have hidden to avoid the carnage. Then you get to blow away Jews as they scream 'Oy Vey!' on your way to the command center." (9).

In another innovation, the Alliance was the first hate group to make spam calls to innocent consumers via 21 hotlines they operated. They used computer programs to make random calls to pagers, leaving the Alliance hotline as the number to call back. On returning the call, the unsuspecting consumer heard a hate message and an invitation to leave their name and phone number. Dad also set up a cyber unit to explore other ways to communicate more effectively. The unit was told to engage readers on public forums but it didn't do much to boost recruitment so unit members were ordered instead to engage in private conversations with individuals they met over the Internet. He even launched a Rapid Response Team of volunteers who could be contacted by email to quickly alert other members if there was an emergency (10).

Email was another weapon. In 1998, hundreds of people received spam messages containing one of Dad's propaganda pieces. Another 16,000 emails were sent to college students and faculties calling on the National Association for the Advancement of Colored People to apologize to "victims of rape and all white women" after three black students were charged with raping two white students at a university party in Texas. The campus NAACP chapter had opposed the filing of charges, according to the Anti-Defamation League.

That same year, hundreds of people received a transcript of a radio broadcast in which Dad claimed that "Jewish media bosses" had ordered their employees to write about a young White House intern, Monica Lewinsky, and her relationship with President Bill Clinton in order to punish Clinton because he had become "a liability" for them. He said the media was exaggerating the danger posed by Saddam Hussein in order to get the U.S. to bomb Iraq and aid Israel. Among the media bosses he cited was Stephen Spielberg, saying his films, such as "Schindler's List," were psychological weapons aimed at making white people feel guilty about the plight of the Jews (11).

At the local level, the California Alliance unit was particularly active. It flooded Los Angeles-area grocery stores with flyers promoting the neo-Nazi cause. Flyers were found tucked into in packages of taco shells, cookies, ice cream bars, and tuna advising shoppers that white culture and racial heritage were being destroyed by a "tribe of hateful control freaks. Will we find the courage to chain Steven Spielberg to a pickup truck and drag him down Sunset Blvd. before we are exterminated through interracial sex and marriage?" (12).

Sales of his books and publications, plus donations, kept enough money rolling in to allow him to travel to Nazi meetings in Europe and cater to the shopping needs of the women he married after deserting my mother — they were bored and unhappy living in the hardscrabble rural isolation of his hilltop compound.

But while he churned out books, articles and speeches for his base, Dad realized he had to bring in new blood, young people who would carry on his movement. He knew, too, that they were unlikely to read his prodigious polemics or be overly interested in current affairs. So, around 1995, Alliance affiliates in the Midwest started reaching out to neo-Nazi Skinhead groups by staging White Power rock concerts with bands known for their violent anti-Semitic and anti-minority lyrics. Skinhead leaders endorsed his American Dissident Voices radio show as "forward-looking and progressive" and Dad decided the best way to reel in new recruits was through the music they listened to. That's where Erich Gliebe displayed a marketing talent that created Dad's biggest money-maker, hate music. Erich so impressed my father that he set up a whole new division for him, complete with its own dedicated publication, Resistance.

It was a move that was more than a little astute.

In 1999, Dad spent $250,000 to acquire a white power music label called Resistance Records, including its CD catalog, inventory, mailing list and publishing arm. The purchase caused a fuss among older Alliance members who questioned the decision, but it was a huge source of income for the Alliance. Erich took the Alliance further into the entertainment business by organizing concerts to attract families to soften the Alliance's public face. The get togethers were disguised as wholesome, white European cultural affairs, with folk music and dance acts, while Skinhead and racist heavy metal bands were reserved to attract young people to Alliance political rallies and protests (13).

The Resistance Records label came to dominate the white power music scene, especially after Dad took over four or five other hate-music entities, making him a major player in the international hate-music business with some of the most popular white-power music bands under his control. Among his purchases was the "Cymophane" label, owned by Hendrik Mobus. A big noise in the national socialist black metal market in Europe, Mobus's band, "Absurd," was classified as "right-wing extremist" in Germany, and Mobus himself was a convicted murderer.

In April, 1993, Mobus and other band members had stabbed and strangled a 15-year-old boy with an electrical cord after he spread rumors about an affair involving a band member. Mobus was sentenced to eight years in prison but was released in 1998 after serving just over five years because of his youth — he was 17 at the time of the crime. His parole was revoked when he posed for photographs for his new album at the Auschwitz death camp, holding up Nazi banners inside a gas chamber. He was ordered to serve the remaining three years of his sentence, plus another 26 months, for mocking his victim in interviews as a "leftist faggot," and including a photo of the boy's grave on the cover of his album.

Mobus, by then 23, fled Germany for the U.S. with the help of Gliebe, a fluent German speaker. He arrived at Dad's compound in June, 2000. A few weeks later, Dad registered Cymophane LLC with state authorities, listing himself as its manager. In August, U.S. marshals arrested Mobus on an international warrant. Never slow to seize a recruitment opportunity, my father campaigned for his release, organizing demonstrations, buying newspaper ads protesting the arrest, and raising funds to pay his legal bills, promoting Mobus's case on his radio program as a First Amendment issue.

Dad claimed that President Bill Clinton's "secret policemen" had jumped Mobus as he bought groceries at a local store. They "jammed a pistol in his ear," smashed his face on the back of their car, broke his arm, and tricked him into signing an agreement that he wouldn't contest deportation to Germany. Dad argued that what Mobus had said in Germany would not be illegal in the U.S., simultaneously bragging about the interviews he'd done with the German press on the issue. Mobus was just "a quiet, skinny, non-violent intellectual" who he had invited to stay at the compound to "help me establish new outlets in Europe for my records," he told listeners to one of his broadcasts.

Dad railed against the U.S., saying that it pretended to favor free speech but secretly use the country as "a cash cow for Israel." Prosecutors were using Mobus's juvenile offense just so they could plant the idea of a "fugitive murderer" and "neo-Nazi" in the public's mind, he said. Mobus returned Dad's flattery in an interview with a Nazi web site from his cell in Buffalo, N.Y., as he awaited deportation to Germany. "Dr. William Pierce is the most impressive American character I've ever encountered, and it's a bloody shame that he can't run this country since this country badly needs people of his personality and mindset," he told fans (14).

Two years before Dad's death in 2002, the Anti-Defamation League declared the National Alliance to be "the single most dangerous organized hate group in the United States." By then, it had an estimated 1,400 to 1,500 dues-paying members and several thousands more listening to its broadcasts and browsing its Internet site. It also had an active presence in 26 states and ties with-Nazi groups in Britain, France, Germany, Holland, Australia, and South Africa. By 2001, with membership growing, Dad was authorizing rallies and demonstrations in conjunction with other white supremacist groups in several states.

In his last speech to his leadership conference on April 20, 2002 — Hitler's birthday — Dad warned about the folly of other white supremacist groups, saying their ranks were filled with "freaks and weaklings" and rejected any suggestion of forming alliances with them. Gliebe joined in, calling members of the other groups "morons," and saying it was time to obliterate the white power movement.

It was a speech that would come back to haunt the Alliance and Erich after Dad died.

CHAPTER 3

BEFORE DAD WAS DAD

After Dad's memorial service, I started to wonder what he had been up to, not only when I was a child, but in the years since he left us. While he was a monster at home, I discovered that Erik and I were lucky in a way — we'd largely lived in blissful ignorance of his activities when he wasn't with us, though my mother was forced into the role of reluctant bit-player.

To this day, I still don't know what made Dad Dad. Was he born with some hate gene, was it nourished by his Southern birth, or did he plant it himself, grow it from a tiny sprout and nurse and nurture it until it bloomed into a raging anger from which he drew inner strength and sustenance? I'm sorry to say that I think that was the case. Now he's dead, I shall never know for sure, but there were definite markers along the way — not least of them the brutal beatings he meted out to us until we were old enough and strong enough to stop him. Then he deserted us.

Looking back, his cruelty now seems like a clear portent of things to come.

But I have learned one surprising thing about him, and it came from his own mouth, or at least his written words. He saw himself as a libertarian or liberal on race, at least for a while. Dad was born in September, 1933, to an alcoholic father and a domineering mother who had trouble showing affection. When he was a young boy, his mother would pay him a small fee to find the bottles of booze his father had hidden around the house. His father died when Dad was still a youngster. Drunk, he was struck by a car driven by a teenager when he got off the bus to walk home. Dad's mother, Marguerite Pierce, decided that they should start a new life. They moved around a few times but eventually settled in Texas, where he was required to work odd jobs to help support the family from the time he was 10 years old. He spent the last two years of high school in a military-style boarding school after his mother embarked on a disastrous love affair that left her heart-broken.

Dad never really experienced the warmth and emotional support that comes from having a loving home. He would entertain himself for hours, reading reams of science fiction, and play around with model rockets and chemistry sets, for which he had an extraordinary aptitude. His favorite author as a kid was Edgar Rice Burroughs and he adored the John Carter of Mars series.

By the time Dad entered college, it was apparent that he had a brilliant mind, winning a full scholarship to Rice University in Houston. He graduated with a degree in physics and started graduate studies at Caltech. He was tall and lean, 6'4" and 200 pounds, with jet-black hair, but was so short-sighted that he had trouble finding the shower controls to turn the water on and off without his glasses. When he wasn't experimenting with chemicals or reading, he'd ski and hike, climb mountains or fly around in his small two-seater plane.

Trying to understand Dad, I talked to my mother at length after he died, quizzing her over several months, trying to gain insight. She patiently sat for what must have seemed to her to be endless questions as I made copious notes, and much of what she told me is incorporated in this book. I hope she would have been happy with the results.

Dad was studying for his PhD in Physics at Caltech and Mom was working at the AT&T office close by when they met in March, 1956. Caltech was an all-male school so they would invite girls from AT&T to come to their dances. Mom had gone to some of the dances but felt the guys were aggressive and not very polite. She had decided not to go again but at the last dance she noticed Dad. He was too shy to approach her but later told a friend how attractive he thought she was. A go-between urged Mom to attend just one more dance so that she could meet Dad.

Mom was 28-years-old by then and had never had a steady boyfriend. Now there was a man actually interested in her. Their meeting was set up as a sort of blind date and Dad came to her house to pick her up. Both her parents were very much against the date because he was an unknown to them. "You are making a big mistake! You know nothing about this guy. He could rape you and throw you out of his car!" her father warned.

Dad did none of those things, though he did almost kill them both.

"He was very polite. He didn't just pull up to the house and blow his horn like other guys. He actually came into the house to collect me," she said. "He took me straight to the dance but then nearly killed us both at a railroad crossing on the way. There were no gates at the crossing, just warning lights and they were blinking red. Your father looked both ways, didn't see anything, and so he went. Just as we started across the tracks a train came around the bend. The train light was suddenly on top of us and I screamed loudly. We barely made it across and his only response to my complaints was a grin, and then, "Well, we made it didn't we?""

They ended up having a great time at the dance and Mom said he really intrigued her. He was smart and he was funny, and not at all like the other Caltech boys.

Mom didn't know at the time that Dad had been put on probation at Caltech because he paid too much attention to having fun instead of working. He breezed through his classes but ignored his research. And he drank way too much. At the end of the semester, Caltech put him on indefinite suspension. He wrote to the head of the Physics Department, told him that he'd met a girl and would change his ways. He begged to be taken back, but his plea was rejected.

While at Caltech, Dad had worked at the Jet Propulsion Laboratory, which Caltech managed for NASA. He was popular but frustrated by his colleagues. He felt that he was far, far ahead of them in his thinking and that they were holding him back, and it made him angry.

Mom and Dad continued to date, hiking, climbing mountains and skiing together. "Your father was an amazing climber," Mom said. "He was just like a billy goat with his long legs and he was very strong. I had a hard time keeping up with him. He could leap over these huge crevasses and boulders effortlessly, while I would be so scared. When I was frozen with fright at the edge of a crevasse, he would urge me to jump and just as I was sure I wasn't going to make it, he would reach over and grab me and pull me the rest of the way across."

Sometimes they would fly up to Sacramento to visit with Mom's sister. "My sister hated him from the beginning because she thought he was an intellectual snob. But to me, he was like a little puppy dog. He would follow me around everywhere because he wanted to be with me, and he was so carefree and exciting to be with," Mom said.

In June, 1956, Mom moved out of her parents' home.

"I was still a virgin," she recalled. "When your dad and I got back from a date at 2:30 in the morning, my father called me a dirty whore. That was the last straw for me." She moved into an apartment close to Dad's place and then, that fall, decided to move to Sacramento, to be close to her sister and put some space between her and her parents. She had actually been considering this before she met Dad. While she enjoyed her time with him, she wasn't really convinced their relationship was going anywhere. "He just wanted to have fun and was never too serious about anything," she said. She told Dad as much.

Three weeks later, the Saturday before she was due to move, Dad proposed to her. They were married a few weeks later, on Thanksgiving Day, 1956.

Dad's frustration with his work at the Jet Propulsion Lab was getting worse. He railed against his superiors and colleagues, and eventually decided to go back to school. He applied to the University of Colorado to pursue his PhD and was accepted, but lied on his application — he never told them that he was being thrown out of Caltech, and that lie came back to bite him.

They moved to Boulder in the fall of 1957 and Dad started work on his doctorate.

Mom was expecting to be transferred to the Boulder AT&T office, a process that was supposed to take about four months. But it was Dad who answered when AT&T finally called to say that her transfer had been approved. Without any consultation with Mom, he told AT&T she wasn't interested anymore. He didn't want her to go back to the phone company, but to go back to school herself. "I didn't know about that until a year later," said Mom. "He said he was concerned that I wouldn't be able to satisfy him intellectually unless I went back to school. "

When she didn't hear back from AT&T, Mom went looking for work. She got a job as a typist at the university but it was boring and the days seemed interminable. Then she had a stroke of luck. She started typing up thesis papers for students and decided to complete the degree in psychology that she had started while in California. Everything went well until the woman who was her professor decided to use her own young twins to conduct a psychology experiment and based her entire class on the results. Mom couldn't believe that any mother would do such a thing to her kids and promptly quit psychology, changing her major to mathematics. She went on to become a mathematics professor at Mary Washington University in Virginia.

Dad, meanwhile, had become a star at Colorado University. His research was getting attention around the world and he was having a great time. Then, disaster struck. In the fall of 1959, a man came to the university and Dad recognized him immediately. He was the son of the dean at Caltech and he promptly told the dean at Colorado about Dad's history at Caltech. Dad was summarily fired and thrown out of school.

Luckily for Dad, he got a second chance when a well-known physicist arrived on campus to deliver some lectures. He met Dad and they hit it off. They sat talking late into the night and the next day the physicist told the dean it would be a mistake to kick Dad out. The physicist encouraged Dad to beg for another chance. He did. He applied for a graduate assistant position and got the job.

"He completely stayed out of trouble after that," Mom recalled. It was probably just as well because Mom found out shortly thereafter that she was pregnant. "I'd had a few miscarriages before, and because of my blood Rh factor and the fact my uterus was tilted, doctors said I'd never have children. I was overjoyed when I found out I was pregnant again."

But Dad was not. He was never interested in having children. The doctor said she would most likely lose this baby, too, and would have to stay in bed to have any chance of going full-term. It was a snowy day in Boulder and the doctor was horrified when he learned that Mom and Dad would leave his office the same way they had arrived — on Dad's scooter. The doctor insisted on taking her home in his car, which was just as well. "While we were following your Dad home, he hit an icy patch on the road and crashed his scooter right in front of us. My doctor just shook his head and muttered something under his breath."

When they got home, Dad asked Mom if she really wanted to try for this baby, and she said she absolutely did. He put her to bed and said that if that was what she wanted, then he guessed he wanted it, too. Mom did her utmost to not exert herself physically. She had lots of bleeding problems and was always scared to death she would lose the baby. She did not know until much later that she was carrying twins.

I was born at the hospital in Boulder in June, 1960, about five minutes before my twin brother, Erik. Dad had made a deal with Mom. If they had boys, he would get to name them, and so he did. He chose Kelvin for me after Lord Kelvin, the eminent British physicist whom he greatly admired. Erik was named after the Viking conqueror, Erik the Red.

"Your Dad was happy in the beginning, and handed out cigars," Mom remembered, sadly. "But he almost never picked you guys up, or fed you or held you, or rocked you or anything like that. The most he would do was to sterilize bottles and mix formula."

Once, when we were first starting to eat solid food, he got excited and wanted to feed me. He put a spoonful of food in my mouth and I spat it right back. That was it for him, although he did take care of us both once, when Mom was sick with amoebic dysentery for two weeks. He even changed our diapers unless they were poopy, and then he would take us into Mom's bedroom so she could change us. We were about six months old at the time.

One of my earliest memories of our life in Boulder was the small house we rented just off the highway ramp, and watching the trucks as they came barreling down the road, shaking the house as they tore by. The house had an undulating floor and it absolutely terrified me. I was about two at the time and I thought if I touched the floor with my feet, it would swallow me up.

To escape the danger I would hop on my rocking horse and stay on her endlessly, rocking and rocking and rocking. I would simply rock the days away, spending countless hours riding her, vanishing into my own world. She was a real beauty with a red, molded plastic body that was painted and with handles mounted by her ears that I would hold onto hard while trying to gallop my fear away. It was truly the only place during the day that I felt safe.

While Dad earned his Ph.D at Colorado in the summer of 1962 and Mom earned her B.A. in mathematics, I continued to rock on my horse. At bedtime, I would rock with my pillow. I was about two years old when Dad started to change. From being a fun, care-free man he slowly turned into a monster. Mom says it was like a psychological switch had been thrown.

After earning his Ph.D., he faced a dilemma. Mom was pushing him to get a job in industry, where he was virtually guaranteed a position with a nice salary. He abhorred the idea. He knew from his days at the Jet Propulsion Lab that he wasn't well-suited for a regular job because he didn't want to work for someone else. He was far more interested in the freedom that came with working at a university somewhere. He had received two offers to teach, one at Michigan State and the other at Oregon State. He was leaning toward Michigan State but Mom preferred Oregon, so she could be closer to her family in California. He finally conceded.

It was the trip to Oregon that made Mom question her marriage for the first time.

"He was so mean and out of character," Mom said. "We left Boulder for Corvallis early one morning in July, 1962, with two Siamese cats and a pair of two-year-old kids. The cats kept getting sick and he felt you two were making too much noise. He just kept yelling at you and your brother and telling you both to shut up. Once you blew up a balloon and let it go, and that made him absolutely furious. I have never seen him like that before."

They drove for seven or eight hours and stopped at a hotel in mid-afternoon. Dad said he was too tired to drive any further. After Mom unpacked the car and moved everything into the room, he told her to take us "and get lost for a while" so he could get some rest. "I took you two to a swing set at a park across the street and played with you for about two hours," Mom said. "When I went back to the room, your father had locked the door and refused to let us back in. I didn't have my purse with me or anything else so I didn't know what to do. I couldn't get food or anything, so we just hung out at the playground. Finally, about 10:00 pm, he unlocked the door and let us back in. He immediately went back to sleep without saying a word to me. I felt like he was never the same person after that."

Mom didn't know what was happening but I think Dad was becoming angry and resentful and was suddenly frightened of the future and the heaviness of it all. He was also beginning to resent the responsibility of being a husband and father. He hated the idea of working for someone else, but here he was on his way to doing exactly that. He never wanted to have to answer to anyone else, not even his wife. It was all too constricting.

Mom and Dad rented a house in Corvallis, Ore., and we stayed there for three years. Dad's job at Oregon State was to teach physics and to do research. He made quite a name for himself and brought lots of recognition to the school, though he didn't earn a lot and we didn't have very much. But the school was pleased with him and he was becoming well known in the scientific world for his work.

After his second year, the physics department promoted him just before his 29th birthday, giving him tenure and reducing his teaching load to only two classes so he could spend more time in the lab. His students appreciated that, too. Dad was a hard professor and a harsh grader, at times giving negative grades, as in below zero points. He did not enjoy teaching at all and really had a hard time relating to his students — they could not think at his level but he nevertheless expected them to. Despite that, the university was delighted to have him doing research for them and wanted to keep him, regardless of what his students thought of him.

I don't remember much positive interaction with Mom or Dad during this time. Mom was usually working. She was anxious and worried much of the time, mostly about money. During the day, she would be at home with us, doing typing jobs for long hours and low pay. As a fairly new professor, Dad wasn't making a great salary either, but he didn't care about money in the least, leaving her to fret about making ends meet and under stress all the time. She was also taking classes in the evening, working toward her Master's degree in mathematics. When she was in class, Dad stayed home to watch us but he was there in body only, deeply engrossed in reading or his university work most of the time.

It was then that he started to take an intense interest in politics and history, especially the Civil Rights Movement. He was beginning to notice changes in society, like the growing popularity of jazz music, which he felt led to increasing integration of African-Americans into white society. He didn't like what he saw. He began reading book after book on European history and the different forms of government. He was fascinated with Adolf Hitler and the Bolshevik Revolution and Communism, and starting to form lasting opinions about race and the role of Jews in our society.

According to Dad, he had been "an ideological virgin" until he was 30. Then he started to notice what was going on around him. While there were no major riots or confrontations on the Corvallis campus, "one could see a microcosm of the racial ferment taking place elsewhere" and the "usual brainless liberal blather about racial matters in the student newspaper," he later wrote in an essay about how he became radicalized. (1)

He said he'd hadn't thought much about non-whites and had very little experience of them as he was growing up. "If anything, I was inclined toward the liberal position on the race question." He recalled during a dormitory bull session as an undergraduate how he had supported the right of a person to marry or cohabit with anyone who would have him, black of white.

And at military school, he had refused an invitation to go with a carload of classmates on what was called a "coon conking" excursion into the local "nigger town." Coon conking consisted of driving close to the curb and poking a closet pole out of the car window to knock down blacks on the sidewalk. "I strongly felt that, as long as blacks were minding their own business, no one had a right to bother them."

He said that at that time he would have been properly categorized as a libertarian because of his "vague feeling that people should be left alone as much as possible." While he felt that blacks should be allowed to do whatever they wanted, he also felt that whites who didn't want to eat with them, hire them or send their kids to school with them should not be forced to do so.

They were contradictory positions, and the media didn't help because they were solidly on the side of the blacks and using every piece of propaganda in their arsenal to sway the public, he believed. He also saw that the "shrillest and pushiest" of those demanding equality were not blacks but another minority group, "which raised for the first time in my life the Jewish question," he said.

He had learnt in military school that there was no such thing as inherent human equality. The 500 students at his school were white but differed enormously. "Some of my classmates were boys of intelligence, character and sensitivity; others were the scum of the earth; and the rest were at various points in between." He concluded that blacks were "manifestly different from whites," and the question was not one of equality, but what the proper relationship between the two races should be.

His conservative colleagues were of no more help in resolving his questions than the liberals, although there were some who would whisper behind closed doors that the Jews were behind the civil rights movement, he said.

It was then that he decided to join the John Birch Society, but the Birchers were of no help either — they believed that the civil rights movement was all part of a Communist plot, so he quit in disgust three months later.

In a condescending letter to Robert W. Welch, a co-founder of the Society, Dad went on at length about the "self-education program" he had undertaken, citing authors he had read, and his conclusion that Communism and Judaism were inextricably linked.

"From Marx, the founder [of Communism] to the leaders and financiers of the Bolshevik revolution in Russia, there was an overwhelming proportion of Jews involved in this movement," he told Welch. The same was true of Germany and Hungary and the U.S. Just a look at those behind Negro agitation, at convicted Communist spies in the U.S., and at left-wing American journalists like Walter Lippmann, reveals a percentage of Jews far exceeding their percentage in the population as a whole, he said. (2)

Yet, the Society had made no similar observations. Why, when it was proclaiming Communism to be the nation's enemy, was there "a deathly silence" on the issue of Jews? It made no sense to adopt such "an ostrich-like attitude." Dad said he had not raised the matter at Society meetings he had attended because it had been pointed out to him that it was the Society's policy "strictly to avoid any stand which might be interpreted as anti-Jewish or anti-Negro." He said he couldn't remain a member of an organization whose leadership ignored such matters through fear, and invited Welch to write to him privately to explain the public stance.

Welch did so a week later, stressing that his reply was private because he didn't have time to get caught up in arguments "with known anti-Semites" but hoped he could prevent Dad from getting involved "with an erroneous approach to the whole problem." (3)

In a letter twice as condescending as Dad's that he outlined to his personal assistant, Welch admitted to being "slightly bothered" by Dad' assertions because "he believes there are not too many people in this country who have read more books on this subject than he has himself." In addition, he said, "for several years now he has given up everything in his life to devote all this time to defeating this conspiracy and to keeping America free. It is his personal opinion that statements accusing the leaders of the Society of fear because they do not blame this whole conspiracy on the Jews is simply proof of the old adage that a little knowledge is a dangerous thing."

While there had been a "high percentage" of people in the "Communist conspiracy" who had been of Jewish ancestry, they were no longer Jews once they became Communists, and since the purges initiated by Stalin in 1937, their numbers had been "constantly decreasing." There is not a single Jew in the top 20 "viceroys" of Communism today, such as Ho Chi Minh, Charles de Gaulle and Tito of Yugoslavia and, further, there "is not a single Jew" in the Praesidium in Russia, Welch argued.

Dad was not impressed.

In Dad's third year at Oregon State, the university hired a new professor, a white man who had an African-American wife and two young children. Dad grew to like and respect him. He found him to be intelligent, engaging and funny and enjoyed working with him a great deal. But when he finally met the man's family, he was taken aback. He hadn't known that the man's wife was African-American. He couldn't understand how the man could find any black woman attractive and was repulsed by the way their children looked. "They are the most hideous looking mulattoes I've ever seen," Dad told Mom after he saw them for the first time.

Dad was suddenly very conflicted about his new friend. He was also questioning more and more the meaning of his life. He wasn't feeling fulfilled by his teaching and research and just didn't see any significant meaning in being a husband or father, either. He was bored with his life. He feared he was destined to work every day at something that had no real meaning and, at the same time, was fast-formulating the belief that Jews were having a massive and negative influence on America. He was convinced that they were the masterminds behind the Civil Rights Movement, and were plotting to mix blacks with whites as part of a plan to dilute the white race and create a society of half-breeds because they feared the idea of a strong white race.

Dad was starting to think that maybe he was meant to do something about this but he had no idea what or how to begin. Then came the evening of the faculty dance. The mixed race couple was there and other professors were asking the woman to dance. He told Mom that he couldn't stay and watch the scene any longer.

"That was on a Saturday and then, on Sunday, the black woman called me and wanted to get acquainted." Mom told me. "Your father asked me who it was, and when I told him, he demanded that I hang up immediately. I made an excuse and ended the call." Mom followed Dad into his study and asked him what was going on. It was the second consecutive day that he had been angry about the man's wife.

"That's when I first saw several articles about George Lincoln Rockwell on his desk. I saw words like 'American Nazi Party' and saw swastikas." She asked why he was interested in this Rockwell guy and Dad said he had heard him speak on TV and agreed with a lot of his ideas.

Then he admitted that he had already spoken at length to Rockwell and even visited with him in Washington, D.C. It was a complete shock to Mom. He had said that he was going to the East Coast for a physics conference and she had no idea that he was there for other reasons.

Mom's first reaction was to ask him if he had considered the possibility that he might lose his job by associating with Rockwell. He was totally unconcerned and said he planned to visit Rockwell again and check him out further. If he was still impressed after his second visit, he might start writing articles for him. Mom was dumbfounded. She was at a loss at what to do.

DAD'S NEW FRIEND, GEORGE LINCOLN ROCKWELL

Dad went to visit Rockwell again around Christmas, 1964. They had long talks about the future of the U.S. and the threat posed by the "Reds" and their Jewish puppets who were trying to undermine the white race. Rockwell's views about Jews and how they were encouraging whites and non-whites to mix particularly resonated with Dad and he decided then and there that he had to help save his people from this Jewish scheme. It was more important to him than anything else — even us. He had finally found the meaning of life that he had been searching for.

Rockwell's views solidified the conclusions Dad had reached through all his hours of reading and his hatred of Jews mushroomed until he came to believe that Hitler's final solution, the mass extermination of the Jews, was the only answer. He used to fantasize about slaughtering Jews and anyone else who supported them and their secret mission to destroy us all. It was an all-consuming malignancy that took root in his psyche and he would spend every hour from that moment until his death waging war on the Jewish people, and the blacks and left-wing students that he believed the Jews were manipulating.

Things only got worse when Dad returned from his second visit to Rockwell. He sat down and had a serious talk with Mom. "After having several more conversations with Mr. Rockwell, I've decided I want to do more writing for his organization," she says he told her. "I've decided to quit Oregon State and move to the East Coast so I can help him in his work."

"Have you lost your mind?" Mom blurted out in complete shock. "What will we do for money? Where will we live? Have you even thought about any of this?" Mom asked, in complete disbelief. "Well, yes, I have. I've actually just accepted a position at Pratt & Whitney in Connecticut," Dad said in his deliberative, reserved manner.

Mom exploded. "Oh, you have, have you? And when were you planning on discussing this with me?" she shouted, in increasing fear and anger. "That's what I am doing now," Dad replied. "Well, are you coming with me or not?" he asked, dispassionately. Mom said later that she realized that he actually didn't care if she went with him to Connecticut or not. In fact, she thought that he secretly wished she wouldn't, so that he could shed himself of the responsibility of being a husband and father, roles he regarded as useless distractions from his work.

In the end, Mom had no choice in the matter — there was no way she could afford to stay in Oregon with two young boys.

"I was somehow hoping that maybe, with his new job and better pay — he'd be getting about three times what he was making at Oregon State — that he would relax and go back to being the man I married. He certainly was not that man now. He had turned into a really frustrated and short-tempered man. It was like we were housemates instead of husband and wife. This whole racial thing came out of the blue," she recalled. "I was absolutely terrified."

Oregon State was very upset when Dad said he was leaving. They did everything they could think of to change his mind, but to no avail.

CHAPTER 5

MOVING CROSS-COUNTRY TO BE CLOSER TO MR. ROCKWELL

We moved to Connecticut in June, 1965. It turned out that Rockwell had been looking for someone who could write and edit a new magazine, National Socialist World, and in walked Dad, just in time. He worked for aircraft engine giant Pratt & Whitney during the day and researched and wrote articles for Rockwell in the evening when he got home. Some weekends, he would even drive all the way down to Virginia, just to spend time discussing politics and the "Jewish problem" with Rockwell. For some reason, Dad always called him "Mr." Rockwell.

When he put out the first edition of the magazine, Dad used to fantasize about what might happen to him as a result. Perhaps, he thought, he would become the target of "black militants or Jewish gangsters" and be killed, he later told Robert S. Griffin, his semi-official biographer. But he was inspired by Rockwell's courage. "My theory is that the printed word doesn't mean all that much to blacks. They will only react when you actually get right in their face and confront them. As for Jews, if they sense a threat, they'll use one of their organizations, or they'll form a new one, and jump on you that way." (1)

At first, things seemed to get better with Dad, Mom recalled. "We had initially rented a house, but after a few months we put a contract on a new home on a big piece of property that even had a duck pond. I was so happy and your father was making a really good salary, so our money worries were over."

But it wasn't to last. Dad grew increasingly frustrated at his new job. Just as he had at the Jet Propulsion Laboratory, he felt his co-workers at Pratt & Whitney were holding him back. He had to get his supervisor's permission before any new idea was pursued and he absolutely hated that. He felt that he was the smartest one there and should not have to answer to anyone else.

At home, he was becoming more violent with Erik and me. He ignored us most of the time, and when he did interact with us, rarely would he use our names. He simply called us both "Smelly." He seemed disgusted with us and preferred not to be around us. He never picked us up nor sat us on his lap, he never hugged or kissed us, or played with us. He didn't even talk to us unless we did something wrong, and when we did make mistakes, like leaving the toilet seat up or not obeying his rules, his typical response was to spank us, and he spanked hard and often.

Many years later I asked Mom why he was like that. "Well, he had really strict rules about his role," she said. "He felt like the father was for discipline and the mother was for nurturing. He strongly felt that nurturing was not his role." At that time, she said, he harbored feelings of personal inadequacy. He thought he lacked the proper discipline to be truly successful in life and blamed his parents for that. He believed they should have been harder on him as a child to force him to develop a more disciplined approach to life, she said.

He was adamant that he wouldn't make the same mistake with us. He hadn't wanted children in the first place but now that he had us, he would be the Aryan disciplinarian. I sensed that he was grossed out by us and that shaped his energy while he was with us. I never felt at ease around him and, over the years, had grown very afraid of him.

His inner rage at events in the outside world would explode into our home in the form of regular beatings that left us bruised and scarred, and in a lot of pain — he'd use a wire coat hanger, an electric razor cord, a belt, or a 2-by-4, or whatever was closest to hand. As he became more violent, I became more detached, hiding inside my head in an imaginary world where I felt safe. Sometimes, I'd reach out into the uncomfortable outer universe, looking for a sign that I was loved and lovable, but I'd always be reminded of my unworthiness and would retreat again.

Every night when he got home, he would sit in his favorite recliner and use a razor blade attached to a long, thin handle to cut articles from newspapers and magazines that he would save for future reference when he wrote for Rockwell's publications. I remember seeing him do this many times, watching him from a safe distance.

Once, when I was five and alone in the living room, I climbed into his chair and pretended to be him, sitting there reading the paper. I picked up the razor and imagined cutting up a newspaper, just as he did. I felt comfortable and safe, and just like Dad. But there was no paper to play with and I wanted to know what it felt like to use this cool razor.

Then I wondered what would happen if I ran the razor across the arm of the chair.

I just had to try it. I slowly and carefully pulled the razor across the vinyl surface. It sliced open the chair with very little effort, exposing the stuffing material beneath. I remember thinking how much fun it was, and spent the next hour slowly and methodically slicing the chair to ribbons, fascinated with every cut I made. By the time I lost interest in my new fantastic game, the chair was completely ruined.

Mom screamed when she saw the chair. I just stared back in silence. I suddenly knew I was going to be in big trouble when Dad got home. It was as if a cloud had lifted and I realized what I had done. I grew more terrified as the afternoon wore on. I could think of nothing else and just sat on the floor under the front window, watching for Dad to drive down the street.

It felt like an eternity and when I did finally see his car coming, I ran to my room and waited. Soon I heard a commotion and loud voices. Then Dad came through the door. He was scary- angry, an anger I'd never seen before. He told me to go down to the basement, take my clothes off and wait. Usually, he would always whip me in my room. He was always quite controlled about it, I suspect because he was trying to convince himself that he was disciplining me, not beating me. He would come in, calmly tell me to remove my clothes and inform me why I was going to be beaten, and then start whaling away.

Suddenly, I was more terrified than I had ever been before.

I went down to the basement and expected Dad to follow me down the stairs, but he didn't. While I was undressing I heard more loud voices. The basement was dark and I waited next to an old mattress that was leaning against the back wall. The basement smelled musty and the floor felt damp and cold under my bare feet. I started shivering and sobbing uncontrollably. Mom was crying upstairs and begging him to calm down. Then I heard the basement door open and Dad start down the stairs. Terrified, I followed each creak as he came down the steps.

Then, I almost blacked out. My vision narrowed and became gray. I saw what looked like a bright white light and began to feel dizzy. By the time Dad reached the bottom of the stairs I felt as if I was no longer in my body. Dad immediately started beating me all over my body with a belt in a fury that I had never experienced before, but for some reason I really didn't feel the blows. It was as if I were standing there watching him hit someone else and I wasn't even crying anymore. I just stood there, taking blow after blow after blow. As I watched what was happening to me, I wondered why it didn't hurt like I was expecting.

Eventually the blows stopped and Dad walked slowly back upstairs. He had not said a word during the entire beating. After several seconds, I slumped to the floor and passed out. The next thing I remember was waking up in my bed in the middle of the night. I hurt all over, from head to toe, and felt utterly alone. I felt that nobody could love anyone like me, and slowly, slowly cried myself back to sleep. It took a couple of weeks for the welts and bruises on me to fade and stop hurting.

That fall I started first grade. I remember being afraid of the other kids and the teachers and almost never spoke to anyone. During recess I would stay at my desk and pull my coat over my head and play imaginary games under the canopy of my coat. My teacher wrote several notes home to Mom, telling her that she was convinced that I was mentally disturbed and that I needed to see a psychiatrist. Mom never took any action though. Maybe she figured that there was no helping me at this point, especially with the way Dad was regularly beating me now.

Mom didn't approve of the way he treated us but she was desperate to regain that closeness she'd had with him before we were born. She tried hard, many times, to change the dynamic between us all, but never could she do so.

I remember once, when we were about five, she convinced us to run and give Dad a big, big hug when he came home. I was scared, but she encouraged me to the point that I became excited and eager for him to walk through that door. I just knew how happy he would be. He would have this big surprised look on his face and hug me back, and everything would be great after that. But when the moment arrived, I just froze. I couldn't do it, but Erik did. He ran up to Dad, jumped up and wrapped his arms around him. Dad, indeed, had a surprised look on his face. He embraced Erik awkwardly and then put him down. He didn't say a word, but walked right by me to eat the dinner he knew was waiting for him, and I crept back into my secret world.

Dad was spending more and more of his time now writing for Rockwell and was losing interest in working at Pratt & Whitney. He wrote long articles about white culture and the threats that he thought Jews and interracial marriage posed, and when he wasn't doing that, he would fire off harassing letters to large corporations, questioning what he perceived as their "support" of Jewish interests.

The letters always asked the same questions — whether the ("U") or "K" symbols displayed on their products was intended to identify them to Jewish consumers, and were the companies paying money to use signs. "I shall be interested in hearing your comment on this matter," he told the recipients, among them Procter & Gamble, General Foods Corp., Purex Corp., and Stop & Shop based in Boston, Mass. (2)

Most responses were very short, but Avram Goldberg, then VP of Stop & Shop, took the time to explain matters to him. "The symbol is that of the Van Harabonim of Massachusetts, which is the official organization of the Orthodox Rabbinate here in Massachusetts," Goldberg wrote. It means that the product in the carton contains no non-kosher ingredients that would violate the dietary laws of the Jewish religion. There is "absolutely no charge whatsoever" for the use of the symbol or the processing of any ingredients for Vaad Harabonim approval.

"We do however, make a contribution to help defray the cost of the inspector who visits our plant from time to time. This is not paid to him nor is it paid to the Vaad Harabonim. It is sent to the Kashruth Commission of the Associated Synagogues of Massachusetts, which is the lay organization supporting the program as a public service,"

Goldberg said. (3). I don't know if Dad ever engaged with Goldberg again, but he went on to denounce the system as "a kosher racket."

Among Dad's things I also discovered letters and memos from "Major" Matthias Koehl, the national secretary of Rockwell's American Nazi Party. They bore dates that puzzled me at first, such as "22 January YF-77 (1966)," until I realized that YF probably meant "Year of the Fuehrer." Hitler was born in 1889 and would have been 77-years-old by 1966, had he not thankfully dispatched himself by gunshot when the Russians advanced on his Berlin bunker.

One memo from Koehl to Rockwell recounted Koehl's first encounter with my father. "I just had an opportunity to discuss the Party with a very interested professor of physics who stopped by Headquarters," Koehl wrote. "He was more than mildly curious; in fact, he was downright sympathetic. In the course of our conversation he mentioned that he was highly impressed by the overall physical appearance of our material. However, he did point out by way of criticism that he had noticed a large number of errors in spelling; which in some instances had caused him to hesitate showing certain items to some of his interested associates." Koehl added that he didn't think the Party could allow "trifles like misspelled words to trip us up. We've got enough odds against us as it is." (4)

Koehl soon struck up a more formal relationship with Dad, sending him copies of articles in French and German that could be included in the magazine and asking him to translate them. He recommended one person in particular, Bruno Ludtke, a German Nazi mentor of Rockwell's, whom he thought might make further contributions. "By this, I mean that he is not only capable of producing real idea material, but also has the willingness — zeal, in fact — to contribute toward an elaboration of National Socialist thought," he said. (5) Ludtke became a major influence on Rockwell, supplying him with information about the nascent Holocaust-denial movement in Europe and providing links to neo-Nazis to help him make connections abroad. (6).

He also recommended Hans-Ulrich Rudel, who had given Rockwell's American Nazi Party permission to reprint his articles. Koehl suggested Dad write to the luminaries of the British Nazi groups to see if they knew where Rudel could be found, suggesting he contact Colin Jordan of the British National Party and anyone in the Union Movement, the

British Fascists led by Sir Oswald Mosley, who was interned by the British during Second World War. In writing to the Mosleyites, he said, Dad was not to mention National Socialism or the Rockwell party. "You might imply that you are a fan of Rudel's, and perhaps want to get an autograph of this famous man. Mosley is professionally jealous of Colin Jordan and us," Koehl explained. (7)

Koehl also wanted Dad to produce a series of "student study aids" that would help spread the American Nazi Party's message of anti-Semitism in schools and colleges by taking advantage of what he believed was the innate laziness of American youth. Students were "becoming notoriously prone toward looking for short-cuts in 'hurdling' a course," and the ANP should be able to "effectively exploit this tendency" by offering a special service — "term-paper topic sheets on a variety of subjects we want discussed in the classroom," he said. (8)

Possible subjects could include material on the causes of WWII, a discussion of aerial warfare, to cover the bombing of Dresden and Hiroshima, the history of National Socialist Germany and the development of anti-Semitism in Germany, in addition to "The Essential Mein Kampf," the objectives of the American Nazi Party, and "social progress under National Socialism." The ANP could suggest a topic on which the student could work, and then provide an extensive outline that could be used almost as is, and a good bibliography. They could also present a guide sheet to questions to be discussed in the term paper. For example, he said, questions could include:

- "In what three basic ways can the charge that German National Socialists allegedly killed six million Jews be discredited?"

- "What percentage of the total world Jewish population were casualties during the Second World war?"

- Was this figure more or less than that suffered by other populations involved in the war?"

- "If it was less, why is there greater concern about Jewish casualties than those suffered by other peoples?"

- "Why are all of the alleged "Extermination" camps behind the Iron Curtain?"

- "In what year did the propaganda media begin using the 'six million' story?"

Koehl said he guessed that Dad "could see the possibilities here. In doing his term paper, the student would have certain points relentlessly driven home into his cranium. Then his term paper would be carried into the classroom, and become the subject of discussion among a larger audience." The ANP could start off with a few subjects only, and then gradually build up the service, one by one, he added.

But it was another of Koehl's missives that really caught my eye — it offered Dad a full-time position at Rockwell's HQ in Arlington, Va., although it never named any salary because the ANP was in no financial position to do so.

The letter started by suggesting Dad include in the magazine simultaneous translations of some articles in German and French, which could attract more written contributions than if the ANP confined itself to the Anglo-Saxon world alone. They would be able to "linguistically cover the entire European, and Aryan, intelligentsia," except for Russia, where they wouldn't make much headway anyway, and make it appear they had a greater appeal across Europe. Running one or more articles simultaneously in two languages would also solve the problem of filling space and allow them to pad the size of the magazine. They could even run articles in the original language if they couldn't get them translated in time, to be seen to have "'something for everybody.'"

Then came the job pitch. Would Dad be willing to run a small book service for the ANP?

With one or two dozen carefully selected titles and a minimum of promotion, "you can develop a regular source of revenue to help defray the overhead of the NSW office," Koehl said.

"We have been approached by two seemingly capable individuals recently who have requested a salaried position with the Party. Although we cannot offer them a salary at the present time, we would be willing to suggest the possibility of their running a Party book service on a commission basis. Before proceeding here, however, we felt it would be more proper and feasible to give you first option on the matter," he said. (9). All the letters ended in the salutation, "Heil Hitler!" with some also offering "Best National Socialist Wishes."

The invitation was all Dad needed to drive South, into the arms of Rockwell and the American Nazi Party. He had reached his breaking point at Pratt & Whitney when workers staged a wild-cat strike. He tried to drive through the picket line, provoking the strikers, who then attacked his car, kicking the fenders, and snapping off the radio antenna.

He went home and told Mom that he was quitting his job and moving south and that she could go with him or not, and he really didn't care which she chose. She reluctantly agreed to follow him to Virginia, where he immersed himself full-time in working for Rockwell. He never held another job or brought home another paycheck after that. When Mom asked what she was going to do for money, Dad replied, "I don't care what you do." Mom was frantic. She had no idea how she was going to support the family now that Dad had concluded that it was no longer his responsibility.

Dad's decision was to have a major impact on our small family, but Rockwell was delighted with his choice, bragging in his publications that a PhD rocket scientist had left his job at Pratt & Whitney to edit "without pay" the party's new magazine, National Socialist World. A short time later, Dad became a firm blip on the FBI's radar. After an anonymous letter was sent to the agency's New Haven, Conn., office, agents were dispatched to Pratt & Whitney's aircraft division to interview a company official, according to FBI files. (10)

The P&W official confirmed Dad had been employed as a senior research associate physicist from July 1965 to June, 1966 at a salary of $15,400. He had a secret clearance issued by the U.S. Department of Defense at Hartford but never actually worked on anything classified, the P&W executive said. He described Dad as a "real loner," but others in the research division were the same way. But Dad "was unusual" in one way — he insisted on receiving and checking all his own packages, did all his own machining, and asked for his own laboratory and machine shop, he said.

Dad took a week's vacation in late May, 1966, but had failed to return for another week. When he did come back, he said he had been at a meeting in Virginia "on personal business." He had been spending hours every night, writing articles for National Socialist World, and would leave physics and P&W in July to start a new career as a writer, he told the company.

When asked whether Rockwell was connected with his new enterprise, Dad described Rockwell as a friend and said the new magazine would be printed on a press Rockwell owned. The American Nazi Party "was the wave of the future," he proclaimed. P&W warned him that if he took just six months off from physics, he couldn't re-enter the field because he would not be able to catch up with new developments. Dad acknowledged as much, but said he had decided to go.

According to the FBI, Dad never displayed anti-Semitic feelings while at work but after he left, several of his Jewish colleagues "expressed their intense dislike of him as a person." One co-worker said Dad was bothered by the complexities of life and was looking for a simple solution to the problems of the world. He never discussed his personal life but once had brought his two sons to the plant. They were very quiet and trained to instant obedience, and when he spoke, "they would jump." It was "impossible to penetrate Pierce," an informant said, but he never made revolutionary statements or indicated that he possessed weapons.

All that was to change. It wasn't only guns, but bombs and dangerous electrical devices that Dad possessed just a few years later.

CHAPTER 6

SO, WHO IS THIS MR. ROCKWELL, ANYWAY?

As kids, we had no idea who this "Mr. Rockwell" was, only that Dad seemed to be captivated by him and preferred to spend most of his time with him, not with us, and Mom wasn't happy.

My father first came across Rockwell when he saw him on the TV news, trying to make a speech at a university campus while students threw bottles and shouted him down. Dad had been writing to well-known people for some time by then, asking how they thought that the anti-Vietnam War and civil rights movements should be dealt with. So he shot off a letter to Rockwell, too. Two weeks later, Rockwell sent him a 12-page handwritten letter spelling out his views in detail. After that, Dad would mentally doff his cap to him every time he spoke about him, referring him "Mr. Rockwell," as a show of great respect.

Rockwell was the self-declared Commander of the American Nazi Party and said he knew exactly how to deal with protestors, those "pasty-faced white peace creeps with their long hair, their fairy-looking clothes, and the big yellow stripe up their spineless back." He had his road to the White House all mapped out and believed that his ragtag band of swaggering, brown-shirted Stormtroopers, modeled on Hitler's paramilitary shock troops, would help him get there. (1)

He theorized that U.S. Sen. Barry Goldwater, a right-wing Republican from Arizona, would be elected president in 1968 as American voters rebelled against the Democrats and President Lyndon

B. Johnson. Of course, Goldwater would go on to betray the American people by causing a depression, which in turn would lead to chaos and race wars. Then, and only then, would people rally to his side and clamor for him to lead them, Rockwell believed.

"I will not have a mass organization until there is an economic catastrophe. Not until people are poor. You can't make a revolutionary out of a guy with two cars and an electric lawn mower and a fur toilet seat," Rockwell said. Until that day, he would keep training his Stormtroopers to be his "elite counter-revolutionary officer corps." (2)

Under his blueprint, he would win election to the governorship of Virginia in 1966, and then use that as a springboard for a run for the presidency in 1972. By then, his American Nazi Party would be strong enough to take advantage of the chaos and take over the government, he said.

He was wrong, on both counts. He won only 5,730 votes, about 1.02% of the count, when he ran for governor in 1965, and he was dead by 1972.

Rockwell's platform was basic Nazi — save the white race and culture from threats posed by Jews, blacks, Communists, liberal "creeps," homosexuals, and other deviants, and break the hold that Jews had on the media that prevented Americans from learning the truth about the dangers of race-mixing. "The Jews Are Through in 72," read a sign over the door at his Party HQ.

The platform of the American Nazi Party reminds me very much of some of the statements and attitudes of our current president, Donald J. Trump, especially when it comes to immigrants, citizenship and the press. For example, Trump in August 2019 started talking about taking away the automatic right to citizenship of anyone born in the U.S., and not granting it until that person was 18 years old. That was one of the key planks of the American Nazi Party's platform. (3)

According to the FBI, Rockwell also wanted to:

- Liquidate all "treasonous" Jews proved to have taken part in Marxist or Zionist plots, which he estimated at about 95% of the Jewish population. Jews were to be removed from any position where they could control non-Jewish thought or action, particularly from the press, the courts, government, education and entertainment. He repeatedly denied that the Holocaust ever took place and believed that Martin Luther King Jr., was part of a Jewish plot to control white people;

- Execute all non-Jews who aided and abetted treasonous Jews. An International Treason Tribunal would investigate, try and publicly hang in front of the United States Capitol all those convicted of having acted as fronts for Jewish treason or subversion, violating their oaths of office, or participating in any form of treason against their nations or humanity. Homosexuals and other deviants would be "purged," along with the Jews and traitors — gas chambers would probably be the most efficient method of mass execution because there were not enough electric chairs available;

- Transport all blacks to Africa, where the U.S. government would build for them a modern, industrialized nation, complete with shopping centers, cities, airlines and other conveniences to attract them, appropriating $10 billion a year over five years to pay for it. As an incentive to leave, every black family of five or more would receive $10,000 to help them migrate to the new country, build a home and establish a business. No black would be forced to go, but those who didn't leave the U.S. would be stripped of their citizenship and confined to special reservations. He didn't name the African country that would accommodate them all;

- Amend the U.S. Constitution to, among other things, establish a National Eugenics Commission to encourage selective breeding and abolish the right of U.S. citizenship at birth, conferring it only at the age of 18;

- Establish a national "free opinion" network of newspapers, TV and radio, books and magazines to stop Jewish control of the media and ensure real freedom of the press;

- Arrest all teenage criminals and put them into paramilitary volunteer Police Youth Auxiliaries to patrol America's crime-ridden streets; and, of course, abolish the "Marxist" United Nations.

Quite what set Rockwell off on his personal path not even the FBI could fathom. There was nothing in his past that would indicate problems with blacks or Jews, said FBI investigators in a declassified, long and scathing report on Rockwell (4).

Rockwell was born in 1918 in Bloomington, Ill., one of three children. His father was a well-known stage and radio comedian who performed under the name "Doc Rockwell" during the 1920s and 1930s, with his wife, Claire Schade, whose father was German. They divorced when Rockwell was six and the young "Link," as he was called, was shuttled between a cottage in Maine where his father had installed a common-law wife, and a "tyrannical" aunt in Illinois.

But life wasn't all misery for him. Entertainment stars such as Jack Benny, Groucho Marx and Fanny Brice, were frequent visitors to his father's home and indulged his various whims, according to Rockwell's autobiography, "This Time the World." The decision by Rhode Island's Ivy League school, Brown University, to admit Rockwell in 1938 surprised just about everyone, including Rockwell. Brown officials told him that he had the worst scholastic record of anyone they had admitted but also had attained the highest grade on the college aptitude test that year. That gave him the first clue "that he might be different from other people," he wrote.

At Brown, Rockwell met his first wife, fellow student Judith Aultman. She was not overly enamored with him and Rockwell, growing frustrated, dropped out of Brown in 1941 and joined the U.S. Navy. He was commissioned as a naval aviator ensign on December 9, two days after the attack on Pearl Harbor. Just before shipping out on the USS Omaha, he returned to Brown to see Judith. He proposed, she accepted, and they were married in March, 1943. But the relationship remained rocky, with loud and violent arguments. Rockwell even blamed Judith's parents for not "training" her properly for her role as wife and mother, according to Federick J. Simonelli's excellent biography of Rockwell, American Fuehrer (5).

During the war, Rockwell had served in support, photo reconnaissance, transport and training roles in the Atlantic and Pacific theaters, but never flew in combat. By the time he was discharged, he was a Lieutenant Commander, a rank he kept as an officer in the Naval Reserve, receiving a small monthly stipend. Like many released servicemen, he had trouble finding work after the war and returned to Maine to eke out a living painting signs and working as a freelance photographer in a shop opened on his father's land, which meant he could live rent-free.

He was a moderately good artist and in 1946, he and Judith moved to New York City, where he enrolled in the Pratt Institute in Brooklyn under the GI Bill. He won a $1,000 first prize for an advertising poster for the American Cancer Society but dropped out of Pratt before his final year and moved back to Maine to set up an advertising agency with two friends. Abandoning projects was to become a pattern in his life. He argued with his friends and they eventually bought out his share of the company. His next move was to start a one-man publishing house, Rockwell Publishing Co., which produced a Maine tourist guide funded by advertisers and distributed free through local hotels. But he grew bored and abandoned that, too. (6).

The Korean War saved him. He was recalled to duty in the Naval Reserve as a pilot training instructor at the Coronado naval base in San Diego. By then, his marriage to Judith was strained to the limit. She stayed with him at the base long enough to become pregnant with their third child. She was persuaded by Rockwell to give the marriage several new tries, but it fell apart. Two years after moving to San Diego, he was transferred to a naval air station in Iceland and Judith and the kids returned to her parents' home in Rhode Island. They were divorced in 1953. (7)

Rockwell had come to greatly admire Gen. Douglas MacArthur, even adopting his trademark corn cob pipe. Another of his heroes was Sen. Joseph McCarthy, whose smear tactics and unfounded accusations against people he claimed were Communists ruined so many lives in the early 1950s. Rockwell was appalled when MacArthur was relieved of his command during the Korean War and furious when the U.S. Senate censured McCarthy in 1954, effectively ending his anti-Communist and anti-homosexual crusade. He was also outraged by the way they were treated by the press and began to believe there was some kind of conspiracy behind it all.

He started making frequent trips to the San Diego public library to look for evidence to bolster his pet theory that Jews controlled the media and slanted the news. He found what he believed was documentary evidence that "Communism is Judaism," and so awakened from "30 years of stupid political sleep," he said. (8)

The more research he did, the more he was convinced of an "international Jewish conspiracy" to destroy the civilization of Gentiles "and quietly conquer and subdue the world." Then, while foraging in San Diego second-hand bookshops, he came across a copy of Adolf Hitler's "Mein Kampf" and it brought everything into focus for him. He now knew beyond doubt that there was a vast Jewish conspiracy to undermine white culture, and "that was the end of 'nice guy' George Lincoln Rockwell," as he put it. (9)

It also led to the end of his Navy career.

While on assignment in Iceland, Rockwell met Thora Hallgrimmsson, the niece of the-then Icelandic ambassador to the U.S. In October 1953, just months after his divorce from Judith, he married Thora in Iceland's national cathedral in a service conducted by her uncle, an archbishop. They honeymooned in Germany, visiting Hitler's former retreat at Berchtesgaden, before settling down in the U.S.

In 1954, he launched another publishing venture in Washington, D.C. This one was a small success, but he again he lost control of it to his business partners. The magazine, "U.S. Lady," was ostensibly for servicemen's wives but he used it as his own political mouthpiece, spreading his views on race and Communism. Eventually, because of what he called a conspiracy by his co-workers, he was forced to sell his interest in the publication.

More failed ventures followed. He tried to use Thora's family connections to get a soda bottling and distributorship franchise in Iceland, but failed. Then he applied for a job with a New York public relations firm but got nowhere there, either. Already out on the far-right fringe, he tried to insinuate himself into the conservative right wing but was rejected because of his fanaticism. (10). He did manage to get a job in 1956 as an organizer for a conservative action group but was fired within a year. He even tried to set up his own conservative umbrella organization, but that collapsed, too.

Then Rockwell had an epiphany, of sorts. In 1958, he met two right-wing activists who encouraged him to come out of the Nazi closet. He remembered that "the ultimate smear of the Jews was 'you're a Nazi.' Rather than disguise his aims, like other neo-Fascists were doing, he decided he would be "an OPEN, ARROGANT, ALL-OUT NAZI," not a sneaky Nazi …with the swastika, storm troops, and open declarations of…intentions to gas the Jew-traitors." (11)

One of the activists was Harold Noel Arrowsmith, Jr., a rabidly anti-Semitic multimillionaire from Baltimore who had been living in Mainz, Germany. In 1950, Arrowsmith had founded the National Committee to Free America from Jewish Domination, which printed and distributed anti-Semitic literature (12). Arrowsmith agreed to fund Rockwell and in 1958 bought a house in Arlington, Va., where Rockwell revived the National Committee and started pumping out hate propaganda on an old printing press. Arrowsmith also funded Rockwell's first public protest, the picketing of the White House with placards decrying "Kikes" to protest what they saw as President Eisenhower's pro-Israeli policies. By September 1958, he had fallen out with Arrowsmith, who evicted him from the house, reclaiming his printing press. (13)

However, Arrowsmith had served his purpose. By then, Rockwell was well on his way to becoming America's Hitler, as the British Broadcasting Corp. once called him. In February 1959, he founded the World Union of Free Enterprises National Socialists — WUFENS, for short — at a meeting attended by six people, supposedly the leadership of the group. He dropped the clumsy WUFENS name in December, 1959, for the snappier American Nazi Party.

1960 turned out to be not the best of years for Rockwell.

That July he was arrested at a demonstration in Washington, D.C., on disorderly conduct charges and committed to a hospital for "mental observation." The next month, psychiatrists judged him sane enough to stand trial. He was fined and released. Spotting a chance for publicity, Rockwell distributed leaflets and pamphlets reflecting on his experience, bragging that he had outwitted hospital authorities and proved his sanity. (14).

Judith, meanwhile, was trying to get him to pay child support for their three daughters and sued him in family court in Arlington, Va., in February, 1960. He was ordered to pay her $80 a month for three months, with the amount increasing to $200 monthly by January, 1961. At the hearing, Rockwell admitted he had no funds and depended for support on the American Nazi Party, but said he hoped to earn more as the organization grew (15).

Thora, too, had had enough of Rockwell. After years of living hand-to-mouth, and tolerating all sorts of protests about Rockwell's activities, she left him. Her father, concerned about her safety and his son-in-law's activities, flew to the U.S. to collect her in 1958. She returned to Iceland with the three children she had borne Rockwell, divorced him in October, 1961 and remarried in 1963.

Rockwell was also in trouble with the Navy.

In 1960, the Secretary of Navy recommended that Rockwell, by then a commander, be discharged from the service because of his association with Nazi-type organizations, his espousal of real and religious hatred, and his improper use of his rank and status to "foster hatred." He had also broken naval rules by visiting Iceland in 1959 in a bid to persuade Thora to come home, without getting permission to leave the U.S. to do so. At a hearing before a Board of Officers, Rockwell claimed there was "organized pressure" on the Navy to get rid of him and said he had 6,000 copies of his statement printed for distribution. He was given an honorable discharge.

Rockwell's American Nazi Party had continued to grow during all this, but his finances had not. In 1961, he took over a house on a 26-acre site on Wilson Boulevard in Arlington that was to become a barracks for his Stormtroopers, complete with a four-feet-long swastika that hung from the second floor of the house. The property was in chronic disrepair and often vandalized. The widow who owned it had rented it to Rockwell in hopes of forcing county authorities to rezone the site for a high-rise apartment project. Rockwell couldn't always afford the $225 monthly rent so he was allowed to stay there for $1 a month (16).

The house with the swastika was called "Hatemonger Hill" by local residents who were greatly offended by Rockwell's presence and frequently complained about it. Teenagers hurled eggs, rocks and insults at the building and relations with the community hit a new low when two Nazis assaulted a 13-year-old boy who had been walking by the house after a dance at the local high school, forcing him into the house at gunpoint and interrogating him (17). The Nazis were jailed for a year.

In 1961, local residents formed an association, Citizens Concerned, and shared information they had garnered from the Anti-Defamation League and other groups with state legislators and Virginia Commonwealth's Attorney William J. Hassan, asking them to enforce zoning and other ordinances against the Nazis. Eventually, in 1962, the Virginia State Assembly ordered the State Corporation Commission to revoke the ANP's business charter and Rockwell had to change the name again. (18) This time, he opted for the George Rockwell Party. He was granted a charter under that name, but the media, and Rockwell himself, continued to refer to the group as the American Nazi Party. (19)

CHAPTER 7

ROCKWELL AND THE "DEFECTIVES"

Every month, when it was time for his magazine to be published, Dad would drive down to old farm buildings in the Virginia backwoods where an ex-Nazi Party member owned a printing press. He would spend several days there, working to get the printing done, then sleep in his car at night. When printing run was finished, he would bring the magazines back to Northern Virginia to be mailed out to the American Nazi Party's membership list.

The owner of the press was John Patler, who was charged with shooting Rockwell a short time later. Dad was not among Patler's fans, always accusing him of trying to sabotage the printing of the NSW magazine. He suspected Patler was jealous of him and saw the magazine as competition for Rockwell's other publication, "The Stormtrooper," a bi-monthly publication which he edited, described by the FBI as full of "scurrilous squibs about Jews and Negroes."

While Dad wholeheartedly agreed with Rockwell's political platform, he was less happy with the way it was being implemented. He disliked all of the Rockwell drama, the Hitler salutes, the uniforms and, most of all, the Party's name. "Nazi" had too many negative connotations, he said, and he despised the kind of people it attracted — people "who for the most part were quite defective in one way or another." (1)

Rockwell had modeled the American Nazi Party along the same military lines that Hitler's Nazi movement used, even down to the khaki shirts and trousers, brown belt, tie and boots, and the swastika armbands. Members were given ranks, from Commander, which was Rockwell, through Lieutenant Colonel, Major and Captain, and down to First Lieutenant, Lieutenant, Storm Leader, Group Leader and, at the bottom, the lowly Stormtrooper.

Recruits attended three-day training courses that included lectures on topics such as "Mass Propaganda," "Counter-Psychiatry," "Picketing Procedure," "Basic Law and Procedure," and "Survey of Right Wing Methods." At the end of the course, there was a ceremony involving lighted candles on an altar with a bust of Hitler in front of a swastika. The names of Nazis currently imprisoned would be read out and each name saluted with a shouted "Sieg Heil!" Troopers were also required to snap to attention and give the Nazi salute whenever they entered HQ and had various codenames and secret handshakes (2).

Every new member had to take the "Trooper's Oath." They had to promise to abstain from alcohol, cigarettes and coffee, and make a candle-lit loyalty pledge to Adolf Hitler, to their Commander (Rockwell), to Party comrades "even unto death," and to live "a clean and manly life of honor" as a leader of the "White Man's fight." For good measure, they also swore to mete out "swift and ruthless justice" to race-traitors and be patient with "ignorant fellow white men" who persecute Nazis because they have been "so cruelly brain-washed."

Early Party rituals were said to include a one-inch vertical razor cut on the right cheek. If a member was found to be a spy or, if he left the organization, he was supposed to receive a horizontal cut across the original scar, signifying a double-cross, and those who broke Party rules were reprimanded or court-martialed, which could lead to confinement to barracks or expulsion from the Party. Breaches cited by the FBI included two troopers caught drinking in barracks and bragging in bars, who were confined to barracks, another trooper who was found to be friendly with a member of a rival extremist group and so expelled, and one who solicited money under false pretenses while not on active duty. He was also shown the door.

Loyal Stormtroopers won mission and merit medals if they were jailed for Party activities. One trooper received the highest medal yet awarded, the "Order of Adolf Hitler Silver Medal" after he hit civil rights leader Dr. Martin Luther King in the head for calling Sammy

Davis Jr., "a great American" in a speech delivered at the Southern Christian Leadership Conference in Birmingham, Ala. in September, 1962. Davis was a popular black American singer who also happened to be Jewish. The city of New Orleans honored the trooper with 30 days in jail.

It was considered a badge of honor for troopers to get arrested and Rockwell used to brag that he had "two or three" Party members in jail somewhere in the U.S. "almost 365 days a year." Every Sunday night, he held a ceremony on the ANP parade ground to honor them, he told writer Alex Haley in an interview for Playboy in 1966. Before agreeing to the interview, Rockwell had asked Haley over the phone if he was Jewish. Haley replied that he was not. But Rockwell neglected to ask Haley about the color of his skin. Haley was black. Stormtroopers were shocked when he arrived at the Party's HQ and Rockwell kept a silver-handled pistol on the table beside him throughout the interview, constantly referring to Haley as a "nigger." (3).

Rockwell always said his troopers never engaged in violence, except in self-defense, but his "garish and theatrical demonstrations" were intended to provoke "riotous action" that frequently led to melees and arrests. Despite his protestations that the ANP was a peaceful lot, Rockwell kept short, combat-lengths of sawed-off iron pipes in a special wooden rack at his HQ, along with revolvers, automatic pistols, shotguns and rifles. At times, he would erupt from his HQ, brandishing a gun at hecklers. He claimed to have been the target of numerous assaults and assassination attempts, with shots fired at his building, and all his troopers received boxing and weapons training (4).

Protests were staged for theater and the publicity they garnered. One of his first demonstrations took place in front of the White House, where the ANP protested President Eisenhower's policies on Israel bearing placards proclaiming "Protect Ike from the Kikes," which Rockwell himself designed and painted. The typical protest involved troopers handcuffing themselves to embassy gates or manning picket lines during visits by foreign dignitaries or the showing of a film like Exodus. Civil rights and Communist Party meetings were also favored targets. His methods were crude and inflammatory — during a visit by an African head of state he sent a truck filled with black-faced costumed troopers around streets parallel to the parade route.

Rockwell had a "hate bus," a battered baby-blue pickup with plywood sides plastered with swastikas and racist messages that he used to dispatch to counter civil rights Freedom Riders who toured around in a "love bus" protesting segregation in the South. In 1961, he filled his "hate bus" with troopers and sent it on a long, bumpy trip to New Orleans. Rockwell himself, of course, traveled to New Orleans in comfort aboard a plane, meeting the bus when it finally arrived. But the authorities would not let the vehicle into the city until the racist signs were removed and when Rockwell and his troopers eventually set up their picket lines, they were arrested and jailed for two weeks. Rockwell later bragged that it was the longest time he ever spent in a cell. He and his troopers staged a hunger strike, which was how they got out of jail. Eleven of them went eight days without food but one man cracked and said he was going to eat, "so we had to let him know that if he did, it would be his last meal. He changed his mind," Rockwell told Haley.

Rockwell's organization was more smoke and mirrors than a national security threat, although his distribution network made his influence seem broader than it really was. ANP literature would turn up in odd spots across the country, tucked under window-shield wipers, handed out to pedestrians, and even stuck inside books in stores and at newsstand, usually by teenage supporters creating the impression that the ANP had a large presence coast-to-coast.

He liked to brag that he had an international operation, with followers in most western countries and beyond the Iron Curtain. However, FBI agents said that the ANP's international ties were mostly limited to correspondence with people holding similar views in Europe, South America and Scandinavia, plus Middle East nations like Egypt and Saudi Arabia.

In an attempt to project himself onto the international scene, Rockwell would write letters to world leaders in hopes of baiting them to respond. In a missive to Egypt's President Gamal Abdel Nasser, he complained about the treatment he received from Nasser's representatives in the U.S., while, in March 1964, he wrote to Premier Nikita Khrushchev asking questions about the Soviet Union's attitude on racial issues. "I consider you a mortal enemy, but I am not ashamed to admit I respect your guts, directness and dedication." (5).

Two years earlier, he had attended a meeting of delegates of various National Socialist international groups in Gloucestershire, England. Shortly afterward he was deported by the British because his presence was deemed not conducive to the "public good." On his return to America he published the so-called "Cotswold Agreements, "which described the formation of a new, international Nazi movement" which he would lead. But when questioned by the FBI later, he admitted that no such movement had been formed. He had inserted the phrase into the documents only "to enhance his own importance."

Although the minimum age for membership of the ANP was 18, one of Rockwell's main targets were teenagers, and he tried hard to gain a following among high-schoolers. Many of those who showed an interest in his organization showed "distinct signs of mental instability or illness," according to the FBI. One 17-year-old from Utah had previously attempted suicide, and in May, 1963, four Long Island teenagers armed with a submachine gun, shot up their high school and the home of a teacher who had given them poor grades. All of them had visited Rockwell's HQ in Virginia and when the police raided one of their homes they found an arsenal of weapons and Nazi hate literature.

Rockwell spent time visiting university campuses, usually at the invitation of student groups who were looking for controversial speakers. "If I can win a small group ….in each college, I can win the youth," he said. During a speech in San Diego in 1962, he was pelted with eggs and his glasses were broken. The next year, a bomb threat was called in during a University of Chicago talk, all of which was grist for his publicity mill. But be didn't always get the protests he sought. When he finished speeches at campuses in Michigan and San Francisco and asked his audience for questions, the students rose silently and filed out. Rockwell was furious.

Dad later followed Rockwell's path to college campuses, sometimes getting the same reception and worse from students. One of his campus critics was Chris Christie, who went on to become the Republican governor of New Jersey and a presidential candidate in the 2016 election. Christie was student government president at the University of Delaware and, together with university officials, objected to the distribution of one of Dad's vilest essays, "Who Rules America?," in leaflet form.

The student newspaper complained that Jewish students suffered "verbal and physical abuse" as a result of the leaflet, which claimed that Jews controlled the U.S. media. In a subsequent essay, Dad described Christie as "flashing a toothy TV smile suitable for a political candidate," saying he was a young man cut out to one day become president of the local Jaycees, "a fellow who will always go along to get along." (6)

Dad went on to call on student sympathizers to hand leaflets openly, instead of tucking them under windshield wipers at night, and to start "challenging apologists for the Jews to public debate." They should be "as insistent and as obnoxious as necessary" to force the student newspaper to give them space. The "Chris Christie types" will then be "forced to either back down and look foolish or they must resort to Jewish methods: lawyerly debating tricks and deception, emotional appeals, organized badgering and heckling, and even physical intimidation — especially if there is a large non-white contingent on the campus."

Looking back at news accounts of Rockwell's antics, it may seem that the ANP was just a bunch of clowns, albeit ugly ones. But they were not — they were brutal, ignorant thugs, happy to bully and beat up any protester in their path and proud to be jailed for doing so.

"George Lincoln Rockwell is a professional bigot, a con man, a malcontent, and a chronic failure who will stop at nothing to gain notoriety and even power," agents said in a 1965 report that was personally approved by Clyde Tolson, then Associate Director of the FBI and long-term friend and protégé of FBI director J. Edgar Hoover.

Rockwell claimed in a speech at California's Stanford University in 1964 that he had "700 hard-core troopers" across the U.S., and another 12,000 active sympathizers. Two years later, he told Haley that he had launched a world union of National Socialists — presumably the Cotswolds deal — of which he was the international commander. In the U.S. alone, there were 1,500 Party members and about 15,000 "correspondents," who were people who write in and donate to his cause, he boasted. While FBI agents were skeptical of his numbers, they had no illusions about the type of person drawn to Rockwell's movement.

The ANP had an especial attraction for "the failures, the misfits, the mentally ill, and the potentially violent," agents said. Almost all

Rockwell's Stormtroopers were under 30, and some had only an elementary education, although most had 1-3 years of high school. Background information from 19 membership applications revealed that 13 of the would-be Nazis had arrest records for charges such as assault, carrying dangerous weapons, attempted rape, armed robbery and burglary. Of those, eight had a history of mental disorders — one was "a paranoid with systematized delusions of persecution," a second suffered from acute paranoid schizophrenia, while a psychiatrist claimed a third one displayed "poorly controlled hostility."

Answering a question about his background, one applicant wrote that he had been dishonorably discharged from the U.S. Army in Korea for "taking it upon myself to exterminate prisoners when captured." Many of the applicants were barely literate. Those able to string sentences together offered various reasons for joining. One said that the wanted "a mighty nation united under the philosophy that might makes right," while another volunteered that he wanted "to save the white race from mixing themselves to death" with minorities.

In December, 1963, Rockwell personally evaluated 27 members and former members of the ANP. "He described them variously as vicious, irresponsible, beset with delusions, thieves, liars, uncontrollable, desperate, irrational, murderers and potential murderers," the FBI said.

While my father spent a great deal of time with Rockwell, he never joined the ANP — he simply could not stomach the type of people Rockwell had around him. He felt that 95% of them were "outright defective" and acted very unprofessionally, and he wanted them gone. Rockwell disagreed and there was some method in his madness, Dad said. Rockwell believed that it was "the losers [and] the social outcasts" who make up the ranks of every revolutionary movement.

"They're the ones who are available, the ones who don't have anything to lose by becoming associated with a politically incorrect cause. Individually they may not be very impressive but large numbers of them, organized and disciplined, would make a revolutionary army," Dad wrote in an essay on Rockwell. (7)

Rockwell told Dad that he had tried appealing to what he called "the winners" — the teachers and professors, doctors, lawyers and engineers, to the writers and artists, businessmen and craftsmen, and to his fellow military officers, to everyone that he considered to be "careful, responsible men and women with steady employment and stable families." While he found that many agreed with him in principle, "almost none had the moral courage to stand up and be counted among the righteous." In short, while they shook his hand after his speeches, Rockwell said, they would scurry away in fright when he talked about taking America back from the Jews.

"They were too comfortable, too corrupted by good living and materialism, too unaccustomed to taking risks and facing opposition," Rockwell complained. Only in the masses could he find the recruits he needed to launch a political campaign to take back America, and the masses could only be reached through mass media, he said.

"The touch of Hollywood in Rockwell's approach to revolutionary politics always was a bone of contention between him and me. I argued that the uniforms, flags, and theatrical behavior —even the name 'American Nazi Party' — made it difficult for serious people to take him seriously. His medium got in the way of his message," Dad wrote. But Rockwell said that if "he put away the flags and armbands and wore a business suit and shunned theatrics, the news media would ignore him and no one would hear what he had to say."

Rockwell's aim was to make people pay attention to his "simple, core message of the need for rebuilding a white, Jew-free America," based on Hitler's Mein Kampf principles, and for that he had to get publicity. But when he tried to present his message in a sober, serious way, no-one had paid any attention to him, Rockwell said in shades of Trump-To-Come.

"The newspapers and television stations wouldn't send reporters to his press conferences, they ignored his press releases, and the public didn't even know he existed. But as soon as he raised the swastika banner, the news media went crazy and swarmed all over him. He was seen on all the TV channels and what he said was reported in the newspapers," Dad said.

Unknown to Dad, the FBI was in some agreement with his views on Rockwell's antics. "George Lincoln Rockwell is an egocentric and a chronic failure who created the shabby, smalltime enterprise which he named the American Nazi Party in order to abate his tormenting ambitions to achieve fame," the FBI said. "Carrying the war-tattered banner of a vanquished enemy the world would like to forget, Rockwell leads his heterogeneous 'army' against an imaginary 'Zionist conspiracy.'

Distasteful costumes, contemptible slogans, and disruptive tactics have brought national attention to Rockwell, inflating him and his group far beyond their due." (8)

CHAPTER 8

SUMMERS IN FREDERICKSBURG

A few days before my sixth birthday we moved into a rental house near Fredericksburg, Va. Mom had got a good job as a mathematics professor at Mary Washington College, the first female Phi Beta Kappa faculty member ever to be hired by the school. She worked hard and did her best to support us, but Dad was ever-more distant, spending most of his time now hanging out with Rockwell at his American Nazi Party HQ in Arlington in affluent Northern Virginia and writing and editing Rockwell's magazine, National Socialist World.

When Dad was at home, he spent all his waking hours, except for meals, holed up in his office or sitting in his chair, reading. We had strict orders never to go into his office, and he always kept the door closed when he was home. I just wanted to be alone and lost in my head and, frankly, that seemed to suit Mom just fine, because she worked all the time. She always seemed anxious and afraid now. Her sole focus was trying to make ends meet and take care of us and Dad, which meant she didn't have time to devote to playing or talking with us.

Dad was never really there when he was home, anyway. He was mostly lost in his own world of work and politics, a bit like me, I suppose, but older. I don't remember him ever having a casual conversation with Mom. He expected a meal to be waiting for him when he got home at night and Mom never failed to meet those expectations. After dinner, he would sit in his easy chair, reading the newspaper and news magazines for hours with his cat, George, sitting on his lap. George was a seal point Siamese and Dad really, really loved him. He would talk to him in a silly, childlike voice and crack jokes, as if George were talking. Sometimes, Dad would fart and then he would start laughing and say something like, "George, you nasty boy, you should warn me before you do that!" The two of them were inseparable when Dad was home.

Dad rarely did any work around the house or in the yard. He believed it was Mom's job to do 100% of the home-making, and anything else in the way of chores was left to Erik and me. He made many demands of us, and if we didn't do as he said, there was always "hell to pay," as he would say, except for when Mom stepped in, and that always made Dad furious.

By now he only referred to us as "Midget." I can't remember when we transitioned from "Smelly" to "Midget," but it was always, "Midget do this" or "Midget do that." We only ever said "Yes, sir" and "No, sir." Thanks to his beatings, we were deathly afraid of him. Whenever I was in the same room as him, I wanted nothing more than to escape. And yet, when he was gone, I would think about him and fantasize about him being different.

It was at this house where Erik and I first learned to ride bikes and I used to spend most of my time outdoors exploring — and avoiding Dad as much as I possibly could.

We had numerous chores, but the worst of all was cutting the grass. It was a huge task because the yard was well over an acre and the only mower we had was a rotary mower with no motor. He felt it would be character-building for us, but at six years old, we could barely reach the handle or push fast enough to get the blades spinning and moving the damned thing through the tall grass was almost impossible. Mom used to complain that he was expecting too much of us, but he wouldn't budge. We would work at it for hours, and then he would come out to inspect, say it wasn't good enough, and tell us to keep working. That cycle would repeat over and over until Mom would finally intervene, telling us it was good enough and that we could go and play. Then she would finish cutting the grass herself, and then Dad would get really mad.

I remember him accusing Mom of "ruining" us. He said we needed to learn the value of hard work and to finish what we started. Instead, she was undercutting his authority and teaching us to be lazy. Then Mom went for him. If he was so concerned about us, she shot back, he should act like a father, not a warden in our house. "They are scared to death of you and you never spend any quality time with them," she said. Dad stared at her silently but never replied. I think he was trying to control the rage boiling within. Mom shook her head and turned away.

Dad wasn't much of a parent at the best of times, even when we were ill.

One day, Mom had to go into work at Mary Washington and left Dad to take care of us. As usual, he shut himself up in his office. We were playing quietly when Erik suddenly hurled the contents of his stomach onto the living room floor. The first thing I noticed was the awful smell, and then he threw up again. Dad must have heard Erik because he came out of his office. He grimaced, looked at Erik, and pointed to the mess, saying "You need to clean that up!" He marched into the kitchen, got a bowl and towel, and gave them to Erik. "The next time you get sick, do it in this bowl or in the toilet." It didn't seem to bother him that his kid was ill. He just turned and went back to his office, slamming the door. Erik tried to clean things up but vomited several more times over the next few hours.

Dad didn't come back out of his office again until Mom got home from work. After relaying her dismay to Dad, she cleaned up and sprayed Lysol all over the room. After that, I was deathly afraid of throwing up, or of anyone else doing so anywhere near me, even well into my adulthood. And to this day, I hate the smell of Lysol.

In summer we would spend hours playing outside in the adjoining fields, riding our bikes and exploring the stream at the back of the property. None of the local roads were paved and there was rarely any traffic. I made forts and flew kites and went barefoot most of the time. I could run across the gravel driveway of the house and never feel a pinch. I also got into trouble, lots of it.

There were just five houses in our development and we sometimes played with two older boys who lived up the road. We were playing in their house one day when I lost interest and went outside. There was a carton of empty glass Coke bottles by the side door and I began to imagine what it would be like to put a bottle under each tire of their car and watch it smash the bottles as the car reversed.

As usual, I never considered the consequences of my actions. I've often wondered since then if my escapades were my subconscious way of trying to get Dad to notice me.

I carefully placed one bottle tightly under each tire. I stood there for the longest time, waiting for one of the parents to come out, get into the car and back up, but they never did. Eventually, I lost interest and went off to play elsewhere. About an hour later I came back to get my brother and that's when I saw it. The car was gone but there were four smashed bottles where the tires had been. My first reaction was a mix of pure fascination — and disappointment that I didn't see it happen. Then, as I reveled in my accomplishment, I slowly realized that maybe what I had done wasn't such a good idea after all.

I ran all the way home and was engrossed in something else when Mom called me. She didn't look pleased and I knew I was in trouble. She asked me if I had put the bottles under the tires and I denied it.

When Dad got home, I lied again. They knew better and just kept asking until I started crying and admitted my guilt. Unfortunately, this was a regular pattern by now. My curiosity always resulted in an appointment with Dad where I lied and then felt the sting of his belt or razor cord. This time, I was also required to apologize to the neighbor. The walk over there was like a death march for me and having to speak to them was worse than any beating. I stood at their door for what seemed like an age and then rang the bell, praying that they wouldn't answer. But they did, both of them. Finally, in a barely audible voice, I said I was sorry for what I had done. They thanked me for apologizing and quickly closed the door. Mom told me later she and Dad had to buy new tires for the car.

By now, I knew beyond all doubt that there was something seriously wrong with me. I was simply bad to the core, and nothing could save me, which is why my Dad never loved me. Unfortunately, my curiosity and lack of impulse control continued to get the better of me.

One summer's day, while Dad was out of town, I was playing down by the stream behind our house. I'd found a book of matches from somewhere and decided to entertain myself by setting individual leaves on fire and then blowing them out. It was grand fun and I did it several times until suddenly a couple of adjacent leaves caught fire and I could no longer blow them out. In a few moments the fire spread to the point that it was out of control. I got up and ran back to my house and shortly after one of our neighbors noticed the blaze and called the fire department. There was quite a large blaze raging behind the house by the time the fire truck arrived. I just stood there, watching all the commotion, in rapt fascination.

Mom was in the shower at the time. When she heard the sirens she got out, grabbed a night gown, and ran out of the house. She was standing in the backyard trying to figure out what the hell was going on when a fireman walked up to her. "Ma'am, you might want to go back inside and get dressed," he suggested. The night gown she'd put on was sheer and she was completely naked underneath. She took one look at herself and ran for cover. It didn't take long for everyone to figure out who was probably responsible for the fire but fortunately it was put out quickly and nothing of real importance was damaged.

Mom was furious with me — and extremely embarrassed by the night gown incident. She was so mad that she decided that she couldn't wait until Dad got home for me to be punished. Dad had always been the one to hit me before, but now Mom decided she was going to do it. But despite her anger, she just wasn't cut out to physically punish anyone, no matter how hard she tried. Her effort at hitting me was pretty pathetic and didn't hurt at all. I pretended to cry and she stopped almost immediately and started crying herself. It was the only time she ever tried to hit me. What really surprised me, though, was that she thankfully decided not to tell Dad about my pyromania when he got home several days later.

It was the first winter that we spent in the Fredericksburg house that I met my cousins on Dad's side of the family. Dad's brother, Uncle Sandy, had four kids and, until then, I had no idea that I had an aunt and an uncle and cousins in Ohio. They came for a visit during Christmas and I remember all of us kids sitting in the living room, staring at each other and not saying a word for the longest time. We were all terribly shy but finally someone broke the ice and soon we were laughing and playing and having a really good time. They were so much fun to have around.

The thing I remember most was how different Dad was when he was around Uncle Sandy and his family. He seemed happy, even playing with two of my cousins, both girls. One was a month older than Erik and me, and the other was a few years younger. He got down on the floor with them, and chased them and grabbed them and tickled them until everyone was giggling. Dad laughed so much and he seemed to genuinely enjoy it. I just stood there in silence, looking at them playing and wondering who this man was. He never once played with us like that. The girls loved it, and he played with them like that several times over the few days they stayed with us.

I was really confused by what I saw but happy, nevertheless, because his energy was different and I didn't feel afraid of him, as I had always been before. I really liked my aunt and uncle. They were nice to me and seemed to like me and enjoy my company. It was a warm feeling I don't ever remember experiencing before. I was comfortable and at ease around them. I didn't get into trouble at all when they were with us, and Dad never got mad at me or hit me. It was all very unusual because I used to have trouble with Dad almost every day. I cried when they left to return to Ohio. I was sad because I knew I could never have what they had with Dad.

CHAPTER 9

DAD'S NAZI FRIENDS

Dad continued to have serious reservations about whether Rockwell could ever build an effective organization with all his flamboyant tactics, and those doubts "made me hold back from whole-hearted support of his efforts," he later recounted in one of his infamous radio broadcasts.

But he grew to believe Rockwell was right, especially about what Dad called the "moral cowardice and servile conventionality" of the majority of Americans. "Most of them would rather lose an arm and a leg than be suspected of thinking a politically incorrect thought." As he argued and worked with Rockwell, his appreciation for what he called the man's "courage and idealism" grew.

By 1967, Dad had finally convinced Rockwell to abandon the American Nazi Party name in favor of the National Socialist White People's Party (NSWPP). By then, his name was on the masthead of the National Socialist World and his writings and radical views were attracting the attention of both the FBI and the press.

And perhaps because I was older now, I paid more attention to the things he talked about. He went on at great length about African-Americans and Jewish people and how much he hated them. It sometimes seemed to me that it was the only thing he thought about during this time, but it didn't take long before it had a profound effect on me, too.

My favorite place to play was in the woods behind our house, and I spent hours there almost every day. I played with box turtles and tried to make forts and log cabins, and paddled in the streams, catching tadpoles and frogs and crayfish.

One day, as I walked home, I encountered the neighborhood bullies for the first time. Four or five older boys surrounded me and one of them picked up a big branch on the ground. "Hey look, it's the Nazi!" he said. "Let's get him!" I couldn't move, I was terrified. The next thing I knew, I was down on the ground, seeing stars. He had hit me in the face with the branch and broken my glasses in half. I felt blood running down my face. Then they laughed and ran off. I slowly picked up the pieces of my glasses and walked home, crying. When I told Mom what had happened, she was really mad. "What is wrong with people?" she asked.

That is when I asked her what a Nazi was, but she didn't answer me.

Dad was really upset when Mom told him that evening what had happened. "Did you fight back?" he asked me. "No, sir," I replied. "Why not?" he asked. "I don't know," I whispered. After a long silence, I quietly asked him, "What is a Nazi?" I knew that Dad hated blacks but I had no idea what a Nazi was. "It's not important," he said, and then proceeded to tell me that I needed to learn how to defend myself. Mom just about exploded.

"How do you expect him to defend himself in a situation like that? You do absolutely nothing with your boys and yet you expect them to magically know how to defend themselves? You've never taken any kind of an interest in them whatsoever, and you call yourself a father!" Mom usually didn't say stuff like that to Dad, at least in front of us, but she was furious that I'd been beaten up because of his political views. Dad just looked at her, then went to his office and shut the door. I dealt with what had happened the same way I always did. I imagined that all those around me were in a separate, parallel universe and I had a world of my own, where I could go on journeys to faraway lands, where I was perfectly normal and no-one would tell me otherwise.

I remember one of those journeys…I am standing on a crowded street corner in the middle of Washington, D.C., with a machine gun. I look around and all I see is blacks, hundreds of them milling about, walking to and fro. With great pleasure I open up and mow them down. "Take that, you stupid Negroes! I hate you, I hate you all! You are all

Dad talks about, and he hates you, too," I was shouting. "Dad will love me now for what I am doing, and he's going to be so proud of me!"

According to FBI files on Dad, Richmond agents had noted that he didn't take part in Rockwell's picketing protests while we lived in Fredericksburg and "remains aloof from the rank and file members." That wasn't quite true, though. We didn't go out much socially because with only Mom earning, we didn't have the money to reciprocate hospitality, but occasionally we went to Nazi shindigs.

I remember once we went to a picnic at Great Falls Park in Virginia. I watched a bunch of men hanging a huge Nazi flag from the trees near the cookout area. Other visitors at the park were disgusted and soon the police arrived and made the men take it down. I remember it so clearly because it was a bad day for me. That evening after we got home, we all were sick from food poisoning.

One of Dad's friends was Louis T. Byers, who was later to provide Dad with the political vehicle that carried him through the rest of his life, though we didn't know that at the time. I remember Byers because he cost me my favorite toy rocket. It was another picnic and he persuaded Dad that I should bring one of my rockets with me. I was pleased to be given such an important task and, of course, selected my very best rocket for display. We set it up and sent it off, but I never got it back because I couldn't find where it landed.

I often wondered what happened to that rocket, especially in light of what I know today.

Apparently, Byers was on the FBI's radar, too. Agency files describe a social affair held at Byers' home, which Dad attended. Obviously, FBI informants were watching from a distance because there was a fairly detailed description of the evening's events. The party went on for some hours and a 15-minute film was shown that included frames of Hitler. Every time Hitler spoke, there was applause from the guests, so much so that the noise irked the neighbors. The FBI also had a description of the cars and the license plates of the guests.

I sometimes wonder if they found my rocket in the bushes as they kept watch that night. Of all the Nazis, Robert Lloyd was Dad's closest friend during this time and for a few more years after that. A captain in the ANP, Lloyd served as Rockwell's security officer but his most notorious role was that of mischief-maker. His racist stunts made headlines, which was Rockwell's intention, of course, and the fines he incurred were paid by the Party.

Lloyd was a former beatnik from Richmond, Va., and one of the few people in the American Nazi Party with whom Dad was content to share his time. Dad admired Lloyd, regarding him as "an intelligent guy who was fearless." (1). After Lloyd dropped out of the Party to help his father run his rest home business, Dad brought him back as circulation manager.

I remember him being quiet but friendly toward us as kids. We hung out a few times with him at his house in Arlington, Va., though I didn't particularly enjoy some of the visits. I recall one at Halloween. Erik and I were all fired up, hot to get into our costumes and out on the street with all the other kids to trick-or-treat. Instead, we were bundled into the car and told we were driving up from Triangle, Va., where we then lived, to see Lloyd. Mom said we could take our costumes with us and she would take us around the houses in his neighborhood instead.

But when we reached Lloyd's house, Dad forbade us to leave. He and Mom disappeared into another part of the house with Lloyd and his wife, and Erik and I were left alone in Lloyd's study for hours. I remember sitting there, looking at all the stuff on his bookshelves. On his desk was a silver dollar. I'm ashamed to say that the young me studied the dollar for some time and then pocketed it to pay him back for stealing our Halloween.

Rockwell called publicity the "lifeblood of any political movement." He knew that without it, no one would know that he and his Nazis existed. His publicity stunts included sending Stormtroopers dressed in ape costumes to the National Zoo in Washington, D.C., carrying placards demanding "Free our Brothers" and "We Equals Want Civil rights."

Lloyd was indispensable to Rockwell when it came to such demonstrations. One of Lloyd's most notorious stunts was pulled off on the floor of the House of Representatives as he leaped around like an ape, evading the Capitol Police and demanding to be seated as a member of the Mississippi Democratic delegation.

The Democrats in Mississippi had split over who should be able to nominate election candidates. The established Democratic Party was run by an old boys' network that allowed only whites to vote. Disenfranchised and disillusioned, in 1964 working class blacks formed the Freedom Democratic Party, organized their own primaries and elected their own representatives who they said were the rightful delegates to Congress from Mississippi, and not the five white men the Democratic Convention had selected.

Rockwell was quick to capitalize on the furor, dispatching Lloyd to Capitol Hill as congressmen took their seats on the opening day that year, January 4, 1965. Three black women who had been elected were barred from entering the chamber by police, while their supporters in coveralls, boots and straw hats protested in the streets, marching on the White House and clogged the corridors of Capitol Hill. (2)

Lloyd managed to slip through security and into a bathroom where he changed from street clothes into a lion skin, put a fake bone through his nose, and donned blackface and an old stove pipe hat. He ran onto the House floor where he danced and cavorted among the seats, singing out, "I'se the Mississippi delegation." He was eventually caught, jailed and fined $19 for disorderly conduct, and Rockefeller got some priceless TV coverage.

Lloyd was involved many times in such antics.

He distributed "boat tickets" for "Coon-Ard Lines" at a meeting of the National Association for the Advancement of Colored People. The tickets promised free trips back to Africa with "all the bananas and choice cuts of missionary desired." According to the FBI, a "similar bit of abhorrent ANP propaganda" offered a "Jew Communist Traitor's Surrender Pass" that entitled the bearer "to be gassed toward the very last." He pulled a similar stunt at a gay rights' convention, pretending to be a delivery man and rushing on stage with a box labeled as an emergency shipment of 24 quarts of Vaseline.

Lloyd also played a part in our very first vacation as a family. Sometimes, in the summer, Mom would take Erik and me to California to visit with her parents but Dad never came with us. Then Lloyd announced that he was going to the beach for a week and invited us to join him. I remember it very well because it was my first encounter with the ocean and Dad terrified me.

I still see and smell that day — the faint fishy odor on the ocean breeze, the sound of surf crashing ashore, gulls squawking, the feel of the hot sand under my bare feet as we walk up from the car. The sun reflecting off the white sand hurts my eyes as I stare at the waves and the flat, distant horizon. There were lots of parents and kids on the beach and sounds of happiness everywhere. I was awestruck, soaking it all in. Then Mom suggested Dad take me down to the water and play for a while. Dad had never played with me before. I was thrilled but he wasn't.

Without saying a word, he grabbed my hand and we walked toward the water. As we got close to the surf I tensed up and pulled back. I was afraid and wanted to slow down. The sand was cooler and dense under my feet and the sound of the waves seemed so much louder. But he didn't slow down. Instead, he picked me up and ran into the water with me over his shoulder. I started crying and pushing away in an effort to get free but Dad held on tight. He was laughing as he ran through the surf. My crying got louder and more frantic and suddenly Dad stopped and looked at me. "Shut up! You are acting like a little sissy," he yelled.

By now I was hysterical. Without warning, Dad heaved me out into the water and walked back to the dry sand. I hit the water head first and immediately tasted salt as I swallowed a mouthful. I tried to stand up but just as I got my feet under me a wave crashed down and I was tumbling again. I felt like a rag doll as the surf pushed and pulled me, my body scraping against the sandy floor and the rocks and shells. I was in a frantic fight to survive. Every time I got my head above the water, I was hit by another wave. Eventually, I ended up tumbling and sort of body-surfing onto shore where I lay stunned, waiting for the next wave to pummel me. When I finally realized I was safe, I picked myself up and ran away from the waves as fast as I could.

Dad never tried playing with me again. I didn't understand why he hated me so much but it must be because I was a sissy, I thought. I remember the feeling of fear and loneliness that overcame me because it became all too familiar over the years. It took me a few days before I would go near the water again but eventually, when Dad was nowhere in sight, I gradually eased my way back to the water's edge and started playing there.

Dad was fast being recognized as a formidable force as a white nationalist, as he later started calling himself, and Mom worried that she might lose her faculty position at Mary Washington because of him. They argued many times but I didn't know then what was going on between them. I know now that Dad only stuck around because it was convenient for him. He needed Mom because he was no longer earning an income. He was getting a free ride, home-cooked meals into the bargain, and could pretty much do whatever he wanted with few consequences.

Mom told me later that she considered leaving him many times but he threatened to go to the dean at Mary Washington and say that she was heavily involved with his work with Rockwell, although that was a lie. While any romance was long gone, Dad wasn't willing to let her go anymore because he needed her salary in order to keep writing for Rockwell. His threat was extremely effective and, in the end, Mom just kept working and taking care of us and Dad.

CHAPTER 10

ROCKWELL'S LAST DAY

Perhaps the least surprised by the events of August 25, 1967, would have been George Rockwell himself. He had twice predicted that he would die violently, and in that he was right.

Not long after the picnic in Great Falls, Rockwell was assassinated by his printer, John Patler, as he left a laundromat in Arlington, Va. where he had planned to do his shirts. He was shot by Patler through the windshield as he got into his car. He managed to crawl out through the passenger side door, pointed to the roof of the building and then collapsed and died, splayed in the street with his box of Ivory Snow Flakes by his side (1). His corn cob pipe and a dirty, brown sock were found on the front seat of the car seat.

Just a year earlier Rockwell had been asked by a journalist if he had ever considered the possibility that he might be killed one day. "I've not only considered it; I expect it. And I'm ready for it," he replied. He said he knew he was "going to go, probably in some violent manner; the only question is when and how." But he was sure that it wouldn't happen until he had completed the mission God had given him. "I believe I was placed here for a purpose and I think God has something to do with it. Our country needs a leader. So I think I'll be spared. As Rommel said, 'Stand next to me; I'm bulletproof,'" he said. (2)

Rockwell made a similar prediction during a question-and-answer session with students at State University in Geneseo, N.Y., in February, 1965. Asked about a possible assassination attempt, he said he hoped it would be "a clean shot," adding flippantly as an afterthought that perhaps a wound would be good, too, because it would garner "world-wide publicity." (3) Shortly before his assassination, Rockwell had petitioned an Arlington Court to be allowed to carry a handgun, according to Earl Shaffer, assistant to then-Commonwealth Attorney William Hassan. Shaffer declined to get involved. "Rockwell knew he was going to get nailed," Shaffer said in an interview with journalist Charles S. Clark. It was Rockwell who coined the term "White Power," but apart from his slogan, he didn't leave much in the way of an estate — $257 in cash, various writings, his corncob pipe, and a pair of gold Navy pilot wings. (4)

Patler had tried to kill Rockwell two months earlier, in June, but his shot went wide. He had laid brush at the end of the driveway leading up to Rockwell's house and then hid behind nearby bushes as Rockwell's bodyguard got out of the car to clear the debris away. The house was frequently the target of vandals and Rockwell's guard was not surprised at the obstruction on the driveway. Patler fired, missed and ran. Rockwell gave chase but lost him. Although he saw his assailant from the back only, Rockwell later told Dad that he thought it was Patler.

On his second attempt, Patler again spied from the bushes at Nazi HQ, watching as Rockwell drove to the nearby "Econ-o-wash" laundromat, this time without his guard. Rockwell went into the building with his shirts, then realized he had forgotten the bleach and returned to his car to drive back to the house to get it. Perched on the rooftop of a beauty salon next door, Patler fired twice, hitting Rockwell in the head and chest as the car rolled backward, hitting another vehicle. Patler was caught 20 minutes later as he stood at a bus-stop, having allegedly discarded the gun as he ran away.

Patler was a 29-year-old ex-marine marksman who had been judged "unsuitable" and honorably discharged after he was seen wearing his uniform at a Nazi rally. He ran a print shop in rural Virginia, producing Rockwell's "Stormtrooper" magazine and crudely drawn cartoons for his hate literature. He also printed Rockwell's children's comic, "Here Comes Whiteman." The hero was Lew Cor, (Rockwell spelled backwards), a deliveryman for a dairy company. When Lew speaks the secret words "Lieh Geis" (Sieg Heil, backwards), there is a flash of lightning and he transforms into "Whiteman," sporting a super-hero costume with a Nazi swastika emblazoned on the chest. Lew duels with "the Jew from Outer Space" and "Supercoon," and makes "Jew Commies tremble," "Nigger criminals quake," and "Liberals head for the hills," the comic said.

Patler's birth name was Yanacki Patsalos but he changed it to Patler to make it sound more like 'Hitler.' Dad disliked him intensely. He called him "a very aggressive little turd," and said Rockwell had told him to watch Patler carefully in case he tried to sabotage the printing operation because there had been "incidents" at the printing shop that Patler had organized. "We used to call Patler the 'animal trainer' because he would gather the most defective people around him, the ones nobody else would put up with," (5).

Patler was one of two sons of Greek immigrants. He had brown eyes and an olive complexion, unlike most of the other ANP members, who were of white European descent, with light-colored hair and eyes. He believed that the "blue-eyed devils" looked down on him and tried to organize a coup by brown-eyed ANP members. Rockwell ended up expelling him from the Party in March 1967 after Matt Koehl, Rockwell's deputy, claimed that Patler had "Bolshevik leanings."

Patler had been a member of a small political group in New York called the National Youth League, which used to march, picket and disrupt Communist meetings. After being arrested for handing out inflammatory leaflets, he was committed to a mental health clinic for observation. After evaluating him, a doctor noted "hatred, impaired judgment, his rigidity, his very immature emotionality, his narcissism, his irrelevant suspiciousness, his belief in his own righteousness." The doctor, Dr. Pierre Rube, thought Patler might be a repressed homosexual and a potential murderer. He diagnosed him as suffering from acute paranoia. (6)

Patler was sentenced to 20 years in prison in February, 1968 after Rockwell's assassination, the lightest term that could be imposed for murder at that time, but was freed on bond while he appealed his conviction. He was eventually ordered to start serving his sentence in 1970 but was paroled less than five years later, in 1975. The judge in his murder trial, Charles S. Russell, wrote a lengthy letter to the parole board supporting his early release. However, when Patler breached the terms of his parole, he was returned to serve another six years. He finally got out in 1983.

The prosecutor at Patler's trial was Commonwealth Attorney William Hassan, who had been involved with Rockwell before on a number of occasions. In one particularly embarrassing incident in 1959, Hassan and Shaffer, his assistant, took part in a police raid on Rockwell's then HQ, a rambler on Williamsburg Boulevard in Arlington, expecting to find a huge weapons cache. All they found was a pistol, a revolver and a few rifles — and some birthday cake. They hadn't realized that that day, April 20, would have been Hitler's 70th birthday and that Rockwell and his troopers would be celebrating it. Never one to miss an opportunity, Rockwell offered them some cake and then snapped their photograph at his home, which he sold to a local newspaper (7). Patler maintained throughout that he was innocent, appealing his case to the U.S. Supreme Court, which in 1972 declined to hear it. Much of the evidence presented at trial was "largely circumstantial," a state court of appeals noted, and there was considerable concern about the conduct of the police during the investigation of the crime.

Patler had been taken out of an interview room and walked past eyewitnesses sitting on a bench without his lawyer being aware of what was happening. Even so, they failed to identify him as the man they had seen running from the scene. Police also searched his father-in-law's farm without a warrant, but the appeals court ruled in 1974 that the land concerned was common ground, 200 feet outside a fenced area around the farmhouse and outbuildings, and therefore Patler had no expectation of privacy. The police recovered spent bullets and shell casings that matched the 7.63 mm Mauser pistol used to kill Rockwell, but Patler said he and others frequently went target-shooting in that area. Robert Lloyd testified that it was his gun and that he had lent it to Patler in 1964. When he asked for its return the following year, Patler told him it was lost or mislaid.

The prosecution also failed to disclose until late into the trial that 17 soil samples taken from Patler's shoes failed to match anything along Patler's alleged escape route and that the shoes didn't match prints found on the beauty salon roof. There were no hairs or anything else to connect him to a cap and a coat found abandoned along the route that witnesses said looked like the clothes Patler had worn, and no fingerprints on the gun. However, the trial court ruled that all that was "neutral," not "exculpatory" evidence. Patler maintained there was no evidence that the gun was in his possession when Rockwell was shot.

His defense attorneys said he had been three miles away at the time of the shooting, running errands with his wife and child.

Some Nazi Party members were skeptical that Patler had shot Rockwell, while others thought that he had not acted alone. According to an FBI memo, one ex-Party member said Rockwell had expressed dissatisfaction with Dad, shortly before he was shot, and that Rockwell believed that Dad "was trying to establish an intellectual coup d'état in the NSWPP."

Frank Smith, Rockwell's bodyguard and an alleged organized crime member who was married to Rockwell's secretary, Claudia, conducted his own investigation of the crime. He claimed he had been tasked by Rockwell himself to do so in the case of his sudden death but he never ended up proving anything. Smith testified for the defense at Patler's trial. Former Nazi Party members who had quit, disaffected with Rockwell's leadership, including Karl Allen, the founder of the American White Party, also believed other Party members were responsible for Rockwell's death (9).

Quite why Patler shot Rockwell, if he did, I don't know, although there were reports that he was angry and felt betrayed at being thrown out of the Party. There were also theories that Rockwell might have been having an affair with Patler's wife, according to a post on "Stormfront," a white nationalist website. Another theory held that Patler might not have killed Rockwell, but was allegedly set up to take the fall for the murder by Robert Lloyd and Matt Koehl.

By some accounts, Patler may have suffered from mental illness. His mother had deserted his father, taking the then-five-year-old boy and his younger brother with her to their grandmother's home in Harlem. His father tracked her down and murdered her, subsequently serving 10 years in prison as a result. When he was released on parole, his sons were sent back to him, despite reports of child abuse.

At the time of writing, Patler is still alive. He is in his 80's and has reverted to his birth name of Patsalos. He lives in New York and was still drawing in 2017, contributing illustrations to High Times magazine for $500 a month (10). At the time of writing, his son, Nick, is a professor of African American history at a university in West Virginia. He wrote in an afterword to a biography of Rockwell that his father is ashamed of the time he spent as a Nazi and calls it "'a period of temporary insanity.'" But with the current climate of hate in America, he may be changing again. "Now it seems, little by little, he's becoming poisoned again," the younger Patler said in an interview after a Nazi demonstrator ran down a young protestor at the rally in Charlottesville, Va. (11).

Patler was by no means the only Nazi upset with Rockwell's leadership style and his lawyer suggested at trial that it could have been another ANP member who pulled the trigger. There had been some reports that two men were involved in the shooting. A year later, a source told the FBI that he believed that my father had something to do with the assassination because he and Koehl had had "an acrimonious showdown" with Rockwell the night before (12).

"Things were in constant chaos. One damn thing after another. People were fighting with each other and organizing mutinies," Dad said. "People had to be gotten out of jail. I thought to myself, 'I couldn't put up with this,' I'm never going to do anything that is dependent on defective people like this. I've got to have normal, moral, capable people around me if I am ever going to get anything done…that was the most important lesson I learned from Rockwell." (13)

Rockwell was a drunk and a hypocrite who flouted his own rules and frittered money away. He required troopers to swear an oath not to smoke, curse or drink "and keep it sacred, as I do myself," he wrote in an issue of his "Rockwell Report." (14). But members complained behind his back that he was drunk much of the time, and smoked and cursed. He defended his smoking by saying his corncob pipe was a "sort of trademark" and that he was exempted on cursing because, for professional appearances, he had to swear to shock people. "But in private conversations, neither I nor any of my members…use foul language," he said. (15).

Money was a constant problem for Rockwell — he had funded the launch of the ANP through donations from sympathizers, mainly from the South. "We operate simply on the little guys in the movement who go out and work, and old ladies who dip in the sugar bowl for a dollar," he said in a radio interview, but when he wanted to impress people, he would brag about the money the Party was receiving in donations. Yet he couldn't afford to keep a promise to hire a pilot to etch a swastika in the sky over Washington, D.C. on Hitler's birthday in 1964. Regardless of his claims of solvency, his most pressing problem was money — the ANP had no logical accounting system. "When there is money in the bank, Rockwell spends it freely. When it is gone, he curtails his activities once again and begins critical campaigns for additional funds." (16)

His income came mainly from dues, initiation fees, sales of mail-order hate literature, and "Hatenanny" records and jamborees on patriotic holidays. Unknown to most of his supporters, he also secretly ran several front organizations that had no overt connection with the Nazi Party so that he could capitalize on anti-Communist sentiment. Members were sent to solicit funds door-to-door and Rockwell raised cash himself on speaking tours. His typical pitch was that he had "big business" backers, such as a brewery-owner in St. Louis, just waiting for the Party to get off the ground before forking over substantial sums. "Many people are unaware of the real nature of the ANP and are duped into contributing to it as a means of fighting communism. One woman in New York contributed $1,500 before she learned the true nature of the group," the FBI said.

But things were so bad at times that Rockwell and his troopers subsisted on cat food, or beans and canned hash. When a supporter occasionally brought over food for them, Rockwell kept the best bits for himself and his troopers had to be satisfied with the leftovers, one complained. Additionally, they were all frequently left sitting in the dark. Utilities at Rockwell's HQ and at the troopers' barracks were constantly being cut off for non-payment and even his "hate bus" was repossessed by the bank. (17)

Rockwell also had problems dealing with dissent. In 1964, six members signed a petition listing their grievances, and seeking redress. They complained that he had not accomplished many of the ANP's goals and took him to task for his "one man rule" and demand for "unbinding loyalty" to himself. They wanted the Party's structure altered to allow it to be governed by a board of directors. They got nowhere. Two of them were expelled and the others resigned, some leaving to form a rival white supremacist group, the White Party of America, in New York.

Even after his death, there was a touch of farce about George Lincoln Rockwell. His family wanted a private funeral in Maine but the NSWPP and Matt Koehl said they had obtained verbal approval from federal officials to bury him at Culpeper National Cemetery with full military honors as accorded to veterans. Dozens of Stormtroopers and supporters accompanied his body to the cemetery but were met at the gates by U.S. Army MPs, backed up by dozens of police officers drafted in from various jurisdictions. They were told that they couldn't bury Rockwell unless they followed Army protocol and would have to remove their Nazi uniforms first. They refused and there was a day-long stand-off before the NSWPP backed down and took Rockwell away, stashing his body at a funeral home. They had him cremated the next morning. (18)

According to the FBI, a source told agents that Dad was the custodian of Rockwell's ashes but I don't believe that was true. I don't think he would even have wanted them.

CHAPTER 11

THINGS FALL APART, THE CENTER CANNOT HOLD

As kids, we knew nothing of Rockwell's murder. My parents never discussed it in our presence; we had no access to TV, and no interest in newspapers. It wasn't until college that I learned what became of the man some called the "American Fuhrer." All we knew at the time was that Dad wasn't home because he was "away on business." I can't say we were saddened by his absence. Mom later admitted that she had lied to us — Dad had gone into hiding because he feared he, too, would become a target. He was right, in a way: FBI agents were busy reporting on all his activities, collecting information from infiltrators, and adding his name to special indexes.

By January 1968, agents were reporting that their sources claimed Dad was trying to take over the National Socialist White People's Party, as it was then called, and planned to remove the "hardcore" members loyal to Rockwell. Then, in April, someone from the NSWPP's National Socialist World voluntarily appeared at the FBI Alexandria, Va., field office and said they hoped to keep undesirables, "such as convicted criminals," out of their organization. Those particular FBI records don't name the person, but I strongly suspect that the informant was my father himself.

It's clear from FBI records that agents had infiltrated the NSWPP and received detailed reports of Party meetings from more than one source. At one meeting, Dad apparently talked about erecting an 8-foot-high chain link fence around the building for security; at another, in late 1969, he was asking for the location of theaters that would be showing a movie about Martin Luther King. He had also discussed joining an anti-Nixon protest march with 12 uniformed troopers but was apparently stopped by the police.

FBI concerns about Dad grew after he addressed students at the University of Scranton, Pa., in April 1970, calling the U.S. "weak, decadent, rotten and corrupt," and led by a President (Richard Nixon) "who should be dragged out of office and shot." He predicted there would be a race war in the U.S. within 10 years but evaded questions when asked exactly how he planned to rid the U.S. of blacks and Jews. "We might ask all the blacks to return to Africa, or else. Of course, it would probably be 'or else.'" (1). "This may come to machine guns and Molotov cocktails, but it must be done," he said. "We invite you to join us." The FBI feared his speech before 450 students would lead to protests, but students just reacted with "laughter but no violence," agents reported.

To the FBI, Dad was not only a menace but a pain in the butt. However, they discovered, to their chagrin, that there wasn't much they could do about some of his activities.

Dad started calling for the assassination of U.S. senators. Agents learned of a message he recorded on an NSWPP phone-in service after they received an angry late-night call from the floor of the U.S. Senate. On the other end of the line was Sen. Claiborne Pell, (D-R.I.), demanding to know why the FBI hadn't "ripped out" the NSWPP phone line. Pell said just that afternoon he had asked the U.S. Justice Department to get an injunction to silence the recording, which urged that Sens. George McGovern (D-S.D.), William Fulbright (D-Ark.) and Mark Hatfield (R-Ore), be shot. "The whole rotten bunch need a bullet between the eyes," callers to the hotline were told. (2)

Alexandria, Va.-based FBI agents were told to get copies of the recording and to ask the U.S. Attorney what could be done. And the answer to that question was not a whole helluva lot. U.S. Asst. Attorney C.P. Montgomery told them that the messages were not prosecutable. There was no evidence to establish a violation of the federal interstate commerce law because Dad had not transmitted the message across state lines, but merely left a recording on the phone line. Also, there was a question as to whether the message actually constituted a threat to do injury, Montgomery advised.

By now, the FBI knew Dad carried a gun and tagged him in their records as "Considered armed and dangerous." Agents wanted to go further, pushing to include him in a special Security Index because of his threats against Nixon and other key figures in the executive, legislature and judicial branches, but FBI HQ said there wasn't enough evidence to justify the move. Instead, Dad was added to the FBI Agitator Index.

Around this time we were living in Triangle, Va., and it was there that Dad started attracting unwelcome press coverage that made life even harder for us and for Mom. Dad had bought a state permit to sell guns, paying all of $5.75 for the privilege, and had set up a company called NS Arms Inc., running ads in his various publications promoting "Guns for Use as Negro Control Equipment." Several brands of lethality could be purchased, new or used, by phone or by mail order, and there were no real security checks.

On offer were pistols, riot guns and semi-automatic rifles. A used Walther P.38 semiautomatic, promoted as the "standard German side arm during WWII," was priced at $69.95, a brand new Derringer was $39.95, and a Remington rapid-fire pump action riot gun — "the perfect weapon for self-defense and crowd control" — could be had for $94.95.

Gun-fanciers could also buy a new "Volunteer" semi-automatic carbine "with nearly unlimited fire power" and a magazine that held 30 rounds and "shoots as fast as you pull the trigger." It was available for $99.95, and the ammo was $7.40 per 100 bullets. Chemical mace was available also in two handy sizes — the largest canister held 80 bursts of mace and would "control a whole crowd," he promised. (3)

And he kept blasting away with his message of violence. He said Americans should arm themselves, and "not just with a pistol under your pillow at night," if they wanted to protect themselves and beat the coming federal ban on mail-order weapons. "You should have at least a semi-automatic rifle with several hundred rounds of ammunition," he advised.

To my delight as a kid, Dad actually did sleep with a gun under his pillow. I used to creep into his room to play with it when he was away. I suppose I'm lucky to have survived. His gun business made it into the papers, including the Washington Post. In answer to the Post's questions, Dad claimed he didn't sell "to just anyone" but took special steps to stop weapons falling into the wrong hands. Those "special steps" turned out to be a statement printed on all order forms that required customers to declare that they were older than 18, had never been convicted of a crime punishable by a year or more in prison, and were not "a fugitive, a drunkard, drug addicted or mentally incompetent." In an interview, he told the Post, "As long as it looks like a legitimate order, we go ahead and fill it. If it looks suspicious, we check with the police …we tend to attract unbalanced people, kooks, as you know." (4)

Years later, he boasted that the inflammatory ads for his gun business were just a ploy to get press attention. "My purpose was not only to supplement my scanty income, but also to attract the attention of those persons most likely to be responsive to my ideological message... The mass media jumped for the bait. Headlines such as 'Extreme Rightists Aiming for Race War' appeared in newspapers all over America and were even picked up by a number of European papers. I became somewhat of a celebrity, and my gun business thrived — until the federal gun control law of 1968 went into effect and virtually outlawed mail-order sales of firearms." (5)

I'm glad Dad was happy with his strategy, because we certainly paid the price for it.

Our neighbors saw the stories and soon Erik and I were being harassed and beaten up by local kids. We became known as the "Neighborhood Nazis" and people told their children not to mix with us. Some of the papers also printed our address. Mom was really scared and wrung out her woes in a letter to my grandmother, Marguerite Pierce, after the stories started appearing. She sent her a copy of an article in the Fredericksburg, Va., paper, noting that a similar piece ran in the weekly Triangle, Va., paper, which would remain on newsstands for a week.

"Unfortunately, the local paper also printed our address here. Another article on the same line appeared in the Washington Post last week. There was another reporter here this morning!" she wrote. "The repercussions for this could be very serious — all these so-called 'kooks,' including Rockwell's murderer, now know where to find us. It also wouldn't surprise me if the owners of this house try to break the lease. Marguerite, I still love Bill very much, but I think he is asking too much of this family. I begged him not to get the gun license at this address, but he wouldn't listen. He realizes now that it was a mistake." (6)

In the immediate aftermath of Rockwell's assassination, Matt Koehl became the new NSWPP leader and took control of the Party's assets. The NSWPP operated under Nazi principles, which said that the Party leader was the sole decision-maker and held all power, as Koehl reminded members at a hastily convened meeting before they voted him in as the new commander. (7)

Lloyd was named No. 2 and Dad was No. 3, serving as the Party's information officer. Dad's role was to produce National Socialist World and record messages for the NSWPP's hotline. The recordings changed weekly but always featured anti-Semitic and anti-black rants. The Party had phone services in Washington, D.C., California, Louisiana, and Ohio, and in early 1970 launched another in Miami. In a press release bragging about the "White Power Message Telephone Service," Dad bemoaned those "misinformed journalists" who called them "hate messages." Rather, he said, he was giving the public "vital information" that they couldn't get elsewhere because Jews controlled the media and distorted the news, and attempting to "foster a feeling of racial consciousness and White racial solidarity." (8)

Dad was also the official NSWPP photographer and bail bondsman, taking pictures at protests, carrying a wad of cash to bail out troopers arrested in brawls, and hitting the college speaker-circuit, picking up $200 fee per speech, plus expenses (9).

When Rockwell died, Dad did something that he had previously resisted: he became a member of the NSWPP, a decision he came to regret. He felt indebted to Rockwell for helping him launch National Socialist World, which gave him a platform for his views on race and eugenics. Rockwell also provided an initial mailing list, and subscriptions were rolling in. He didn't want "everything to fall apart" and tried to help Koehl keep things going. "In retrospect, that was a mistake. I should have quit and gone my own course," he said later. (10)

There had been splits in the American Nazi Party before Rockwell's assassination. Among those to quit was Karl Allen, a Harvard graduate who had joined the party in 1961 but left three years later to form the White Party of America after an argument with Rockwell. Allen acquired the ANP's printing plant in Spotsylvania, Va., and used it to print books and run a smear campaign against Rockwell — after which the plant suffered two mysterious fires. Allen initially accepted police reports of Rockwell's murder but then came to believe that the Anti-Defamation League may have been behind the killing and set up a defense fund for Patler. (11).

Three years of mayhem followed the assassination. There were squabbles and purges, potshots taken at members' homes, burglaries, and obscene phone calls, all of which my father described as a "cadre-building" phase that consolidated the NSWPP into "a serious revolutionary organization with professionals." Koehl, Lloyd and Dad tried to keep the Party together but without Rockwell as its figurehead, the NSWPP imploded. Dad himself was expelled by Koehl at a rancorous meeting where he was threatened with physical harm, according to FBI agents, who dismissed the threats as just talk by people trying to "look tough."

Dad was regarded by some Party members as an elitist; some even called him a traitor to Rockwell's ideals. He was always pushing for a new look to the Party, to make it less clownish and more appealing to the college-educated. He sought unsuccessfully to persuade Rockwell to abandon the brown Stormtrooper uniforms, the swastika flags and the Nazi salutes at public demonstrations, and continued to campaign for those ideas after Rockwell died.

Relations with Koehl had been strained for some time. Koehl suspected Dad and Lloyd were in cahoots, working against him, coup-plotting being a common pastime in the NSWPP. The feud finally exploded in the summer of 1970, when Dad sent Koehl a 12-page memo saying that they should build a new U.S.-style NSWPP and forsake the old German model. There were no more Hitlers; a leader like Hitler came along only once in a lifetime, and Koehl should relinquish some of his control of the Party so that potential new leaders could be identified and developed, he said.

Dad's June 1 memo detailed his plan for a new National Socialist Party, and added for good measure allegations of theft and fraud. (12)

After receiving the memo, Koehl retaliated, writing to members portraying himself as a strong and capable leader and accusing Dad of being a "clever and conspiratorial weakling challenging his authority." Lloyd, who Koehl hoped to retain in the Party, was just a "good natured fool" duped by Dad into conspiring against him.

Dad had said that his big concern was the lack of progress. They were three years into Rockwell's four-part plan to win power and had barely started on Phase II, a cadre-building exercise to convince the American public that they were a legitimate party. There would be more mutinies and declining membership and dues if they didn't see some successes. "And by 'successes,' I do not mean the drumming up of any more Phase I newspaper or TV publicity through Storm Troop-type fiascoes." For 11 years they had relied on protests to show people that the Party was still active, he said, actions that revved up the base but projected "a weak and ineffective image" elsewhere.

They should stop parading around in brown shirts, boots and armbands and instead adopt "more of the humble attitude of missionaries" if they wanted to win converts "who are racially sound, whether liberal or conservative, hippies, truck drivers, or businessmen," he said. "We will need fighters in the future…real fighters who must be prepared to kill and be killed, for we will certainly face some real brawls…in which hardened fighters with real armament will give us a lot rougher time than the couple of scuffles with college kids we've seen so far." The Party should also abandon the one-man leadership concept and give officers individual responsibility and autonomy. "If, by remote chance, a man with abilities approaching those of Hitler's came to us now, he would take one look and then begin building a separate party of his own from scratch," he said. Officers should be free to make decisions and there should be a regular exchange of information among the top echelon — Dad, Lloyd and Koehl — so the Party could "serve as a revolutionary instrument for the liberation of the [white] race."

Then, in a memo to Party members whom he considered loyal to him, Dad dropped a bombshell — he claimed that Koehl had transferred Party funds to a secret deposit box that he held under his own name (13). Dad had found a receipt for the safety deposit box Koehl had rented three days after receiving Dad's memo. The Party had only started keeping regular financial records after a raid by the Internal

Revenue Service in 1965 and before then, it had operated on "a hand-to-mouth basis," which was a "chaotic state of affairs," he said.

By 1968, the Party's finances had been looking healthier. Income had reached $3,500 a month, increasing to $4,000 monthly in the first half of 1969. Then, in June, there was "a substantial fall-off" in weekly deposits — Koehl had been skimming as much as $400 a week and squirreling it away in his safety deposit box, Dad alleged. Over the next six months, the shortage rose to $500/monthly. Then Koehl took out $2,000, almost all the money in the Party's account, and put it into his deposit box. Dad had unwittingly written checks against that money. When they bounced, Koehl admitted what he had done but refused to return the cash and Dad ended up having to cover the loss with the $1,000 he kept in an office safe for bail bond payments.

For any one man to decide he is answerable for his actions to no-one is "intolerable," Dad wrote. "Today we have no Adolf Hitler, inspired by Providence, in our movement and we must get along somehow with more-or-less ordinary men and women," none of whom can be allowed to do as he pleases with the Party funds. Not surprisingly, Koehl didn't appreciate Dad's memo. He waited until Lloyd was out of town, then called a meeting of about a dozen people, not all of whom were Party members. "I was then accused of attempting to usurp the Party's leadership, organize mutiny, and several other things," Dad wrote. The meeting degenerated into "a disgusting and embarrassing" shouting match. "An attempt was made to intimidate me, with thinly veiled threats on my life." When he refused to resign, he was expelled from the Party.

Returning the next day, he found the lock on his office had been changed and Lloyd's house had been broken into. He posted armed guards at the house and the Party bookstore, which Lloyd operated and which was a source of revenue for the Party. When Lloyd returned, he discovered that several hundred dollars' worth of private property had been taken. (13). An inside look at the events that followed was provided to me by H. Michael Barrett, one of Dad's early supporters, who was present that night. (14).

Barrett said he wasn't a Party member but was Dad's first street activist, breaking the bones in his hands in fights against so-called left-wing demonstrators. He was also Lloyd's bodyguard during a tour of TV and radio stations and had been asked by Koehl to go with Lloyd to visit Frank Collin, the NSWPP's Chicago leader. Koehl believed Collin was secretly "an ethnic Jew" after Collin's father published a book in which he said he was Jewish and that his real name was Cohn. Koehl wanted Collin to quickly and quietly resign. On their return journey from Chicago, a wheel nearly fell off their car "because of mysteriously loosened lug nuts," Barrett said.

Meanwhile, Koehl started to undercut Dad by criticizing those who supported him, including his secretary, Earl, who he pressured to resign. The next day, Koehl's security chief, Chris Vidnjevich, tried to physically push Earl out of the front door but ended up going through the glass paneled door himself. Koehl reassigned Earl to the NSWPP's bookstore and circulated a rumor that he was insane. Then he scheduled the surprise meeting, excluding Dad's most obvious supporters. A messenger was sent to order Barrett to go on a one-man demonstration. "I was to be asked to handcuff myself to the White House fence and spend a night in the D.C jail, which was populated nearly 100% by black inmates," Barrett found out later. Barrett was in the bookstore with Earl and Koehl's messenger couldn't find him.

Next, Koehl sent someone to seize the book store's cash receipts. Before Barrett could close the door, another six NSWPP members arrived, one armed with a shotgun, but all they did was recite what they'd heard and seen at the meeting. After an hour, Barrett was able to get rid of them and lock the door. With Earl armed and the store secure, Dad asked Barrett to help him take possession of Lloyd's house. The printing press that the Party used was in the basement of Lloyd's house and some of the NSWPP troopers had keys to the place.

Since Dad was the only one armed, he searched the house and came back to report that there were three Party members working in the basement. He suggested Barrett casually send them on their way, telling them that he was taking armed possession of the house. Dad gave Barrett his own revolver, "a .38 with an extremely unusual, light aluminum frame," and left. As Barrett went to get rid of the men in the basement, he bumped into Koehl's messenger. The man wasn't armed and Barrett said there would be a physical risk to anyone forcing their way into the house. He told him to tell Koehl that he wouldn't be accepting any more "suicide missions" and that if anyone tried to break into Lloyd's house, he would have no choice but to shoot them.

Barrett secured the house but soon realized that it would be unsafe to wander too far from the front room. Vidnjevich had been through the house with a group of loyalists who had searched all the living accommodations, including Barrett's. They had been into Lloyd's office, looking for paperwork that might reveal what Lloyd and Dad had been communicating. The diary of Lloyd's wife had also been examined, but revealed nothing more than her spiritual contemplations. Lloyd had a large gun collection in the house, including the Mauser used by Patler to kill Rockwell, which had been returned to him by the court. He also had some of Rockwell's personal effects. Later that night, a Party supporter climbed over the fence to try to find out what Barrett was doing. Barrett kept the lights off and the man left, perhaps suspecting that Barrett had a gun trained on him. Two more attempts were made that night, one by Vidnjevich. Barrett said he slammed an inner door with as much force as he could muster to make it sound like a gunshot. Vidnjevich leapt off the steps and chambered a round into his automatic, but did nothing more.

Dad told Barrett to answer any phone calls to the house and explain to Party members what was going on. Among the callers was Joe Tomassi, a prominent member of the California Nazi unit. Occasionally, Vidnjevich also came on the line, threatening Barrett. Later, a Party supporter, Richard Bierderman, threw a large rock at the front door, but then left. When Lloyd got home, he asked Barrett for one last favor: to remain at the house while he took an axe to break into his office across the street at HQ. Lloyd chopped his way through the door, and once in, called Koehl and loudly demanded an explanation, punctuating one point by punching his fist through a plaster wall into Koehl's office that bore a long picture of a Nuremberg rally.

Conversations in the following days led to a truce of sorts, during which Lloyd went about his normal business, moving between headquarters and his home, testifying in court against Patler, and running the book shop, where he owned most of the stock. It was decided that Dad would move on, for he would have found it too suffocating to remain under the now more assertive Koehl, who had issued his own memo about obeying "the leadership principle."

Dad's focus was now on advocating revolution and Koehl's on founding a National Socialist religion, Barrett said. Dad and Lloyd decided to move to new offices in Washington, D.C. and Koehl's people watched as they moved the book stock out, at one point hurling a brick through the window. Lloyd later replaced the window with a plastic one and the next time a rock was aimed, it bounced back on the young man who had thrown it. They used the books to form the stock of a new store, Western Destiny Books, located on the first floor of Dad's new office. According to the FBI, in 1971 Lloyd and Dad had a falling out — Lloyd couldn't pay the rent on the bookshop and my father kicked him out because he needed the rent money to keep himself afloat. He leased the space to someone else and Lloyd left radical politics altogether.

Of the people involved in the aftermath of Dad's expulsion, Bierderman was killed while serving in the Rhodesian (now Zimbabwean) military when a bomb blew up under his military vehicle. Tomassi, who played a minor role in a dirty tricks campaign organized by the Watergate conspirators, was gunned down in the street by a Party member during a split in the Los Angeles Nazi group. (15)

Vidnjevich had several run-ins with law enforcement and at one point was arrested after firing 55 shots during a half-hour gunfight with Frank "Boston Blackie" Smith III and his wife, who were then living in Maine. A white supremascist, Smith was still calling himself a "bishop" of his tax-exempt Church of Christ in Israel as of January, 2019. He set up the church following his 1964 release from prison after serving a long sentence for a bombing the home of a civic leader in Massachusetts — the police believed that he got the wrong address. He was associated with Rockwell, who once said that he was thinking of naming Smith the Nazis' chaplain. He married Rockwell's secretary, Claudia, who was 20 years his junior. Smith was a figure in multiple FBI investigations, was a known associate of mobsters, and had links to Rhode Island mayor Brian J. Sarault, who was sentenced to five years in prison for racketeering. Vidnjevich's attempt on Smith's life was not the first — previously, Smith was hit with five bullets during a mob war. After Vidnjevich's attack, Smith said he was targeted because he had tried to prove that someone else had shot Rockwell. He believed Dad, Lloyd and Koehl masterminded the assassination, and that Vidnjevich had pulled the trigger. Vidnjevich was later convicted on a lesser charge of assault and fined (16).

As for Barrett, he helped run a white nationalist mail order business for a while with Earl, Dad's secretary, and eventually moved away from the NSWPP to form another white nationalist group.

Dad predicted to all who would listen that the American Nazi Party under Koehl would collapse and fade away because Koehl didn't have the character or brains to lead it. The party did splinter, with one faction breaking off and forming the National Socialist Party of America in Chicago. In 1982, faced with recruiting problems that they blamed on the concentration of military and government employees in the Washington, D.C., area, Koehl moved to the Midwest. He bought an 88-acre property in a Milwaukee, Wis., suburb — appropriately called New Berlin - and changed the NSWPP name to The New Order. He announced that National Socialism was a religion, that Hitler had been sent by God to rescue the white race, and that his suicide in 1945 was "a voluntary, Christ-like sacrifice" to prepare for the return of National Socialism. He then gave up all the swastika garbage and disbanded his Stormtroopers. After his death in 2014, the group was led by a former Rockwell disciple, Martin Kerr.

CHAPTER 12

A FAREWELL TO ARMS AND A NEW ALLIANCE

In his farewell to the NSWPP troops, Dad said he was withdrawing from the field of battle but it wasn't a promise he would keep for long —actually, for only about two months.

In a letter to those he deemed loyal to him, Dad warned that the Party had been "seriously damaged" by Koehl's incompetency and insistence on being the one and only leader. If a revolutionary movement is not fortunate enough to have someone of Hitler's caliber to lead it, "it had damned well better find some other way of governing itself," he said. Knowing Koehl's propensities, "I will not be at all surprised to see the Party retrench into a sort of Matt Koehl Nazi Fan Club, consisting of a few dozen members and supporters within the next few months."

"I am planning no further Party activities for myself and I can imagine the disgusted reaction of Party members and supporters everywhere," wrote Dad. "…I have no intention of attempting to form a separate faction in the Party or of founding a rival Party. My immediate problem after four years on a Party salary of only $50 a month is to find some remunerative work for myself inside the Movement, which will allow me to once again to support my family and relieve my wife of that burden." He signed the letter "Heil Hitler!" (1)

Dad folded National Socialist World magazine after only six issues, saying it had "just too small an audience," and began casting around for another venue for his views. Then he saw a TV interview with the head of a group said to be fighting the 1960s "counterculture" and trying to recruit students to take on left-wing activists, including the Students for a Democratic Society.

The camera was focused on Louis T. Byers, an organizer for the Wallace campaign in Pennsylvania and front man for the National Youth Alliance (NYA), a right-wing group set up by Willis Carto. A virulent anti-Semite and shady moneyman, Carto was bankrolling several ultra-conservative groups, including his well-known Liberty Lobby organization. Later, he was found to have been playing shell games with the millions in donations and fees he was raking in, such as by asking donors to help him pay off mortgages on property he already owned and for which he had been charging them rent.

The NYA grew out of an earlier entity called Youth for Wallace, which Carto created to support the presidential ambitions of George C. Wallace, the segregationist governor of Alabama who was running as an independent in the 1968 election. Carto campaigned for Wallace but when Wallace lost the race, Carto lost interest in him. He turned the remnants of the Wallace group into the National Youth Alliance and handed day-to-day operations over to Byers, a longtime friend, giving him a mailing list of 24,000 sympathizers to tap for donations. (2).

Byers led the National Youth Alliance from 1969 to 1971 but by the time he met Dad, the organization was all but moribund and Byers wanted to unload it. He said he would soon have to fold it because he couldn't raise enough money in donations to cover the costs. It was already $500,000 in debt and within a couple of months would run out of credit (3).

It was just too good an opportunity for Dad to pass up. He told Byers that he had to give something in order to get something from donors, such as demos, campus activities, and a paper geared to young radicals. Dad said he could deliver all that and more, and offered to pick up the group. In December, 1970, he registered the NYA as a corporation in Virginia, rented office space in Arlington, Va., and put Byers' name on the letterhead as leading the NYA advisory board. Next, he used $2,000 he borrowed from Byers to print a new tabloid called "Attack!" and mailed it to 15,000 of the names on Carto's list. To Dad's great delight, it brought in $6,000 in donations.

A few months later, Dad took over the operation. It was to consume the rest of his life, stealing all that he had left to give and leaving not a shred for his wife and kids. Even when he died, the only reference to us was a line in his will acknowledging that he had had two sons.

The NYA had been splitting into factions, even as Dad appeared on the scene, riven by rival groups supporting different racists. One bunch remained loyal to George Wallace, while another bloc backed Carto and his latest fascination, the recently deceased Francis Parker Yockey.

Byers had started a society dedicated to the memory of Yockey, an American attorney and polemicist who travelled the world preaching his Fascist philosophy and proclaiming that the U.S. was run by Zionist Jews. The FBI had been tracking Yockey for years and finally caught up with him in California after his suitcase was sent to the wrong airport. When authorities opened it, they found seven false birth certificates and U.S., Canadian and British passports under seven different names. It was enough for the FBI to arrest Yockey on charges of using a false passport. He committed suicide in a San Francisco jail cell in 1960 at the age of 42. A week before his death, Carto had visited him in jail and promised that he would promote his book, "Imperium," which claimed that Germany would one day rule the West. It was never clear how Yockey got hold of the cyanide he swallowed, only that a capsule was found next to his body, but his book became a seminal work for the Far-Right after Carto re-published it.

When my father and his supporters joined the National Youth Alliance, it split in two. Wallace supporters quit first, and then the Yockey disciples and Carto's loyalists protested the influence of the National Socialist wing and were ousted by Dad's supporters, leaving him in control of the whole shebang (4).

Dad went on to play a minor, but meaningful part in Carto's eventual downfall. After firing spitballs at each other for some time, Carto sent an invoice for $40,000, saying it was his rental fee for the mailing list that Byers had given to Dad. Carto also had theft charges filed against Dad, accusing him of stealing Liberty Lobby mailing lists and selling them, even though they were the same lists he had given to Byers. Carto complained that Dad had used the lists to send "poison pen letters" criticizing Liberty Lobby's chiefs, and the upshot was that Dad was charged with receiving stolen goods.

Dad sued Carto for libel, saying Carto had routinely rented out his mailing lists, while promising his donors that he would never do such a thing. Dad claimed Carto had bilked his followers out of at least $50,000, citing an emergency appeal for funds Carto had made to donors, claiming that the Liberty Lobby could no longer afford the rent on the building it leased. Donors responded generously, with Carto subsequently telling them that he had received so many contributions that he had been able to buy the building outright. Dad produced a copy of a Liberty Lobby newsletter showing Carto presenting a $55,000 check to the bank that held the mortgage. Trouble was, he said, the photo was a fake. He had found documents showing that a different Carto front group, the Government Educational Foundation, owned the building. In effect, Carto had been collecting rent from the Liberty Lobby for premises he already owned, and then more cash from donors to buy it all over again.

Carto's case against Dad went to trial on Nov. 16, 1971. Judge Alfred Burka dismissed the case because the U.S Attorney dropped the criminal charges. Dad didn't bother pursuing his libel case against Carto. By then, the Liberty Lobby's influence in Washington, D.C. was waning (5).

I don't think Erik and I ever met Carto, but we were chased around the Virginia suburbs by 'Carto's men," at least, that's what we were told at the time. Either way, it was a thrilling ride.

Mom had to be at school on a Saturday, so Dad took Erik and me to Northern Virginia with him. He didn't speak to us at all during the drive up and I spent the entire trip up Interstate 95 staring out the window and taking in the sights. When we arrived at his office in Arlington he told us to sit down and be quiet and then disappeared. After about an hour, a couple of young men who were hanging out at the office came up to us and said, "Hello, boys, why don't you come with us. Your dad said we should keep you occupied for a while." The men were in their 20's and kind of looked like thugs, wearing dirty slacks and white t-shirts, with tattoos on their arms. Neither of us felt comfortable with the idea of going with them and didn't move. Then one of them said that we shouldn't be afraid because we were just going to go for a ride around town.

We followed them hesitantly, climbing into the back seat of the station wagon. After driving for only a few minutes, the man in the passenger seat told "Jim," who was driving, that we were being followed. Jim focused on his rear view mirror, and said, "I think you're right, it looks like some of Carto's men. Let's try and lose them." He then mashed his foot against the gas pedal and we raced off down the street, tires squealing. He made sudden turns without braking and we were sliding side to side, all over the back seat. Jim and his buddy were laughing, but seemed deadly serious about losing whoever was following us.

Soon we were all caught up in the game of cat-and-mouse and having a grand time. It was a real adventure and we were as involved in the chase as the men in the front seat. It went on for about an hour or so. To be honest, I was never really sure that we were being followed at all but it was great fun. Soon after we got back to Dad's office he told us it was time to go back home. Excited, I tried to tell him about our adventure but he simply wasn't interested, so I just shut up and we were quiet the rest of the way home.

I remember being puzzled by the two men in Dad's office because they didn't seem to be all that intelligent. Over the years, I would see similar people at Dad's gatherings. It was as if he were surrounded by weirdos, mostly young men who had nothing better to do than hang out with other small-minded thugs, making themselves feel better by putting down other people.

"Attack!" was now Dad's monthly newspaper. It was pretty much the primary focus of the National Youth Alliance at that time and was supposed to incite young people to wake up and get involved with White Nationalism. Every month he would come home with his car full of freshly printed newspapers and envelopes and set them up on a painted plywood table in the living room, where Erik and I had to put a newspaper into each envelope and then seal it with a wet sponge. He called it "stuffing and sealing" and I absolutely hated it.

We would spend hours indoors after school, several days each month, stuffing and sealing thousands of envelopes. Sometimes, he would surprise us and come home in the middle of the month with a special issue and demand that we start work immediately. We would look pleadingly at Mom, begging her to intervene, but she wouldn't. She explained once that the Carto guy had launched a smear campaign against Dad and that he needed to respond with a special issue of

"Attack!" I remember feeling really mad about it all and scratching the words "I hate Carto" into the top of the plywood table. Erik told Dad, who came over to look at what I'd done. I hoped he might be proud of me, but he just growled and told me to get back to work.

At least he didn't beat me.

Carto seems to have spent much of his life in courts. After Dad's claims against him, an article in the National Review exposed the web of organizations that Carto secretly controlled and the revenues of "at least a million dollars" a year that they brought in. Carto sued, and William F. Buckley Jr., the editor of the Review, sued him right back. The case dragged on for 14 years, but the magazine won in the end. Carto lost in court again after he failed to pay a promised $50,000 to anyone who could prove that Jews had been gassed in Auschwitz. A California survivor produced evidence and eyewitness testimony — including his own account of seeing his mother and sister gassed —and sued when Carto didn't cough up.

Later, Carto declared personal bankruptcy after he and the Liberty Lobby were sued over who was the rightful owner of a $16 million estate. The money was left to another Carto entity but Carto claimed it was left to him personally. After years in court, Carto lost again and was threatened with forced liquidation of his personal assets (6). But although his conservative empire had been defanged, he kept going, setting up yet more organizations until he died in October, 2015.

As for Dad, in August, 1970, two months after being booted out by Koehl, he published a 4,000-word document, "Prospectus for a National Front" that became the not-so-successful blueprint for the National Youth Alliance. He had grand ideas on how to build a National Front that could seize power but things didn't quite work out the way he hoped, as he admitted a few years later in an article that partially blamed Carto for his failures.

In his prospectus, he argued that a "large-scale revolutionary movement" was needed to save the white race from extinction but existing radical groups were not capable of building it, as their "unbroken record of failure" showed. They were mostly "overgrown children" who spent their time talking about what things will be like "when we come to power," but never did anything about it. He said any tactics would be acceptable —even "illegality and terrorism."

He believed that Communists were behind the massive anti-Vietnam demonstrations in the streets but most of the people giving clenched-fist salutes were ordinary, decent Americans who didn't realize how they were being manipulated and thought they were simply showing their opposition to an unpopular war. Brainwashed by Communists, he said, college liberals think they're fighting for individual freedom, "parlor pinks" believe they're struggling for social justice, and frustrated women feel they need to be liberated. Pacifists are working for peace and priests hope they're helping "humanity." Mixed in with all those are kids who only want to smash things and opportunists who see "a Judaized, Bolshevized, and mongrelized world" as the future, he argued.

As the Communists use diverse groups, so could the National Front. They could steer people in the direction they wanted them to go by representing — "or even misrepresenting" — their goals. When organizing policemen who hate revolutionaries, the Front should talk not about building a "White people's revolution," but rather about fighting Bolshevism and anarchy. On the other hand, when talking to radicalized university students, "we can speak much more freely of smashing the System and building a new order," while being more discreet when talking about racial matters to students than to policemen. "We must carefully consider and then use – not ignore – the prejudices and special interests of each element in the population to which we wish to appeal. We must always remember that our immediate aim is power — the capability for mobilizing and directing the energies of large masses of people," he maintained.

Lording over the whole National Front would be a supergroup of leaders — organizers, propagandists, fundraisers, and other competent people dedicated to building a broad-based white people's revolution of "liberals and conservatives, longhairs and hardhats, policemen and student radicals, truck-drivers, businessmen, and housewives."

The base would consist of separate groups, linked only through the superstructure, which the Front could use to exploit specific situations. Unseen, they could coordinate the activities of middle-class property owners in, say, New Jersey, for whom "respectability" was all-important, with blue-collar workers in Michigan, for whom rough-and-ready activism was the key. Coordinating various groups would allow them to seize new opportunities to build the revolution. Organizers would help solve problems, like how to hold rallies, run a political bookstore or a revolutionary print shop, install a recorded-message phone service or produce a newspaper. Front staffers, meanwhile, would train the organizers at special workshops, helping to spot new talent for HQ.

As for propaganda, National Front staffers would help local groups print their own monthly tabloids by providing content, including national and international news items, editorial cartoons, features, and even local news stories. In effect, local groups would have their own newspapers to promote their grassroots cause, while the Front controlled the essential thread of unity of purpose among all affiliated groups. If his followers moved now, they could build "the largest possible power base with the greatest possible speed," Dad concluded.

Of course, the prospectus was meant to be an internal document only, laying out his grand strategy. For public consumption, the NYA promoted just a four-point program. It would banish from campuses dangerous drugs and narcotics, which, of course, it said was associated with black students; neutralize "black power" and the "unjust demands" it made on the educational community; fight "anarchist groups" like Students for a Democratic Society; and oppose U.S intervention in foreign wars, such as the "no-win" war in Vietnam.

CHAPTER 13

DAD AND MARGUERITE

Dad married five times in all, but there was only one woman he truly cared about and to whom he was loyal to the end: his mother, Marguerite Pierce. She wasn't terribly affectionate in return, which perhaps is one reason why he was never able to show love to Erik and myself. My mother was terrified of her but, to her credit, Grandma did urge Dad to think again when he told her he was dumping us for his new, all-consuming love — National Socialism.

Dad never had any money to speak of after he decided to go full-time Nazi but Grandma Maggie was always a reliable source of funds. She even paid for the train tickets he used to bring his then-latest amour, Olga Skerlecz, down to Virginia from New Haven, Conn., where she had been living with relatives after arriving from Hungary. He found her, like all his subsequent wives, by advertising in a magazine. She was Wife No. 3.

I'd like to say that Grandma was a sweet, white-haired old lady without a racist bone in her body, but that wouldn't be true. She shared all Dad's anti-Semitic views and didn't hesitate to let you know that. If it's possible to be an active accomplice while standing on the side lines, she was certainly that. Dad told her of his loves and woes, and she offered her opinions and advice.

Grandma was born in 1910 in Richland, Ga. Her parents were both schoolteachers and her father was the son of Irish immigrants. She preferred to believe, however, that she was a member of the Southern aristocracy because her great grandfather, Thomas Hill Watts, had served as Attorney General in the cabinet of the Confederate President Jefferson Davis, and later as Governor of Alabama for a year. However, the family fortune was destroyed by the Civil War and all that was left was the old Watts family home in Montgomery, Ala., the place she grew up.

Her parents separated when she was not quite two-years-old and her mother took her back to the Watts family home to live with her grandparents, who both died within the next two years. While her mother worked, Grandma was raised by two maiden aunts, her mother's unmarried sisters. When the First World War came, the family rented out rooms to servicemen and their families. One of the soldiers was Alan Stern, a mess sergeant from New York who married Grandma's mother. Grandma was eight-years-old at the time. He died when she was 11.

"He was a man of bad character and repeatedly betrayed the family and squandered what little resources it had with his drinking and gambling," Dad wrote in Grandma's obituary. "On one occasion he forged Marguerite's mother's name on a check and ran off with every penny the family had. He also attempted to sexually molest Marguerite."

Stern was Jewish and some people have claimed that her relationship with him was the cause of her virulent anti-Semitism. Dad always disputed that suggestion, saying she had only mentioned that her stepfather was Jewish toward the end of her life. Either way, he said, the three years she spent with Stern had made a "lasting impression on her, which contributed to the difficulties she had with personal relationships for the remainder of her life."

Alcohol played a prominent and tragic role throughout Grandma's life. For some reason, she seemed strangely attracted to heavy drinkers — her father and stepfather were both alcoholics, and so was her first husband and her last, whose love of the bottle eventually killed him. Grandma was 19 when she married. She started work at an insurance company when she was 17, straight out of high school. Two years later, she married my grandfather, William Luther Pierce II. He was 37, worked for Aetna Casualty Co., and his best friend was the bottle. He hated the insurance business and wanted to return to the Merchant Marine, where he had served three years when he was younger and happier.

Talking to Uncle Sandy last year, I can see where Dad learned some of his habits, at least in the parenting department. Grandfather Pierce never played with his sons when they were young, or even interacted with them, and was drunk much of the time. Alcoholism runs in the family. Uncle Sandy remembers when his father took them for a ride in their car. His dad was so drunk that he passed out at the wheel, ran off the road, careened into a ditch and then into a tree. Uncle Sandy and my Dad weren't hurt and the police just took them home. They never arrested his father. Uncle Sandy remembers, too, when his father died. He was drunk again, on his way home from a bar. He got off the bus and walked straight into traffic, into the path of a car driven by a teenager who couldn't stop in time. It was 1943, and Grandma Maggie suddenly was a 32year-old widow with two young sons to raise. Just a year before his death, my grandfather had quit Aetna and set up his own business, the Pierce Insurance Agency in Norfolk, Va. He left her with a life insurance policy that helped supplement her $25 weekly salary as a secretary, but little else.

Grandma had no choice but to return with my father, then aged nine, and Uncle Sandy, six, to live with their uncle in Montgomery, Ala. Uncle Sandy says he remembers his uncle quite well. He was the head of road construction for the state and had a black man, an ex-convict who had murdered a fellow black man, as his personal servant. Uncle Sandy remembers the servant going out into the back yard to kill a chicken. He cleaned it out, throwing the innards into the woods. When he returned to the house with the chicken, Uncle Sandy's uncle asked where the liver was because he wanted to eat it. The servant said it was out in the woods, with the rest of the guts, and was promptly sent back out to crawl around with a flashlight until he could retrieve the liver and bring it back. Perhaps unsurprisingly, Uncle Sandy and Dad did not like living in the house. At night, there were huge rats running around in the bathroom, and they were scared to go to the toilet. He recalls, too, he and Dad getting into terrible trouble when they got bored and sat on the driveway, tossing pebbles at passing cars.

After about six months, Grandma Maggie's uncle said it was time for her to leave. She loaded her sons and their few possessions into an old Chevy and drove west, ending up in Dallas, Tex., a few weeks later. Uncle Sandy says he never had any real relationship with Dad when they were growing up because Dad was interested only in his own hobbies, like chemistry, to the exclusion of everyone and everything else. He never wanted to play in the woods or do normal kid stuff and he believes to this day that Dad didn't care much about him.

Listening to him talk about Dad now, I can see my father again. He just never grew out of being the selfish, self-absorbed kid he was, he just got bigger and older. Dad helped out at their new Dallas home by washing the family's clothes in the bathtub with a washboard, and earned money for himself by delivering newspapers and mowing lawns. With his earnings, he built model rockets and radios and bought chemicals and apparatus for a small lab that he built in his bedroom — that is, until he set fire to his bedroom curtains and sent a friend to the hospital with second- and third-degree burns. After that, he and his lab were banished to the garage.

Six years later, Grandma fell quite madly in love with her new and very married boss, Cyrus Weller, the owner of a struggling refrigerated trucking company. They began an affair that lasted nine years. He was the "one great love of her life," Dad said. He promised to divorce his wife and marry her, but never did.

Grandma was heartbroken when the liaison ended. She packed off Dad, then 15, and Uncle Sandy, 12, to military school and moved 350 miles west to Midland where, lonely, she married Lanford DeVeny, "a man wholly unsuited to her," Dad said. She had been married to DeVeny for three years when she heard that Weller had divorced his wife. She quickly did the same to DeVeny and contacted Weller. Not only did he decline to marry her, but went off and married another woman. Her heart in smithereens for a second time, Grandma fled to South America where she stayed for four months.

Dad hated every minute he spent at Allen Military Academy but learned a skill that was to serve him well — how to manipulate others while pretending to be their friend. He even managed to finagle a job cleaning up the stockroom of the chemistry lab and, as he put it, "used the opportunity to continue my self-education in matters scientific." He'd been an avid consumer of science fiction until his teens, when he graduated to reading Scientific American.

He talked about his new-found ability in a letter to Grandma in February, 1950, as his graduation neared. Thanking her for money she had sent him, he celebrated the fact that he had only 90 days left before he could get home to Midland, Tex. "It will certainly be a relief to be out. The boredom of Allen Military Academy is driving me crazy," he said. "In my two years at Allen, I have developed a thorough dislike for this place, its society, noisiness, dirtiness, military uniform and activities, and especially its absolute lack of freedom and independence."

Nevertheless, he was grateful for his time at Allen. He had matured mentally and emotionally more than he could in twice the time elsewhere. He had learned, too, about different kinds of people, "how to act around them and how to control them. (This will help me a lot)," he noted.

He had also developed a new philosophy of life.

"… I have found that the most successful policy is to have as a prime objective one's own self-betterment by any means possible. Besides the few close friends, it pays to have contacts, or tools, in other persons who think you like them, whether you do or not. It also pays to have society keep the idea of you that you want them to," he wrote.

"I have tried to learn how to not show off and how to keep my eyes and ears open, but my mouth shut. One can use society for his own self-betterment, if society has the right opinion of him, yet one need not constantly associate with one's contacts and tools for them to have the right opinion. If someone sees too much of you, and knows all about you, he is likely to find you uninteresting and boring. He is also likely to find faults which he didn't know about previously."

At first it seemed to be an un-Christian attitude but "I lost my conscience" at Allen. "The main thing is not to let any of the tools or contacts realize your true feelings," he said. He went on to win a full academic scholarship to Rice University in Texas and the check from his father's life insurance policy paid for his accommodation and living expenses.

Dad used to have robust debates with Grandma over her views on scientists and physicists. She thought that they lived in a world of their own — Dad assured her that they usually did. She was particularly hostile about J. Robert Oppenheimer, the American son of German-Jewish immigrants, who researched and designed the atomic bomb. She compared him to Klaus Fuchs, a German-born British scientist who helped develop the A-bomb and was sentenced to 14 years in a British prison for passing information to the Soviet Union. She regarded them both as dangerous and feared that, somehow, her son would be lured into Communism, too. "Look at Klaus Fuchs — he sold out to Russia, and he was quite a scientist," she wrote.

"I don't see what Klaus Fuchs has to do with the case," said Dad. It was 1954 and by then he was studying at Rice. "Could I justly say that all office-workers are of doubtful integrity because I read about 3 or 4 who were traitors and heard about 200 more who once were Communists? Oppenheimer is not even accused of being guilty of treachery, yet you say he may be innocent???????? It has come to a point now where a person is considered comparable to a Communist spy if he is merely controversial." Oppenheimer is "quite a long way from being 'a thug,'" he said. "He is one of the most highly respected men in the world, among scientists. His contributions to modern science (including U.S. defense) rank among the greatest of his time. He is one of the few responsible for the U.S. being able to end WWII with the A-bomb."

Dad never approved of any form of help for the working class, even then. One of the things "that burns me most" is that men like Franklin Delano Roosevelt "are held in high esteem, while men who are responsible for the progress of humanity are generally looked upon with contempt and quite often are even in danger of the stake," he said.

As for Grandma's lament that scientists seemed to live in a cloud, apart from everyday life, Dad told her that, to a large extent, that couldn't be helped.

"Research physicists are required to devote their whole lives to almost nothing but physics. There is so much to learn and the nature of the material is so complex and completely foreign to everyday life that any person who really wants to do anything in the field must more or less isolate himself from everything but physics," he said.

Most of the physics professors at Rice would be considered 'characters' elsewhere, he said. "The typical physicist is not susceptible to communist ideology. Such things as the 'plight of the poor labor classes,' etc. are of no concern to the average physicist. In general, physicists are violently opposed to any attempt to limit their freedom of action, speech or thought, and therefore the Soviet type of government would appeal to them even less than the U.S. type."

"You certainly needn't worry about my naivety leading me into communist sympathies," he told her. He was critical of the government because of the "totalitarian ideas" being favored, such as Social Security, progressive income taxes, and the increasing power of trade unions. "I certainly have no desire to see these things grow worse, but I believe they will, mainly because of increasing populations."

Grandma really piqued his interest when she told him in one letter that she was sharing accommodation with a woman physicist. Dad, who was at Caltech by then, was surprised. "This is another example of the perversity of nature in general, or in particular, an illustration of the fact (?) that when one needs something, it is never available, but on the other hand, if one can't use something, there is plenty of it," he wrote.

"In this case, the something is women physicists. I have always wanted to meet a woman who could speak my language, but have never had the opportunity. At Los Alamos, I saw one once but never had a chance to do anything about it. It would be nice to have a woman here in Pasadena with the same sort of problems I have."

While his question seems wistful, his remarks give no hint of his views in later years — that was that women should stay at home, tend the house and family, and help continue the species.

In another letter, he told her that he had heard Supreme Court Justice William Douglas on a panel at Caltech, giving his views on civil liberties and conditions in the Far East. "Seemed considerably more frank and intelligent than any other political figure I have heard before. I wouldn't mind seeing such a man President, if he weren't a Democrat."

When we were kids, Grandma would visit us once a year, usually at Christmas. She was always neat and well-dressed, with lots of jewelry and bracelets that she picked up on her international travels, usually to Africa. She was tanned, thin and athletic-looking and wore lots of makeup. Her hair was white but she always looked great and very wealthy, at least to me.

Grandma never liked Mom. When Mom and Dad were courting, she advised him to bed my mother if he must, but, for God's sake, don't marry her. For once, Dad didn't listen to her. She was hard on Mom all the years I knew her. She would sweep in and immediately start criticizing Mom's housekeeping, her personal appearance, her weight, and how the house wasn't up to her standards of cleanliness, always upsetting Mom and sometimes reducing her to tears. Once, after I started college, I heard Grandma rip into Mom and it made me furious. I told her to stop being such a bitch. She never spoke to me again after that, but I have no regrets over standing up for Mom.

Grandma was a veritable fount of advice, especially when it came to Dad's articles and exhortations about Hitler — she always spelled his name "Adolph" — and Jews. In one classic Grandma letter, she enclosed a recipe for sweet potato-apple casserole that she'd found in a newspaper. She said she hadn't tried it, but thought it looked good. She also sent a clipping about J. Edgar Hoover and mentioned in the same breath that her 99-year-old mother-in-law had pneumonia and that her heart might not hold out for long.

Then, with the standard pleasantries over, she moved onto my father's latest articles for Rockwell's magazine, hectoring him about his Hitler worship. His writing was "exceptionally good" and his editorial was excellent — "up to the long quote of Adolph Hitler." Stop going on about the man, she said. "Hitler is presumably dead and buried. People have been brain-washed about him for twenty years, more or less. HE IS NOT THE ISSUE, NOR IS HIS HISTORY THE STORY YOU HAVE TO TELL. Besides capitals, that statement needs underscoring and bold lettering. The story you have to tell is HISTORY ITSELF."

Dad should be writing a book telling the story of "Jewish conniving from beginning to end — or present," she said. "Tell it in an interesting, readable style. Don't be too intellectual for the general public, but, principally, DON'T ADOPT THE STYLE OF ROCKWELL by haranguing and trying to arouse the ignorant...." With all the information and intelligence Dad possessed, and the writing ability he demonstrated, he could influence a lot of people. "But believe me, honey, you've got to forget Hitler. Let him take his place in your historical account, but quit trying to make the world worship him," she urged.

Then it was back to being sweet-old-lady Grandma. She had bought "two darling little wool jackets for the boys" for our birthdays, she said. "In the meantime, take an evening out on the town occasionally. Life's not worth living without a little fun and loving."

Grandma Maggie started sending us plane tickets when we were about 10 years old so we could visit her in Texas. Mom and Dad would never go on these trips with us, but sometimes our cousins would go along. On one trip, she took us all camping in the wilderness at Carlsbad Caverns National Park to see the caverns. We also rode into Mexico on the back of donkeys with her. You couldn't say she wasn't adventurous.

She became interested in creative writing while in Texas and spent two years as a student at the University of Texas in Austin. In 1964, she moved to Odessa, 30 miles west of Midland, and founded a monthly social magazine called "Odessan." I was in high school and had gone to visit her but she had nothing planned for me to do when I got there, so I ended up helping her as she chronicled the social life of influential people in and around Odessa. She would go around and visit small businesses, attend social affairs and take pictures, documenting the happenings around town and selling advertising for the magazine as a way to fund it. She edited and published the magazine for 14 years. She also managed to write two novels and a number of short stories, but she was never able to get them published.

I found unintended humor in some of Dad's letters to her, of the-pot-calling-kettle-black variety, though I'm sure that he would ever have seen the irony.

In one letter, Dad thanked her for a copy of a publication called "The Councilor" that she had sent, then dismissed the publisher as "an all too common sort among professional conservatives" and slammed his efforts as a mere bid to enrich himself. The man was Ned Touchstone, a former Democratic congressional aide who published several weekly newspapers in Louisiana and Texas. He was a professional researcher and one-time journalist who opposed the civil rights movement and a board member of Carto's radical right Liberty Lobby.

According to Dad, Touchstone's publication had "at least a partially correct orientation on race and Jews," and was "generally more accurate than other right-wing papers (which isn't saying much)," and has the largest circulation of publications "which are unfriendly to the Jews."

Touchstone was "apparently a patriot for profit" who had "become wealthy by learning what conservatives want to hear and then telling it to them." He went on to castigate Touchstone because "he also takes in quite a bit of money through various sidelines: the sales of books and gadgets via his paper and an investment-counseling service." Of course, Dad did much the same thing but that, apparently, was different. "I have not, however, heard that he is a crook or a pervert like Willis Carto — only that he is out to make as much money as he can."

Grandma also needed to "be wary of investment advice from professional right wingers," Dad wrote. "There are an awful lot of nuts in that crowd, and the ones who are not nuts themselves cater to a clientele which is a bit nutty." While Touchstone was undoubtedly a good businessman, "he does peddle some screwy financial ideas because he's found that conservatives will buy them." Touchstone tends toward the conspiratorial, Dad said. Everything is a conspiracy, from the suppression of various cancer cures by the AMA so doctors can make more money carving up cancer patients, to water fluoridation, which Touchstone saw as a communist plot to poison everyone. "I don't know whether the man you met has sound advice to offer or not, but I'd be careful," he warned Grandma.

Grandma had two male friends that I recall. One was very nice and I remember him being there when we visited her one year in Texas. He took us to a giant slide park and to a 'Whataburger' eatery to get burgers and I was happy for a change. They were going to get married but he developed cancer and died shortly before their wedding. The other man was Balie Griffith, who was older and very rich. Grandma had bought a struggling travel agency in Odessa in 1983 and tried unsuccessfully to turn it into a profitable operation. She met him in 1984 when she sold him some airline tickets. His wife had died the previous year and she married him soon afterwards, when she was 74 years old. The marriage was rocky and lasted fewer than five years. Balie drank, she scolded, and Balie drank more.

But Balie was very generous, and that helped to grease the marital skids. I remember that he accompanied Grandma when she came to our house one year during my college break. He gave me $500 in cash, which was a fortune to me at the time. But by 1988 his alcoholism was keeping him hospitalized for weeks at a time. In January 1989, a month before he died, he and Grandma were divorced. He left her a house in Odessa and a monthly stipend that covered her living expenses.

Grandma died in May, 1999, at Uncle Sandy's house in North Carolina. She was 88, had Alzheimer's disease, and had suffered at least two strokes. She showed increasingly severe symptoms between 1995 and 1997, including loss of memory of recent events and flashes of uncontrollable rage, and injured herself in falls. She broke her shoulder while working in her garden in Odessa and, unable to get up, remained outdoors in the rain all night and nearly died from hypothermia. When she broke her hip in another fall, Dad and Uncle Sandy put her in a nursing home in North Carolina in 1996. The next year she had a third accident. She lost control of her wheelchair, which then ran down the driveway and into a fence. She never recovered from the third episode. When Dad visited her later the same month, she was conscious but couldn't speak and didn't recognize him. A few months later, she was moved to Uncle Sandy's home. She spent her last year there, unaware of her surroundings. She was unconscious and fed through a tube for several days before dying quietly and without pain.

Through all her travails, Grandma remained a tenacious, strong-spirited woman. Many of her views were and are still abhorrent to me but I cannot say that she was ever boring.

CHAPTER 14

GUERRILLA WARFARE AND THINGS THAT GO BANG IN THE WOODS

It wasn't until much later that I realized that I may have been Dad's unwitting accomplice in some dangerous and dubious experiments in our basement and in the woods behind our home. But I have to admit that, dubious or not, I enjoyed playing my part in them very much at the time. The FBI probably would have been happy to know, too — by this time, agents were going to some lengths to discover what Dad was doing with the chemicals he was buying, and where he was doing it. They believed he kept at least some of them at the Alliance bookshop in Washington, D.C., but actually he stored them in the crawl space of our house.

Given all I've learned since about his calls for mayhem and murder, I have to wonder why he was messing around with such things at home. I'd like to think Mom's constant pleading with him to be a better father might have been one reason, but maybe I served a dual purpose for him.

My involvement in his experiments started when he came home one day and handed me a box. I was 9 years old, I think. He seemed very pleased with himself. I looked carefully at the box but couldn't figure out what it was. "It's a chemistry set," he said, eventually. "You mix chemicals together and observe what happens."

Of course, Dad being Dad, he said I'd have to learn all about chemicals and their properties before I could even open it, and then handed me a copy of the "Periodic Table of Elements" and told me to memorize it. Every day after that, he would sit down with me and quiz me on the elements. I pretty much hated it. I tried my best, but really wanted to be outside, playing in the woods.

A few weeks later, he gave me a brand new slide rule and told me how to use it. I tried hard to understand what he was teaching me, but I just couldn't get it and I could tell he was growing frustrated. Perhaps he thought that by cramming science down my throat he could make me into a mini-him, and get Mom off his back about being such a terrible father.

Anyway, after I learned most of the elements, he started showing me some simple chemistry experiments using the chemicals from my set. He would explain to me what each chemical was and how to measure proper portions and how to use a beaker and test tube to mix and observe reactions. But it was never in a nurturing way; it felt like punishment because he would get so impatient all the time. He wanted me to love chemistry, as he did as a kid, but I just couldn't.

He continued for a few more weeks trying to get me interested by telling me stories about the fun he had with chemistry when he was a kid. He told me how he would mix up a substance using iodine crystals. It was stable when it was wet but became very unstable as soon as it dried and would explode if you disturbed it at all.

"All you have to do is touch it, and then POW!" he explained. Now this was more interesting. He told me that he'd make a small batch of the stuff and apply it to a classmate's school book cover. "When the kid opened up his book in class it would explode and blow the cover off the book," he said. "I would also put it under the legs of a school desk and when a kid sat down, there would be an explosion that would lift the end of the desk off the floor." We were both laughing at that and I found it hard to imagine he did such fun stuff.

"I would sneak over to my neighbor's house and smear this stuff onto their doormat or into their front door key hole and then run away," he told me. "When the neighbor got home it would explode when he stuck the key into the door, or the mailman stood on the mat. It was great fun!" I was amazed, and asked, "How did you know if it actually worked?" It was simple, he said. "I would read in the paper the next day about the guy being rushed to the hospital with a key stuck in his abdomen!" I laughed so hard when he said that, and I still smile about it to this day. It was a side of him that I'd never seen before.

Dad sharing stories with me and laughing like that was the closest I ever felt to him and, in all honesty, it is the only memory I have up to that point when he interacted with me in this way. I really admired him but was also very afraid of him. He still never touched me unless it was to hurt me and never said how he felt about me, except to explain to me why he was going to hit me. The only other thing he would talk about were the racist facts of life. I just wanted him to be proud of me but for some reason it was more important to Dad to hate blacks and Jews.

Occasionally, Dad would tinker with experiments at home. One day, when I was 9 or 10, he was at the dining room table working on something. He had a car battery and a car spark coil hooked up to it with a few other gadgets. I was in my room listening to the radio when I heard Dad yell "Midget, come here!" I wondered what I had done this time as I reluctantly shuffled my way to the dining room.

"Midget, I need you for a second to see if this works," he said, pointing to the contraption on the table. I stood there for a second in surprise that he wasn't about to beat me. "Sit down and put your finger right here," he said, indicating a small metal screw fastened to some wires. I reached forward hesitantly — I wasn't the least bit sure that it was something I wanted to do.

"Go ahead, it won't hurt you," he barked impatiently. I placed my finger tip on the screw head and immediately felt an incredible jolt of electricity shoot up through my hand and into my arm. The muscles in my arm locked and I felt an intense pain as I instinctively yanked my hand back.

The jolt was pretty severe and I recoiled so violently that I fell backward and ended up on my back on the floor, still in my chair and with my feet sticking up in the air. I lay there for a few seconds, dazed by the jolt. By this time Dad was laughing so hard that I thought he'd bust a seam. I picked myself up slowly and kind of looked at him, wondering why he would do that to me. Between fits of laughter, he said, "Yep, it works, thanks Midget." Then, without another word he turned his attention back to his experiment and proceeded as if I wasn't there. I went back to my room feeling hurt, but also with some satisfaction. Dad had just shocked the crap out of me but I had a good feeling because I was able to make him laugh, which he rarely ever did.

I remember another neat experience with Dad when he decided to teach me how to make a bomb. First, he showed me how to make gunpowder. He had me collect charred chunks of wood from the fireplace and showed me how to use a mortar and pestle to grind them into a fine powder to produce carbon. Next, he got sulphur and potassium nitrate, which he called saltpeter, from my chemistry set, grinding them up too, and mixed the three compounds together. Then he produced a thick cardboard tube, glued D-size batteries into each end of it, and drilled a hole in the center, filling the tube with the gunpowder mixture. He made a fuse by soaking a string in a wet substance (I seem to recall he said it was glycerin) and rolled it in the gunpowder until it was fully coated. He stuck the end of the string into the hole in the cardboard tube and the bomb was finished.

I enjoyed watching him do it and I was very impressed at his patience and the precision of his work. It was one of the rare times when I wasn't afraid or felt threatened. I think in his own way Dad wanted to have a relationship with me but just didn't know how. Most of the time during my childhood, his mind was elsewhere, so our relationship was never able to develop normally.

"What are you going to do with it?" I asked when he'd finished making the bomb. "Well, I'm going to blow something up," he replied with a devilish grin. We went outside with the bomb. He looked around for a few minutes until his gaze settled on our firewood pile in the backyard. He carefully placed the bomb into a gap between the logs near the bottom of the pile and lit the fuse. We ran about 100 feet away and waited. Suddenly, there was an incredible explosion and dozens of logs went flying into the air and rained down over the backyard. I know that I had a huge grin plastered on my face and Dad was laughing. We looked at each other and smiled from ear to ear. I thought it was just the coolest thing ever.

Eventually, after a few months his interest in playing 'chemist' waned. The last experiment I remember was when he had me help make a small batch of nitro-glycerin in our living room. I remember it vividly because Mom stood out in the hallway, sobbing and holding onto a fire extinguisher, pleading with him to stop. We worked with the nitro for about an hour, then he told me to get lost. He took it to the basement and I don't know what happened after that. I do remember that Mom was furious, but Dad just thought it was funny.

Unfortunately, the time we shared doing experiments together changed nothing between us. Dad went right back to being the same man he had always been, but those experiments were a time that I looked back on later as something very special that we did together. While we were blowing up things in the woods, the FBI was investigating Dad's involvement in the handling of explosives.

In the summer of 1971, he had embarked on an extraordinary series of articles that delivered detailed diagrams and instructions on how to make weapons that could kill and maim, explaining patiently in a professorial tone how to use each one efficiently. The articles, under the title "Revolutionary Notes" and "Patriot's Notebook," appeared in "Attack!" his publication aimed at high school and college students. He wrote that they were part of a new phase in the development of the Alliance that would involve "intensive organizing using the most radical and aggressive methods we can devise."

Reading them today, years later, they are still shocking.

There were cold-blooded discussions of the relative merits of various weapons, which were the most suitable for "urban firefights," the best ammunition to use, and how to make improvised firearms, including a cyanide gun. Another article covered the use of explosives, expounding on how to make a Molotov cocktail, the effectiveness of bombing churches, synagogues and theaters as a revolutionary tactic, and the steps needed to build a 100 lb. bomb using fertilizer.

He introduced the articles by saying that they were meant to "arm the patriot with detailed information on urban guerrilla warfare techniques and materiel, thus overcoming the monopoly Marxists presently enjoy in this area." He lifted at least some of the information from publications promoting the very left-wing causes that he so much despised. Other parts of the instructions were available in non-classified government manuals, I learned later.

There were also tips and worldly-wise comments on assassination techniques. He noted, for example, that most assassins are "amateur zealots," while professional Marxists can kill and get away with it. A gun with a silencer would be good, but Israeli and Soviet police use cyanide guns that are "quieter and deadlier." Then he gave instructions on how to make one that involved a piston in a gun that would rupture an ampoule of prussic hydrocyanic acid and expel it in a fine spray. The range of dispersal was six feet and the victim would only have "time to gasp once before collapsing," he wrote.

The one danger was that the assassin would get too close and die, too, he said, citing what he claimed was a case in Argentina where an Israeli policeman's body was found next to the victim. He even offered a recipe for avoiding that. It involved a tablet that was to be swallowed an hour before the attack, and an amyl-nitrate ampoule that was to be sniffed after firing the gun. I doubt very much that his proposed remedy would have worked.

As for firearms, the availability of ammunition was a primary consideration, he said. While guerrillas might be tempted to look for super-power cartridges, they were almost impossible to obtain. Instead, fighters should use ammo that could be "scavenged" from military units, the National Guard or the police. Urban firefights nearly always involve ranges of 100 to a maximum of 200 yards, he wrote, so "except for sniping, long-range killing ability isn't critical."

Semi-automatic weapons would be best, preferably with a detachable box magazine that could be rapidly replaced with a fully-loaded spare. The .30 M1 and M2 carbines were good but several different kinds of rifles should be available with common ammunition, he opined. Shotguns are "a satisfactory substitute," since they are more readily available in homes, stores and police armories and have "an adequate kill-capability at most urban firefight ranges" — an auto-loading shotgun could get off five shots in less than three seconds. As for sidearms, opt for the Walther P.38 or Smith & Wesson Model 39, he advised. Another article, "Survival Tips for the American Jungle," explained how to improvise firearms like a single-shot 12-gauge shotgun which could be "thoroughly lethal at short-to-moderate ranges."

And, of course, there was his advice on how to make a 100-pound fertilizer bomb, which was almost identical to what Timothy McVeigh later used to blow up the Murrah Building in Oklahoma City. Dad said the material "is very cheap, very safe and very readily available in large quantities without red tape or questions for the purchaser." He gave precise instructions on how to make a large or medium-sized bomb, even down to checking the nitrogen content described on the fertilizer label. The fertilizer could be bought at retail for just $3.75 or so in 100-lb sacks at seed and feed stores in rural areas, especially in spring and summer, he said.

The psychology of picking a target was also important. The bombing of a synagogue or a church used by Leftists "does more to relieve the bomber's frustrations than advance the revolution." Marxists made a mistake when they bombed buildings in New York City in 1970, wrecking the offices of Mobil Oil, IBM and others, because the man-in-the-street doesn't lay awake at night stewing about the military-industrial complex, like a revolutionary does. "Proper targets" would be a federal judge who had just made a controversial business ruling, a white school board chairman who had "sold his race down the river," a Washington Post or New York Times editor, or a state legislator pushing for gun control because they all symbolize some aspect of the system with which the average Joe could identify.

According to FBI files, the police in Washington, D.C. said that two incendiary devices had been purchased from the National Youth Alliance. The FBI's National Office Laboratory examined the devices toward the end of October, 1971 and described them as tubular in shape and between 2.5 to 3.0 inches long. The FBI's informant believed that Dad was the chemist who made the devices. He said they were priced at $7.50 each and that the seller had claimed he could also get dynamite caps, fragmentation and smoke grenades, stink bombs and other small incendiary devices from my father. The seller was an ex-NSWPP member who had quit the party because he thought they were not "true Nazis," one FBI report said.

Meanwhile, the firearms enforcement agency, then called ATFD, was conducting its own investigation and had two people under surveillance. They had discovered that Dad was operating a company called ECO LABS, which they said was a fictitious firm with a mail drop address where chemicals and other paraphernalia were delivered.

According to the FBI, ECO LABS was getting shipments from two dealers in scientific equipment. One firm was identified as VWR Scientific, based in Baltimore, Md. The second was Wills Scientific. Both were owned by the same entity and advertised themselves as dealers in lab supplies, equipment and chemicals. The FBI informant said he felt certain that Dad didn't actually conduct chemical experiments at the National Youth Alliance HQ, but that some unassembled explosive devices were kept at Western Destiny Books, the Alliance's bookstore. He also reported Dad had "professional associates" whom he could call on for technical advice.

Dad had placed at least 13 orders for equipment and chemicals, beginning in November 1971 and continuing through March, 1972. One of the shipments indicated that it was a restricted item, potassium chloride, agents said. VWR Scientific sales reps visited customers regularly and the FBI wanted to get access to Dad's lab and get a professional opinion on the set-up. But the VWR executive interviewed by the FBI seemed reluctant to become involved. Dad was "a good customer," he said, and there was nothing unusual or restrictive in most of the shipments he received. "However, he did indicate that the proper combination of several chemicals received could be potentially dangerous," the FBI noted (1).

The FBI did eventually get access to the lab but concluded that no experiments involving the manufacture of incendiary or explosive devices were being carried out there. It was strange reading all the FBI reports on Dad's activities, in part because I remember seeing several jars of chemicals and beakers and flasks with the Wills label on them at home.

Dad had been stockpiling explosives in the crawl space of our house, in readiness for the race war he hoped would start soon. Mom knew about the cache and wanted it gone. She begged him time and again to get rid of it but, as usual, he ignored her. Then something happened, I don't know what, but suddenly Dad gathered up all the explosives and dumped them in the Potomac River. Less than a week later, while he was at work, the doorbell rang. It was the FBI with a search warrant. Luckily for Dad, there was nothing to be found. Of course, Mom never let him hear the end of that, and how stupid and careless he had been to have explosives in the house in the first place. Dad never acknowledged it but I think he was grateful to her for forcing him to act when he did. He had come very close to doing jail time.

Dad did put his chemistry skills to good on one occasion, perhaps. Our cats suddenly started to get sick and in the end we lost them all to feline leukemia. Our youngest, Herman, was less than a year-old and was dying. Dad put him in a box and fed a chemical through a tube he inserted in the lid. We were all very sad but Dad felt that he did the right thing euthanizing Herman — and saved us money by not paying the vet to do it.

He also continued with his role as the disciplinarian. I remember the first time Mom and Dad left me and my brother home alone. We were 9 years old. Dad wanted to go see a movie and, despite Mom's objections, we were left alone at home by ourselves for the very first time. It was a hot and steamy summer night and just as they were getting ready to leave Dad ordered, "Midgets, go to your rooms and get into bed and do not leave your rooms for any reason!" "Yes, sir" we replied in unison, and went to bed.

About an hour later I was awakened by a loud clap of thunder. A large thunder storm was approaching the area and soon the thunder and lightning was lighting up the night sky and shaking the house almost uninterrupted. After a few minutes my brother appeared in my doorway and said he was scared. I was also frightened and so we both ran to Mom and Dad's bedroom and crawled into their bed together and hid under the covers. We were asleep before the storm finally subsided.

The first thing Mom did when she got home a couple of hours later was to check on us. Of course, our rooms were empty. They started searching for us and eventually found us sleeping in their bed. "Those little bastards!" Dad shouted. "I told them to not leave their rooms and just look at them!" He immediately grabbed his razor cord off the dresser and pulled back the covers and started wailing away on our backs and legs. "Bill, stop it!" screamed Mom. By then we were screaming out in fear and excruciating pain. "I told you not to leave your rooms!" Dad yelled as he continued beating us.

By now Mom was crying hysterically and she grabbed Dad and did her best to restrain him while we continued to howl out in pain and confusion. Mom then screamed at Dad "What the hell is wrong with you? They didn't do anything wrong!" Dad looked at me and demanded to know why we had disobeyed him. I just stared at him, blinking through my tears, trying to figure out what we'd done wrong. "We were scared of the thunder," Erik finally whimpered. "Get back to your rooms right now!" Dad ordered. We ran back to our rooms and cried ourselves to sleep. "That was completely uncalled for!" Mom screamed. "You have got to stop brutalizing the boys!"

Mom told me that Dad said he was only trying to teach us to obey orders and have proper discipline. "It's for their own good! I wish you could understand how important it is that they're brought up properly. They need strict discipline in order to become fully functioning and responsible adults." Mom said she just stared at him in total disbelief, then finally shook her head and repeated "What is wrong with you?"

Dad didn't answer. He turned and went to his study, feeling completely misunderstood, and didn't speak to Mom for several days after that.

CHAPTER 15

THE ALLIANCE STUMBLES, DAD TAKES TO DRINK AND KILLS BETSEY

When Dad was gone, I shed my chemistry-set shackles and played in the woods as much as I could. One day, as I trekked up the hill behind my house, I saw a large machine parked at the top of the hill. It was a bulldozer left by construction workers who were clearing the edge of the woods for a new house that was to be built there. It was after school and they were gone for the day. There were neighborhood kids playing in the dirt pile the bulldozer had created, but I was far more interested in the big yellow monster and the raw, earthy smell of its power.

I inspected every inch of it before hopping up into the seat to look at the levers and dials. The seat had a black vinyl cover that was split in a few places and you could see the yellow foam padding underneath. There was the smell of fresh dirt and diesel fuel and hydraulic fluid, all equally fascinating. Then I spotted a small key in a round port on the control panel. I reached down and turned it, and to my surprise and delight, the engine started right up. I was thrilled.

I sat there, pretending that I was the boss and it was my machine. Just as I reached to grab one of the levers beside the seat, a neighborhood parent came running, screaming at the kids in front of

128

the bulldozer, "Get away, get away!" Then he lunged and yanked me off the seat and quickly turned off the engine. "What is wrong with you?" he yelled at me. "You could have killed someone; can't you see other children are playing here?" I stared at the ground and didn't say anything. He grabbed my hand and walked me briskly home where he told Mom what had just happened. I knew I was in trouble and waited for Dad to get home to give me a beating.

Dad looked at Mom. "What did he do this time?" It was his standard question when he got home because I invariably was into some sort of mischief. She told him about the bulldozer and then the strangest thing happened. He started laughing and actually smiled at me with a look that, to me, held a hint of pride. "Well, I guess boys will be boys. No one got hurt, so no harm done," he said. He then asked Mom, "What's for dinner?" I was shocked but happy.

To my extreme good fortune, Dad had come home in a rare, good mood.

Dad had a very bad temper and at times he seemed to explode in rage. He had an old Pontiac Tempest and one morning it wouldn't start. He tried everything, but nothing worked. As I played in the driveway, I heard him cuss over and over again. Then, suddenly he slammed his foot into the dashboard as hard as he could. The dash was made of plastic and it smashed into pieces. We found out later that the car wouldn't start because someone had put sugar in the gas tank. He ended up having to replace the engine, and taped up the dash with a whole roll of tape.

In one of his worst outbursts, he killed Betsey, one of our outdoor Siamese cats.

Dad was making a sandwich for himself in the kitchen and went to the refrigerator to get something. When his back was turned, Betsey jumped up onto the table and snatched a piece of meat from of his bread. Dad turned around just as she leapt from the table with the meat in her mouth. He grabbed her and snapped her neck. It had to be a moment of uncontrollable rage because he adored our cats — in fact, he seemed to love them more than he cared for us, so I guess we were lucky that all he ever did was beat us.

When we got home, Dad said nothing, but it wasn't long before we noticed Betsey was missing. We spent the next few weeks searching the neighborhood for her, desperately hoping she would return. All the while, poor little Betsey was buried in the backyard. Dad eventually confessed to Mom but she chose not to tell us until years later. Erik and I always thought that Betsey had run away or had been hit by a car.

Not too long after Betsey, it was Buckwheat's turn. He killed her in a similar rage, but this time, Mom was there to witness it. Unfortunately for Buckwheat, she didn't die fast. Buckwheat was their very first Siamese cat. Dad got her when she was just a kitten and Mom was pregnant with us, and they both loved her dearly. She was a sweet cat but she was getting old and had started losing weight. Mom took her to the vet who prescribed medication because Buckwheat's thyroid was acting up. The first night they tried to give her the pill, Buckwheat fought back and ended up biting Dad on his hand. Dad flew into a rage and threw Buckwheat into the wall as hard as he could. Mom screamed and he instantly felt bad for what he had done, but it was too late for remorse. Buckwheat was mortally injured from the impact with the wall and died a slow and painful death over the next couple of days. Mom cried for days over the loss of her Buckwheat.

Dad carried a terrible rage inside him and it didn't take much to light his fuse. He would cuss like crazy when things went wrong, which was often. The smallest thing set him off, even having to replace a light bulb would spark a blue cuss-storm. But when he was discussing his beliefs, he never raised his voice. He was thoughtful with his choice of words, articulate and persuasive. When he explained things to me I was certain that he was right because he always seemed to make perfect sense. He had me completely convinced that Hitler was a hero, the author of great deeds, and that the Holocaust never happened. It was the invention of the Jews, who spread massive lies about him and what happened during WWII, he would say.

It was the same when he had disagreements with Mom. He never raised his voice to her and never, ever came close to hitting her, even though they argued many times over the years. But when his temper erupted, he had to throw or break or things. We would get a whipping if we forgot to lift the toilet seat before peeing, or if we didn't say "excuse me" before getting up from the dinner table. I was often the focus of his rage and while he never smashed me to pieces physically, he came close to it a few times. My physical scars have faded but the emotional scars are still healing to this day

Around this time, he started drinking more heavily and sometimes came home pretty drunk, Mom told me later. I never actually saw him that way, but we certainly had visual and olfactory evidence of his new habits.

One morning when I got up, Mom said Dad was sick and still in bed, but had left orders that we were to empty a trash can he'd left in his car. We went outside and opened the car door. There, on the floor in front of the passenger seat, sat his office trash can. I reached in and grabbed it and the first thing that hit me was the terrible smell. The second was that the can was half full of puke, puke as I'd never seen before, orange and almost glowing. I recoiled, dropping the can. Looking at Erik, I said, "You do it!" He took one look and shook his head. "No way!"

We stood there for quite a while trying to figure a way around this chore but we knew what would happen if we disobeyed Dad. Finally, we used one hand each to pinch our noses and the other to carefully remove the can and dump it out in the yard. We then had to wash it out to make sure it was spotless before we put it back in the car. It was an extremely unpleasant experience. At the time, Mom told us that he was sick with a stomach bug instead of telling us the truth — that he'd driven home, totally and utterly drunk.

His favorite tipple was Black Label beer and he would buy it in quart-sized bottles. I guess his habit was becoming pretty expensive because I remember him trying his hand at brewing his own beer at home. He had saved at least 100 empty Black Label bottles and filled them with his homemade hooch. That didn't last long, though, because one night he came home terribly drunk and threw up all over their bed. Not surprisingly, Mom was furious and perhaps he felt some shame, because after that night, he never had another drink, at least as far as we could tell.

Getting lost in the bottle may have been his escape from the troubles besetting the National Youth Alliance that was, from all accounts, collapsing around his ears. He beavered away, trying to breathe new life into the ailing organization, but was not too successful.

He had been building ties with European Nazi groups that he considered to be on a par with the National Alliance, notably Germany's National Democratic Party (NPD) and Britain's National Front, now the British National Party. In 1970, he was due to address an NPD meeting near Munich but local police said they'd arrest him if he tried to speak to the assembled Nazis, so he backed off. Similarly, he had been warned by the British that an exclusion order was to be issued against him and he was not welcome in the U.K. (1) He was reputed to have sneaked into Britain to meet British National Party head John Tyndall more than once after that, but none of his European jaunts helped him that much with the Alliance in the U.S.

In 1970 and 1971, Alliance activities consisted mainly of publishing and distributing "Attack," holding a few demonstrations, and addressing student groups at universities — one student leader who opposed him was Chris Christie, who went on to become the Republican governor of New Jersey. It wasn't much but it kept a steady stream of $100 contributions coming in until the war with Carto burst into full bloom.

Carto had launched a "mass-mail smear campaign," as Dad described it, and his most loyal followers fled, taking their cash with them and creating great financial angst for the Alliance.

What was left were the "run-of-the-mill" conservatives who were largely lacking any "ideological discrimination" and would support anything or anyone that they deemed to be "pro-American," Dad wrote a few years later. (2)

"They boosted the shallowest and most transparent hucksters with the same mindless enthusiasm they bestowed on the NYA," he said. Trying to explain fundamental concepts to them "was like casting pearls before swine," he complained.

Believing he had to do more to mobilize the masses, he began writing his "Revolutionary Notes" series, preaching that "bullets, not ballots" would be required to set things right. But the switch in tone terrified many of the remaining conservatives and they deserted in droves, leaving him with enthusiastic but mostly penniless young radicals. While he gained "bolder, more militant supporters," he realized that there were not enough white Americans to start a revolution and his calls to smash the system "began to sound hollow."

"The radicals may give us their hearts, but conservatives give their money," he noted. The NYA was fast going out onto a limb, with declining conservative support and not enough radical support to replace it. No matter what he wrote or the stunts he pulled, he couldn't seem to boost membership in any significant way. Nevertheless, he kept trying.

His political proselytizing on college campuses was an important part of his strategy but even that wasn't going well. Many of the invitations he received came from student leaders anxious to spice things up for their groups and to brag that they'd bagged a real live Nazi to address their members. But for him, it was still an opportunity to spread his gospel of hate.

In February, 1972, he accepted an invitation to speak at George Washington University and walked straight into a trap. He was pelted with eggs and threatened with physical assault, and the whole event descended into chaos. Students had lured him onto the campus "in order to assault him," said an FBI agent's report. A grey-haired, bearded man at the back of the room had repeatedly baited Dad. "You think you're a pretty smart kike, don't you?" Dad yelled at him. The man then pushed his way to the front of the room, waving his umbrella and pointing it at Dad, telling him to leave. That was supposedly the signal for the attack.

"Suddenly, from all points of the room came a barrage of eggs, which splattered" his head, neck and chest (3). Then, orange smoke from a stink bomb left under a chair began to fill the room. Dad and the student who had invited him stayed behind while the others ran, continuing their eggy onslaught through the slightly open door until security men arrived to disperse them. The Jewish Defense League claimed responsibility and Dad sued the university for $50,000 in damages. He won but he it was a pyrrhic victory. He was awarded only the cost of cleaning his suit (4).

The FBI, meanwhile, was busy investigating him for suspected violations of the Civil Rights Act of 1968, among other laws. They were particularly disturbed by his Revolutionary Notes series and what they called his efforts to establish a "German-type national socialism of the Hitler era, his white racist and anti-Semitic policies, and all the calls for guerrilla warfare.

In one memorandum, agents noted that he had called for the assassination of federal judges, the burning of retail stores, the dynamiting of TV transmitters and newspaper presses, and harsh punishments for whites who fraternized sexually with non-whites in one of his essays (5). They also knew that he kept a fully-loaded .38 Smith & Wesson revolver in his desk and took it home at night. They even had its serial number, thanks to an Alliance informer.

Dad did all he could to attract attention to the Alliance to grow its membership. Some of his actions were almost as crude as those of George Lincoln Rockwell, which he had condemned so heartily, while other initiatives relied on exploiting the law and courts to fight opponents.

He even called for someone to shoot the actress Jane Fonda — the "sleazy heroine of the New Left" — because of her propaganda broadcasts on Radio Hanoi during the Vietnam War. The British had hanged William Joyce, "Lord Haw Haw," for his broadcasts from Berlin during the Second World War, while the American poet Ezra Pound was imprisoned and locked away in an asylum for his Italian broadcasts. Fonda, "a loathsome Communist bitch," had committed treason. As the U.S. government had failed to act, "the people must take that responsibility on themselves," he said.

Even an apparent victory over another of his bêtes-noir, NBC, didn't help recruitment. The NBC affiliate in Washington, D.C. had run an editorial on gun confiscation that didn't sit well with him. He wrote to both NBC and the Federal Communications Commission demanding equal airtime to respond, and got it. It was around Christmas, so I shouldn't think many people turned on their TVs to hear him. Still, it was a weapon that Alliance members could use again — too often, "patriots" mistakenly overlooked the "fairness doctrine" as a way to spread the message, he said.

The biggest gift to him politically came courtesy of the 1973-1974 oil embargo imposed by the Organization of Petroleum Exporting Countries (OPEC) on the U.S. and some European countries in retaliation for the U.S. decision to resupply the Israeli military. Dad eagerly jumped into the fray, writing congratulatory and encouraging letters to the governments of Syria and Egypt and supporting the embargo, the FBI noted. He also sued, seeking an injunction to stop the

U.S. from supplying arms and military equipment to Israel and an order requiring the Department of Defense to retrieve all the arms it had already delivered. He raised $2,000 to fund the litigation but had a hard time finding a lawyer to take on the case. He and two co-plaintiffs, a retired U.S. Army Lt. Colonel and the boss of a conservative magazine, finally got the case into court, only to see it quickly dismissed, a ruling Dad blamed on judicial bias and bad publicity.

"It was a pure stroke of fortune that the latest Middle East flare-up came when it did," he said in a leaflet entitled "Blackmail!" that the Alliance distributed in November, 1974. Millions of Americans understand that they are being asked to walk and shiver "so that Jews can hold onto their stolen real estate in the Middle East," he wrote. OPEC's move to turn off the oil spigot provided the perfect entree for him to establish contacts with Arab groups, the FBI noted.

Dad ascribed to the idea that any publicity was good publicity, whether the headlines were good or bad, and so was thrilled when Russia's official Communist Party paper, Pravda, devoted a full page to an advertisement denouncing the NYA. "It is the most prestigious paper in the

Communist world" and the attack on the NYA "is absolutely unprecedented," he crowed.

He tried to expand his reach to the man-on-the street by selling copies of "Attack!" at commercial newsstands but didn't meet with huge success there, either. The Alliance couldn't sell it through drugstores because store suppliers would not allow retailers to sell independent publications, he said, blaming the Jews who "tightly controlled" the wholesale news business. Alliance members were told to try to get local newsstands to sell the publication but only 80-100 copies were distributed daily on the streets, only about a third of which were paid for.

Then, investigative reporter Jack Anderson dealt a crippling blow to Dad's wallet, asking in a December 1973 column why the NYA was able to get a tax exemption from the Nixon IRS, while genuine public interest groups were refused. Anderson detailed what taxpayers were subsidizing for Dad, including his "dial-a-hate" message service. A recent message at the time offered ideas on how to deal with black student protests on campuses. "There is only one way to deal with rampaging blacks on our campuses and in our cities and that is to kill them," Dad was recorded as saying. Anderson also cited an Alliance fund-raising letter that said "a well-aimed bullet could have stopped the confirmation of Henry Kissinger as Secretary of State."

The Alliance had been given a tax exemption in October, 1973 and Dad marched off to the Post Office straight away, presenting the official notification letter as proof that the Alliance was entitled to the reduced mailing rate that was usually reserved for non-profits. Thus, he saved $100 on every 10,000 pieces of hate mail he sent out. The latest issue of "Attack!" carried a picture of Kissinger in the crosshairs of a rifle scope, advertised copies of "Mein Kampf" and offered how-to books on the construction of booby-traps and explosives, Anderson said.

Anderson's column spurred angry demands in Congress for an explanation from IRS. Rep. Hugh L. Carey, D-NY, noted that the application from the Alliance, an anti-black and anti-Semitic group, was approved just a month before the IRS had revoked the tax-exempt status of a group dedicated to good government. IRS said in its defense that it couldn't check every entity that claimed they were exempt. Following the furor, it launched an audit and then yanked the Alliance's tax exemption. Strangely, the ensuing litigation pitted the American Civil Liberties Union against the IRS, with the ACLU taking up the cudgels on Dad's behalf, citing "free speech" issues.

In 1974, Dad thought a name change might help end the NYA slump, so he renamed the group the National Alliance and lifted the previous age restriction that barred people over 30 years old from joining. But by December that year, the membership boost he hoped for hadn't materialized. He even resorted to Sunday night film shows at Alliance HQ, where he expounded on how wonderful life would be under National Socialism. Then he expanded regular meetings to twice a month to recruit new members. Attendance was mandatory and each member was supposed to bring friends and relatives with them. But the hall he hired for the first meeting ended up only half-full and some of those present were already Alliance contacts. In fact, according to an FBI informant, the composition of the National Alliance membership seemed much the same as when it was the National Youth Alliance — those at the meetings being "mostly long-time, hard-right activists and sympathizers."

CHAPTER 16

THE SEEKER OF TRUTH

Dad's political principles waxed and waned, depending on his needs at the time. I suppose you might say that he was flexible, if you wanted to be kind.

When it suited his pocket, he portrayed himself as a revolutionary who would lead the White Race to the promised land and wouldn't hesitate to use violence to wipe his enemies from the earth. It was an image he sought to perpetuate through his "Revolutionary Notes," telling his followers how to make guns, bombs and other forms of lethality, and the best way to use them. He stole the instructions from left-wing publications but never admitted to that, of course.

Typical of his offerings were calls for the assassination of those he didn't agree with, from government figures to Hollywood celebrities. One target was then-U.S. Asst. Attorney General J. Stanley Pottinger, whose job was to enforce anti-segregation and minority rights laws. Dad's main venue for his venom was Attack!, his crudely written tabloid that the FBI read closely. In one issue, he ran a picture of Pottinger, branding him "Public Enemy No. 1." There was a "Wanted Dead or Alive" headline above it, with the word "Alive" crossed out, and Pottinger's home address and a list of his "crimes" against the white race were included.

But when donation dollars dwindled, he changed his tune. In a long retrospective in National Vanguard, he conceded that readers might have been "misled" because Attack! packaged the truth in a "flamboyant and abrasive wrapper." He never mentioned his role as misleader-in-chief or the years he had spent fomenting fear about Jews and the "festering sore" that was Israel.

He admitted that "to thunder about overthrowing the government when an organization is clearly in no position to do so robs it of credibility," and sometimes Attack! "ventured a bit too close to this pitfall." His new magazine, National Vanguard, would "avoid misleading" readers into believing the Alliance was building a mass movement, a guerrilla army or a secret organization, or that it planned to use direct action against blacks or Jews or the government, except in self-defense.

Instead, he opted for warning that all Jews would be killed, though avoiding any suggestion that the Alliance would do it itself. He talked in one infamous essay about starting an armed revolution against Jewish people. It would mean sacrifice but would be worth it, he said.

"Yes, the great cleansing which must come may destroy millions of our own people, the innocent along with the guilty, the good along with the bad ...but eventually it must come, because otherwise our people will die, and everything that has gone before, as well as everything that might come in the future, will be lost forever," he said in What is a Patriot To Do? "The great cleansing must come, and we must do whatever it takes to ensure that it does, so that our people will live. We should not flinch from this. We should not focus on the fact that it will be horrible and bloody, but on the fact that it is necessary, and because it is necessary it is good."

Sometimes, I think he was totally mad. Or, perhaps he had just found a way to appeal to the sickest fringes of society, so that he could pocket enough in donations to keep himself in funds.

Dad was flexible when it came to the media, too. Like an early Donald Trump, he reviled every journalist who ever drew breath, but courted their coverage at every turn. He would eagerly take calls from print reporters, play his part in documentaries and sit for interviews — especially if there were TV cameras present. It was as if he needed the attention, like some kind of validation of his value and his views.

At the same time, he'd claim that the media was controlled by Jews bent on destroying the White Race and its culture, and fulminated mightily on the matter every chance he got. In one of his most notorious essays, Who Rules America?, he cites what he clearly thought was the proof of his claims — namely, that all the top media executives of the day had Jewish names.

"The Jewish control of the mass media is the single most important fact of life, not just in America, but in the world today. There is nothing — plague, famine, economic collapse, even nuclear war — more dangerous to the future of our people," he proclaimed at one point.

Everything Americans know about events outside their own neighborhood comes from the press, news magazines, radio and TV. Journalists manipulated information by their use of words and tone of voice, by downplaying some stories and emphasizing others, their choice of headline and illustrations, and their slavishly pro-Israeli commentaries. Even dramas, like "Roots" and "Holocaust," are "blatant propagandizing" to mold public opinion, he said.

Then came his 'big reveal,' as they say on TV these days, on how the Jews run the world.

The major networks, ABC, CBS, NBC, are all controlled by bosses who are Jewish, he said, naming CEOs and directors whom he claimed were the "key control points" and had the ultimate decision-making authority. Then he went through the same "spot-the-Jew" exercise with radio and public television executives, followed by the print media, singling out those whose name sounded Jewish to him.

Somehow, he managed to knit together an entire four-page essay through searching out Jewish names and linking them all together. He provides no proof whatsoever for this theory, yet it seems to have gone down well in some circles. For example, he bragged that the Alliance received lots of congratulatory calls and notes when copies of the essay were handed out at community meetings, such as PTA powwows, by Alliance supporters. He despised Jews even more than blacks. They should be herded into "10,000 railroad cattle cars" and sent plunging down deep mine shafts, he said.

Jews exaggerated their losses and embellished the details of the concentration camps just to horrify Gentiles. As for Germans who confessed to their deeds after the war, they did so under torture. The gas chambers were merely "delousing chambers used for sanitation purposes" and

Jews could not have died in the numbers they claimed because crematoria at Auschwitz couldn't process that many bodies. "Auschwitz was primarily a work camp where they produced synthetic rubber," he wrote.

Yet, despite his disdain for journalists and Jews, he gave not one, but two, interviews to Mike Wallace of the CBS news program Sixty Minutes, spaced five years apart, then complained bitterly after each that Wallace had not treated him fairly because he was a Jew.

I must say it amused me to see that he took off his glasses during the interviews. Dad was incredibly short-sighted and would not have been able to even distinguish Wallace's features without them. Obviously he decided he'd rather be half-blind and look better to the audience than appear bespectacled.

Dad said Wallace had expressed "hatred" of his statements and said they were "vile" to him, as a Jew. He was astonished that Wallace would identify himself as a Jew before an audience that he assumed would be was largely white Americans who could be expected to sympathize with his aims, rather than those of a Jew whose bosses, he said, used channels like MTV to popularize elements of black culture that encouraged young white girls to have sex with blacks.

Dad complained that Wallace "grinned his very Jewish grin" and called him "insane" because of the views he held. "I don't think I'm a crackpot or a nut case but feel I am a seeker of truth," he wrote (1).

I have wrestled with myself over what I'm about to say next, but my conscience won't let it slide.

If there is one person who could readily believe Dad's "seeker of truth" fantasy, it was Robert S. Griffin, a tenured professor of education at the University of Vermont. He wrote a hugely controversial book on Dad, which I have cited several times in this book, and quoted verbatim large tracts of my father's venomous views. He was rebuked by the Southern Poverty Law Center for his "tedious regurgitation" of Dad's words, and for being nothing more than a "fawning admirer" who let my father to get away with asserting that the Alliance was not a hate group, but simply "dedicated to the welfare and progress of our people." I found the book almost impossible to finish, although it was amusing in parts to hear Dad spin his version of events and try to justify his behavior and beliefs. However, I cannot allow Griffin get away with his portrayal of my father as some benign, absent-minded professor with a fascinating insight into how the world really is.

Dad believed modern-day university academics were "lickspittles and hypocrites, liars and wimps without the slightest trace of manliness, honor or self-respect," who "grovel at the feet of Jews and other minorities in order to keep their jobs. It is pitiful to behold, truly disgusting."

Apparently he decided Griffin was the exception to the rule.

Griffin contacted Dad in 1997, saying he wanted to write a book exploring where "culture and society" were headed and the role my father and his views played in it. Dad let Griffin stay with him at the compound for six weeks in the summer of 1998 while Griffin asked him softball questions for 30 hours and taped his answers for posterity. The result was a book titled "The Fame of a Dead Man's Deeds," taken from a line in an old Norse poem, which Griffin self-published in May, 2001. It was all a matter of ego for my father, but Griffin thought Dad saw him as a fellow academic who understood his views.

For a while, Griffin claimed to be "simply a conduit" for Dad's views and dismissed the idea that he was a racist himself. He said he was only an objective observer painting a portrait of my father and called his approach "cultural anthropology," but as time has passed, his racist colors came shining through. Or, as Griffin calls it, his "ethnic pride."

Griffin has a website on which he promotes his articles, books and random thoughts. On watching white supremacists and neo-Nazis march in Charlottesville, Va., in August 2017 to chants of "the Jews will not replace us" and the old Nazi slogan of "Blood and Soil," Griffin said his first reaction was "elation and gratitude" at how white people had organized, "standing up for their heritage and race, standing up for people like me, standing up for me." It didn't seem to matter to him that the marchers wore khaki uniforms and carried flaming torches and Nazi flags. He lauded their leadership, and their "remarkable dedication and courage," and for putting themselves in "physical peril" where "they could have been shot," he said.

Griffin noted that his grandfather fought for the South in the Civil War and said that the counter-protestors that day had mounted "a calculated assault on my race and my ancestors." But not once in his essay did he mention 32-year-old Heather Heyer who died that day when she was mown down by a car driven by James Field, a Donald Trump supporter who had earlier marched around carrying a black shield bearing the emblem of Vanguard America, a neo-Nazi group. Field was sentenced to life in prison for her murder and the injuries he caused to 19 other people.

Likewise, Griffin expressed no grief for the 77 adults and children shot in Norway by far right terrorist Anders Breivik in July, 2011, but likened some of the kids who died to "sheep." Breivik had triggered a bomb outside the office of the Norwegian Prime Minister in Oslo, killing eight, before moving to a nearby island where he shot dead 69 others, mainly teenagers, at a youth camp. He had previously written a manifesto about what he called the cultural genocide of the indigenous people of Western Europe and the increasing number of Muslims in Norway.

Griffin noted that 11 kids Breivik cornered had neither run nor fought back, but huddled against a fence, holding hands. One boy shouted, "Lie down!" And so they did, close together. Breivik stood on a small rise and shot them all. Only one survived.

"These are sheep being slaughtered," Griffin wrote. He went on to question whether people of European heritage, "white people...my people," might have changed. "Have we become sheep, docile, helpless? If this had happened in, say 1850 or 1930, would my people, even teenagers, have responded as the people did in this instance? Would they have lay (sic) down on the ground huddled together, holding hands, both boys and girls? Has something tragic happened to us? Have we somehow as a people become domesticated, weakened, softened? Have we become herd creatures?" He decided that white people in 1850 or 1930 wouldn't have done the same thing. (3)

Griffin's books and essays have been popular with white supremacists and he has received rave reviews on Amazon from some of my father's admirers, who praise his book as "an invaluable service" to my father and as a history of "an insightful man." Griffin estimates that has had sold 12,000 copies of the book worldwide.

But even in his adulation of Dad, he spotted "a menacing quality" about him. "There seems to be a pressure inside him, something brewing just beneath the surface, an anger perhaps," Griffin wrote. "There is a hardness, a coldness, a potential for violence that I feel in him, and it makes me uneasy and uncomfortable."

His discomfort clearly didn't last long.

Two months before Dad died, Griffin spoke glowingly of his attributes. "He's the most fascinating human being I've ever been around — ever," he said. "Whatever you think of him, I found him to be a man of integrity and courage and dedication. And in his eyes he is doing the most important thing he can think of with his life. Those have become standards that I've applied to my own life." (4)

The SPLC called on the University of Vermont to condemn his writings and investigate his classroom activities. The university declined to do so. It said it had an obligation to protect "our faculty's right to academic freedom and freedom of speech."

Griffin sees himself in a favorable light. Anyone who says he is a neo-Nazi is merely "name calling." He describes himself as "curious and perceptive and thoughtful...an honorable person, persevering and courageous." His tenured position at the university, he wrote on his website, "gives me more protection from attack than anybody I can think of."

PHOTOS

Dad (2nd from left) with Uncle Sandy and Marguerite and their dad shortly before his dad was killed

Dad in his Allen Military Academy uniform

Dad and Uncle Sandy with Marguerite on Christmas Eve 1952

Dad and mom on their wedding day Thanksgiving 1956

Dad and mom in Boulder, Colorado 1957

Mom with her beloved Buckwheat early 1960's

Author (standing) with Erik and mom and dad 1961

Dad giving a speech in late 1960's

Dad sitting on the chair author ruined with razor blade

Dad and Uncle Sandy with Marguerite at author's wedding 1986

Dad (on ladder) working on new building at his WV compound

Completed main building at WV compound

Dad's trailer where he lived at his WV compound

Author and Dad during visit to WV compound

Dad at his WV compound

Dad in his office at his WV compound

Dad's memorial service

Author with Uncle Sandy just after speaking at Dad's memorial service

Dad at his WV compound podium

Author meeting his daughters for the first time in Tbilisi, Georgia

DAD BANS CHRISTMAS AND SPORTS, MOM BANS BEATINGS

Dad was an equal-opportunity hater. He would rail against Jews and rant against blacks, measure-for-measure. Jews were "germ-carrying kikes" and blacks were "damned Jigaboos" and "uppity niggers." The fact that they even existed offended him, and so he banned Christmas, outlawed baseball and barred swimming if blacks were in the pool.

I was taught from an early age that white people were superior to all races and non-whites were low knuckle-dragging sub-humans. I learned that it was wrong for races to mix and that one of the worst things in the world was an interracial marriage, especially between whites and blacks. I remember looking at black people and being glad that I didn't have their skin color or condition.

Erik and I loved to go swimming and we'd spend hours on summer days splashing around in the local public pool, but then Dad announced a new rule: if a Negro got into the water while we were in the pool, we had to immediately get out and come home. I hated this rule and it made me wonder what was wrong with swimming with black people. I thought that maybe they would somehow spoil the water and that it would make me sick or something.

The only experience I'd had with black kids up to this point was at school. There was a neighborhood across the street from our school that Dad called "the ghetto." Several kids from there went to my school and I began noticing their features more keenly than before. I marveled at the color of their skin and the texture of their hair and wondered what it would like to be them. I would look at my skin and be grateful I wasn't black. I began to believe that perhaps Dad was right, and that they weren't human like us. But if they weren't human, what were they?

My first real interaction with a black person came in 4th grade. I was sitting in my seat in Mrs. Carden's class when she told us to go to the back of the room to retrieve our mid-morning snacks and then stepped out for a minute. I had just gotten my snack when I felt a staggering blow to my right jaw. I saw stars and my knees buckled. Clarence, a much bigger and older black boy in my class, threw the punch. I was terrified. I just stood there crying, my jaw throbbing, trying to process what had happened. Clarence was a trouble-maker and had been held back a couple of times but I'd never had a run-in with him and had done nothing to incite him.

Several kids told Mrs. Carden what had happened when she came back into the room. She was a tough, no-nonsense teacher whose favorite phrase was to tell any kid misbehaving that "if you don't knock that off right now I'll smack you into the middle of next week!" But she didn't do that to Clarence. Instead, she just gave me a troubled look and told me to stop crying and for everyone to get back to their seats. I was stunned. Why didn't she do anything about it? I went back to my seat and tried my best to pull myself together and ignore the pain in my jaw. I felt completely alone in the room. I wondered what I had done to deserve this, and why I was so bad and disliked by everyone, even my teacher. When I got home I didn't tell Mom because I was ashamed and I was sure that if she knew, she would be ashamed of me, too. Besides, she had become so preoccupied with her own fears that she wasn't present enough to notice when something happened to us. She was just trying to survive her own nightmare.

It turned out that Clarence lived in "the ghetto" and I started seeing him a lot as I explored our neighborhood. I was scared to death of him and was always on the lookout for him, wherever I went. But sometimes that wasn't enough. I would run into him while I was alone and far from home, then he would chase me and beat me up. He seemed to delight in terrorizing me. I started to hate blacks, just like Dad, but I kept my mouth shut. By then, I had an afternoon paper route and was out on my bike alone for hours, delivering papers. I felt safer on my bike because Clarence didn't have a bike, so it was easier for me to escape.

Then, as Erik and I were leaving school one day, we were cornered by Clarence and his friends, and I did something completely out of character for me. I put up my fists and stared at him, waiting for him to come at me. He was surprised and paused for a moment, until his friends egged him on. I thought for sure they were all going to jump us, but instead it was only Clarence, with his friends forming a circle around us. As soon as he came close to me, I started swinging frantically. I was flailing around wildly because I'd never used my fists before and had no idea how to fight. I just went berserk. Clarence landed a few blows, and I landed some too. After a few seconds, he backed up and told his friends, "C'mon, let's go." They turned and walked away. I was left there, buzzing with adrenaline. Erik was shaking but unhurt and we walked home without saying a word. Clarence never bothered me again after that.

Another data point in my view on blacks was added when my bike was stolen after I ran home one day to get a snack during my paper route. Mom said she thought she knew where it was. We got into the car and she drove straight to "the ghetto." She drove around slowly for a few minutes and then I saw a small black kid riding my bike on the sidewalk. Mom stopped the car and told me to grab my bike and ride home as fast as I could. The kid was quite a bit smaller than me. I ran up to him and pushed him over. By the time he picked himself up, I was away, pedaling as fast as I could. Mom followed me slowly in the car. I saw adults coming out of their houses and thought they were going to come after me, but they didn't. Afterwards, I was amazed at how Mom just knew where my bike would be and how easy it was to get it back. Maybe Dad was right? Perhaps blacks were to be feared because of how they behaved?

Dad was always coming up with new rules. One day he decided we couldn't have Christmas anymore because he wasn't going to have us worshipping some Jew. Mom pitched a fit. She just couldn't imagine not letting her boys celebrate Christmas and get presents. And, to be honest, she also really enjoyed the whole commercial aspect of the holiday, like having a Christmas tree and playing carols and giving and receiving presents. She begged and pleaded, but Dad wouldn't budge. She was upset for a very long time and eventually he compromised, saying we could mark the winter solstice instead. The solstice normally occurs on Dec. 21, so that's when we opened our presents. It felt weird. On one hand, it was cool to get presents early but on the other, it was strange to open presents four days before everyone else.

He also banned sports. Mom knew we were both terribly shy and sheltered and decided it would be good for us to be involved in a team sport, to expose us to other kids our age outside of our school activities. She thought Little League baseball would be a good start and filled out an application form that both parents had to sign. She knew Dad would be opposed but was sure he'd eventually agree because it didn't involve a lot of interaction with blacks. She fretted about it for days before approaching him. It would only be a few days a week, she said, and it would be good for us and make us feel more comfortable around other kids.

"What do you think?" she asked him. He didn't need to think. "Absolutely not!" he said. "There will most likely be Negroes in this league and I will not allow it. I will not have them associating with Niggers unless absolutely necessary." Despite her pleading, he said he didn't want to hear another word on the matter, burying his head in the newspaper again. Then Mom then did something brave — she forged his signature on the application and we played baseball for two summers. She was there at every practice and every game. She swore us to secrecy and Dad was too busy in his own world to be any the wiser. I can only imagine what would have happened if he had found out. Luckily for all of us, he did not. When we finished 6th grade, we had to say goodbye to our wonderful woods in Triangle, Va., because our landlord, a colonel in the Marines, returned from overseas and wanted his house back. We rented a house near Fredericksburg, Va., and shortly after Mom took us to California to visit her parents. While we were gone, Hurricane Agnes struck. The entire lower level of the house was under six feet of water. Dad did nothing to clean up the mess, but just waited for us to get home, whereupon he handed us a wet/dry vacuum and we spent days and days sucking water out of the basement. Soon there was mold everywhere but again, he did nothing about it. The landlord was furious. He refused to renew our lease and we had to move again the next summer.

Dad was still beating me in seventh grade. I hated him for it and regularly fantasized about his death. By now, I knew many people loathed and despised him because of his beliefs and activities and I often prayed that someone would murder him, but no-one ever obliged me.

My chores included burning his old work papers and documents every couple of weeks in a 55-gallon metal drum in the backyard. I wondered what would happen if I tossed a can of spray paint in the drum. I'd heard it would cause an explosion and was curious to see if that were true. I got the fire going really hot, tossed in the can, and then ran back to a safe distance and waited. Sure enough, after a few minutes there was a loud explosion and soon there were dozens of burning pieces of paper floating down from the sky. I started running around frantically, stomping on them, trying to put them out. Dad appeared and asked what I had done but, as usual, I lied. He walked over and picked up the charred can and, of course, I denied any knowledge of it. Lying was my only way of dealing with him, despite the fact that it never worked. Anyway, the one time I did tell him the truth — it was about how I got sand in my watch — I still got a beating, so what did it matter?

I went to John J. Wright Middle School for seventh grade and the bus ride to and from school was about an hour each way. The older kids on the bus pretty much made my life a misery. I had buck teeth, wore awful-looking glasses, had huge Dumbo ears and a bowl haircut. Plus, I was quiet. I was the perfect target. One of the older kids gave me the nickname "Bruno" and for the rest of the school year, that was what all the older kids called me. I hated it.

The bully constantly threatened to beat me up and I spent hours contemplating how to deal with him and his friends. Then, one day he told me that he was going to get me after school. I knew I couldn't fight him because he was so much bigger than me and I needed an advantage. I found a large, flat rock with a sharp edge in our driveway and discovered I could just about fold my fist around it to where the sharp edge of the rock was sticking out about an inch.

When I got off the bus the next day, the bully was waiting for me. I started swinging, just as he did, and landed a few blows. He felt the rock and backed off, saying I wasn't fighting fair. But my adrenaline was pumping and I was shaking almost uncontrollably. I lunged at him but he wanted no more of me and my rock. He took a few steps back, told me I was crazy, and turned and walked away. I stood there thinking that maybe he was right. I threw the rock down and walked home. He never threatened me again, although he did continue to call me Bruno. I hated 7th grade, I hated my Dad and, most of all, I hated myself.

It was during this time that I began to understand how sheltered we were. I heard kids discussing the Vietnam War but had no idea what they were talking about. We were not allowed to watch TV and didn't know there was a war going on, and our parents never talked to us about it looked like it bore the words Coca-Cola, only it didn't. Spelled out in the same font and style as Coca-Cola was the word Co-Caine. I finally got up the courage to ask him what that was. He told me it was a drug and I wondered why a kid would want to wear a shirt with the name of a drug on it — I had never heard of recreational drugs or what they were used for.

Dad, of course, was very much aware of the Vietnam War and very much against how it was being fought. He believed war was a deadly serious affair and if you decided to fight one, you should use every resource at your disposal. He thought we should either nuke North Vietnam or pull out, there should be no in-between. He hated the way we were fighting the war, despised anti-war protestors and considered them to be traitors. He also loathed the government. He was convinced that Jews were pulling the strings, making policy decisions with the goal of hurting the white race. It was the same with World War WII, he said.

Powerful Jews orchestrated our involvement because they wanted to see Germany destroyed. The media was 100%-owned by Jews and they were brainwashing Americans into supporting Israel and the Civil Rights Movement, and anything else that would bring us down.

All this time, Mom and Dad's relationship had been slowly deteriorating and six months after the start of 7th grade, Dad suddenly stopped coming home every night. Mom explained it by saying they couldn't afford to pay for him to drive from Arlington every night, so he had a new schedule, basically coming home every other evening. I didn't know where he went when he didn't come home, but it was a wonderful liberation for me. I loved it when he was gone and dreaded the day he was due to come home again. I wished every day that he would die.

For a long time, Mom had been a reluctant participant in Dad's work. She did all of his accounting and all of his typing. He wrote a lot and it was all hand-written. Whenever he needed anything typed, he would bring it home and ask her to do it for him, and she did it straight away, despite being exhausted from her full-time teaching job and being completely responsible for keeping the house clean and handling all family affairs.

Dad wanted Mom to quit her job and work for him and his cause full-time. She refused because she knew we would end up living in or near poverty and she didn't want that for herself or her boys. That didn't please Dad at all. He hated commuting everyday so it was a fairly easy decision for him not to come home. Mom knew her marriage had long since ended but believed in her marriage vows, so she kept teaching and taking care of Dad's needs. I believe the only reason he still came home was to get a home-cooked meal and his laundry and typing done. But she loved him to the very end. She just wasn't willing to throw away our future for him.

The last time he beat me was because of a fire extinguisher, although he said it wasn't. He had put a fire extinguisher on top of the refrigerator in the kitchen. I would see it sitting there and wanted to know what this shiny chrome cylinder could do. Unfortunately, I took it down for a closer look. I was fascinated by the double handle and the gauge with green and red markings, and I just had to see what would happen if I squeezed the handles.

I went out into the back yard and gave the handles a gentle squeeze. Nothing. I squeezed a little harder and a yellowish-white powder squirted out. I immediately released the pressure on the handles but it kept spewing powder and I couldn't make it stop. In a minute or two, the extinguisher was empty and the backyard covered in the powder. I tried to grind the powder into the earth with my feet, but it didn't really hide it. Then I spent an hour scraping up leaves from the woods and spreading them over the powder. When I'd covered up my crime, I put the extinguisher back on the refrigerator. Thankfully, it started to rain and washed the evidence away.

About two weeks later, Dad yelled for my presence. He was holding the extinguisher in his hand. I tried to lie my way out of the situation but Dad said he had checked the gauge a few weeks ago and it was full, and now it read empty. I hadn't thought at all about the gauge and knew I was busted. He grabbed me by the arm, marched me to my room, and beat the living daylights out of me. He said it was because I lied, not because I messed with the extinguisher.

But it was what he did to Erik that finally made Mom stop the beatings.

Dad was sitting in his chair reading, and we were in the dining room doing homework when Mom told us to set the table for dinner. "Just a second, Mom, I want to finish this last question first," Erik said. Suddenly, Dad threw down the newspaper and stormed into the room. "Did you just hear what your Mother said?" he screamed at Erik. "Yes sir, I just wanted to finish this last question real quick," Erik replied quietly.

Dad grabbed him by the arm, hauled him out of his chair, and dragged him toward the stairs. Just as they got to the bottom of the stairs, Erik pulled away. It really surprised Dad because neither of us had ever stood up to him before. Then Erik gave him a look that said something like, "Get off me!" It was a huge mistake. Dad made a fist and reached back and came very close to punching him in the face. He stopped just short and instead grabbed Erik by the arm again, harder than ever, and yanked him around like a rag doll as he forced him upstairs.

When Dad got Erik into his room, he told him to remove all his clothes and then he grabbed a metal coat hanger out of the closet and beat him up and down his entire backside until he looked like a piece of raw meat. It was by far the worst beating he had ever given either of us. Erik was in a state of shock. He crawled out of his bedroom dormer window and stayed out on the roof for hours. Mom was worried sick and looked all over for him. When she figured out where he was, she pleaded with him to come back inside.

"No! I'm never coming back in," Erik screamed. "He made me take my clothes off! I'm 13 years old and he made me take my clothes off! Just look what he did to me! What is wrong with him? I hate him! I hate him! I hate him! I just want him to die!" Erik sobbed. Mom was crying, too. Finally, after a couple of hours, Erik crawled back in. Mom was horrified by the bloody marks on his back and legs. She got first aid cream and applied it gently to his open wounds, then bandaged him up.

She was crying the whole time and her anger brought her to breaking point. She put on the last bandage, then said quietly, "Never again!"

Mom confronted Dad and said simply that he had beaten us for the last time. He said if he ever laid a finger on either of us again, she would leave and he would never see us again. "And that's a promise," she added. He just turned and walked away. A few days later, Mom says, he tried to explain to her how important it was that he be allowed to continue to punish us as he saw fit. "These boys need discipline and it's my job to provide that for them. You can't take this away from me," he told her. But Mom wasn't interested. She said what he was doing to us wasn't discipline, but plain abuse, and she would no longer tolerate it. It was an affront to his manhood and he accused her of trying to "emasculate" him. "If you do this to me, then how am I supposed to be their father?" Mom said he asked her. Then he grew silent and at that moment, what was left of their relationship died. "When I did that to him, whatever affection he had left for me disappeared for good," Mom recalled. "That was pretty much the final blow."

Looking back on it now, I guess Dad somehow derived strength from beating us up. He was like all the bullies at school, I realized. And, just like a bully, when Mom finally stood up to him, it sapped him of his strength, much as I had found out for myself at school. We didn't know what had transpired between Mom and Dad at the time, but he suddenly seemed different after that, even more detached, as if he didn't care at all, and I suppose he didn't. It was as if he no longer felt responsible for making us into what he was not, the perfect Aryan male. We were no longer his hunk of clay for molding, and he was no longer the creator. I stopped fantasizing about him dying because he wasn't around much and didn't seem the same anymore. Over time, he became a bit more approachable and slowly our relationship changed.

I first noticed things were different when I decided I just couldn't live another moment without a motorcycle. I begged and pleaded with Mom for months to let me buy one with my paper route money, but she was absolutely against it, terrified that I would crash and hurt myself, or even die. But I didn't give up. On my 14th birthday I wrote her a note telling her that the only thing I wanted for my birthday was her permission to buy a motorbike. Evidently, she showed the note to Dad and he proceeded to tell her how he much he had loved to tinker with motors when he was a kid and that it would be good for me, too.

Mom made me promise me that I would take Dad with me to look over any motorcycle before I bought it. I agreed instantly, although I privately wondered how that would work, since Dad never showed much interest in my company. I found a used Honda XL 100 that a friend was selling for $100. I approached Dad and there was a long, long pause. Then he agreed to go with me. I was so excited that I wouldn't have found anything wrong with it, even if it had no wheels. I bought it on the spot and for the next two years I lived on that rattily old boneshaker, free as the wind as I rode it along the power line trails around Fredericksburg and around the golf course at Mary Washington College. The campus police would give chase, but they never caught me.

CHAPTER 18

LUNCH AND A RECIPE FOR THE OKLAHOMA BOMBING

Dad was down in the dumps. It seemed no matter what he wrote or how he wrote it, he couldn't stir the masses to revolt, he moaned over lunch with Revilo P. Oliver. It was 1974 and they were sitting in a restaurant in Washington, D.C. Oliver was a controversial classics professor at the University of Illinois, a leading white supremacist, and a founder of the John Birch Society, until he was expelled for his racist views. And no, I don't know why he had a palindrome for a name, except that he claimed that it was a six-generation family tradition.

After listening to Dad complain, Oliver asked if he had ever tried writing fiction. Dad admitted that it had never occurred to him. Oliver opined that Dad would never be able to get his message across to the masses because most of the people he was trying to reach occupied "the lower rungs of society" and simply did not read non-fiction. But they might well read light, action-packed fiction, he said, and promised to send Dad an example of what he was talking about. (1) A little later, Dad received by mail a book called "The John Franklin Letters," which Oliver is believed to have penned under a pseudonym years before. It was published in 1959 by the Birch Society and detailed the bloody deeds of one John Franklin, who forms an underground military group called the Rangers dedicated to killing bureaucrats, whom he called

"Buros." (Oliver shot himself in 1994, at age 86, suffering from leukemia and emphysema).

Skimming through Oliver's book, Dad realized how easy it would be for him to write something similar. He wouldn't have to work at creating a lot of characters or loads of different plot lines, but merely present his own views through the eyes of his own protagonist. And that is where he got the idea for The Turner Diaries, which Timothy McVeigh used as a tactical blueprint for his 1995 bombing of the Murrah Building in Oklahoma City and the resulting murder, in mere moments, of 168 people and the maiming another 680.

It took him four years to write The Turner Diaries, one of the most infamous and hate-filled books of our time —perhaps with the exception of his second offering, Hunter. He carefully followed Oliver's advice, making sure to include some form of bloody action in each of the 26 chapters in order to hold the reader's interest. He serialized the book first in his paper, "Attack!" in an effort to gin up subscriptions. Dad named his protagonist Earl Turner and had him kill at will.

The story is set in the 1990s, which was the distant future at that time. Turner is a member of The Organization, an underground white supremacist group that rises up against the government of the day, known as "The System." Those in power are Jewish politicians who use African American gangs to enforce cruel and unjust laws. The revolution is sparked when the System tries to confiscate all guns in the U.S. Turner's exploits in fighting them are deemed so courageous that he is invited to join a secret, elite group within the Organization, called "The Order." The book reads like Quentin Tarantino on steroids, brutality bleeding from every page. Black Americans barbeque white children, a Jewish Washington Post writer is blown in half by a shotgun blast, blacks are marched into the desert and killed, and Jews worldwide are shot, stabbed, clubbed or killed in various violent ways. In the now most-infamous scene, The Organization brands as race traitors thousands of white politicians, liberals and journalists and strings them up from trees and lampposts in Los Angeles during the "Day of The Rope" chapter.

Turner dies in a suicide mission, flying a crop-duster armed with a nuclear warhead into the Pentagon. It is an act of contrition to atone for selling out members of The Order when he was tortured by The

System, instead of taking the cyanide pill The Order had given him — Dad later said that it was the only "responsible thing for him to do" to make amends. Having beaten The System in the U.S., The Order goes on to conquer the world on April 20, 1999 — the anniversary of Hitler's birth, of course. In the end, all non-whites in the world are eliminated and Asia has been turned into a nuclear wasteland inhabited by mutants. The Order rules benevolently, naturally, and a "Special One," the new Hitler, emerges to lead everyone in peace and harmony.

In a deliberate provocation, Dad did his best to convince his members that the scenarios in his book were about to come true. The first episode of The Turner Diaries ran in a 1975 issue of "Attack!" in which he claimed that the U.S. government was about to start a citizen disarmament program that would lead to house-to-house searches for personally owned weapons, and then offered readers tips on where and how to hide their guns. It was a blatant lie.

The first white nationalist organization to adopt the book as its bible called itself The Order. The brains behind the group was Robert Jay Mathews, a young electrical worker who joined the John Birch Society when he was just 11 years old. He later served six months' probation for tax resistance and converted to Mormonism before starting to identify with the white Christian movement, attending church services and socials at a National Aryan Compound in Idaho.

Mathews was 27 when he joined the National Alliance in 1980 and by 1983 he was a star, receiving a standing ovation at an Alliance meeting after describing his attempts to get farmers and independent truckers to join the white nationalist movement. Later that year, he built a barracks on his land in Metaline, Wash., and with eight liked-minded friends, two of them members of the National Alliance, formed The Order.

It was dedicated to overthrowing the "Zionist Occupation Government" or ZOG, a white supremacist euphemism for the U.S. government. All new recruits were given a copy of the Diaries and required to read it (2). It was also required reading for new Alliance members and other white supremacist groups and remains a neo-Nazi cult favorite to this day. Led by Mathews, The Order launched a year-long campaign of murder and mayhem.

Their first murder was of one of their own members who was hit in the head with a hammer and shot in the face for drunkenly bragging about their plans. Their most infamous killing was that of Alan Berg, a Jewish-American radio talk-show host in Denver who liked to bait rightwing callers to his show. Their first attempt at robbery was of a porn store, but it was a poor payday — only $369. For a while after that, they spent their time tailing blacks driving flashy cars, whom they assumed were pimps or drug dealers, but that also yielded little. Then, taking a page from the Turner Diaries, they began to hit armored cars, sometimes planting small bombs in cinemas and a synagogue to divert police attention from their robberies. They also started a counterfeiting operation, which was eventually to lead to their downfall.

Mathews also made a clumsy mistake. In 1984, The Order robbed a Brinks armored truck near Ukiah, Calif., getting away with $3.6 million, their biggest haul yet. During the robbery, Mathews dropped a gun, which gave FBI agents their first solid lead. Then, one of his friends, Thomas Martinez, started spending counterfeit money too freely. He had been told to spread the fake money around in New Jersey but instead went on a spending spree in his local Philadelphia neighborhood. Worse, he hit the same store twice. He was easily identified and arrested.

In December, 1984, after Martinez turned informant, FBI agents were able to track Mathews down to a house on Whidbey, Island, Wash. They surrounded the house but Mathews refused to come out. After a day of negotiations, they fired smoke grenades into the house but couldn't dislodge Mathews, who was wearing a gas mask and, when they tried to enter the house, he fired on them. As night fell, the FBI brought in a helicopter. More shots were exchanged, to no avail. Then an agent fired flares into the house, setting off a box of hand grenades and ammunition, ending the 36-hour siege. Mathews died as the house burned around him. He was 31-years-old, his charred body found with a pistol still in his hand. An autopsy determined he died from smoke inhalation.

Eleven members of The Order were found guilty at trial and given long prison terms. Another 12 pleaded guilty before trial and 11 of those were imprisoned. Several former members testified for the government, including Martinez, who was sentenced to three years of probation on the counterfeiting charge. According to testimony at a subsequent trial of some Order members, more than $650,000 of the stolen cash was distributed to six men representing white nationalist groups. Dad was said to have received $50,000. I always wondered how he could afford to buy the land for his West Virginia compound — a source at the compound claimed to have seen him receive a bag containing bank notes. He always denied that, as did four of the other alleged recipients named in court.

After Mathews was killed in the shootout, coded notes of telephone numbers were found in his car. The code was deciphered and the telephone number of the National Alliance was identified, as well as the code name 'Cookie.'

The FBI was keen to find out how Dad was paying his operating expenses "to attempt to establish a connection between these funds and those obtained by the Order during the robberies perpetrated by that group," says one FBI memo. Agents repeatedly tried to serve a subpoena at the Alliance's Arlington, Va., office but could only ever find one person, a woman, in the building. They never talked to her but trawled her neighborhood looking for information about her. I'm guessing, but she may have been Liz Prostel, who became my father's second wife. Either way, neighbors said she was a pleasant woman but never said where she worked, except that it was for "an educational group."

I don't think agents ever did trace all the money that the Order stole.

Among those found guilty in subsequent trials was Order member David Lane, who became a prolific writer in prison and coined the term "white genocide," now the "overwhelmingly dominant meme" of the modern white nationalist movement, according to J.M. Berger, author and expert on extremism (3).

These days, white nationalists honor Mathews on December 8, the anniversary of his death, which they call Martyr's Day. My father contributed his two cents-worth to all the eulogies, writing a glowing tribute and quoting from a declaration of war Mathews penned prior to his death. In it, Mathews cited threats the FBI allegedly made against his family and likened himself to a soldier, concluding that his tour of duty was now over and he would "leave knowing that I have made the ultimate sacrifice to ensure the future of my children." In the final showdown, my father wrote, "there will be no other way but Bob Mathews' way." (4).

"'The Turner Diaries' is a Rorschach test for racists of all stripes, pedestrian or ideological," Berg says. It changed white nationalism and helped inspire decades of violence, including dozens of armed robberies and more than 200 murders. My father wanted to appeal to "normal" people, so he made Turner an easy read. It didn't push any political doctrine, which meant people could bring their own ideologies and justifications to the narrative, or none at all. (5)

Dad realized how easy it was to use fiction to get his message across when he saw the impact the Diaries had. If people identified with characters in books, you would have a powerful teaching tool, he reasoned. So, in Hunter, his second book, Dad has Oscar Yeager, the protagonist, talk to other characters in the book and help them solve their problems. He dedicated the book to Joseph Paul Franklin, whom he called "the lone hunter" who "saw his duty as a White man." Franklin was a neo-Nazi serial killer who killed at least 18 mainly black and Jewish people in 10 states. Among his victims were NAACP leader Vernon Jordan, who Franklin shot and seriously injured, and Larry Flynt, the publisher of Hustler magazine, who was shot and paralyzed from the waist down.

Yeager, is a 40-year-old consulting engineer, a former Vietnam fighter pilot and a graduate of Dad's alma mater, the University of Colorado. He sees whites as weak and decadent and kills an interracial couple in a Pentagon parking lot, sending blood and brain tissue flying. It's his sixth kill in three weeks. In short order, he murders a Washington Post columnist, garrotes a congressman, bombs a church, and kills another 41 people. After teaming up with a rogue FBI agent, hundreds more people are slaughtered before he kills the agent and goes underground to continue his campaign. Reading Internet reviews, some people who had liked the Diaries hated Hunter, including a soldier in Iraq who burned it in the trash pit to stop other troops reading it.

Dad thought Hunter was far superior to the Diaries, but The Washington Post described his prose style as "dense, flat, artless," his imagination "bloodthirsty yet drained of passion," and his "ideology is insane." The paper added, "It's hard to imagine Pierce ever capturing the hearts and minds of the American masses." (6). Franklin was executed by lethal injection in 2013. Dad said he dedicated the book to him "because he is the kind of person I would like to be." (7).

The two books were products of my father's feverish mind, his sick, secret fantasies laid bare upon the page, but he didn't have the courage to use his real name, instead writing under the pseudonym Andrew McDonald. He dreamed that his writings would spark a race war and he often fantasized about walking the streets at night, quietly, efficiently dispatching mixed-race couples, Jews, gays, and anyone else who didn't fit his Aryan mold, mentally mapping out the route he would take each night. To quench that volcanic hatred inside him would have been a great therapeutic release but he knew it would be just too risky. Writing a book describing what could be done was the next best thing, he decided.

He admitted as much in a National Alliance radio broadcast in 1997. When he began writing the Diaries, he said, "I wanted to take all of the feminist agitators and propagandists and all the race-mixing fanatics and all of the media bosses and all of the bureaucrats and all of the politicians who were collaborating with them, and I wanted to put them up against a wall, in batches of a thousand or so at a time, and machine-gun them. And I still want to do that. I am convinced that one day we will have to do that before we can get our civilizations back on track, and I look forward to that day."

Rejected by multiple publishers, Dad published the books himself, selling them at gun shows and through survivalist magazines and the Alliance's own book catalog. His keenest salesman was McVeigh himself. A sergeant in the U.S. army, McVeigh sold copies at his cost and gave copies away to friends and his fellow soldiers, according to testimony at his trial. Copies of pages from the Diaries were found in his car after the bombing and he mailed a letter to his sister a few days before the bombing containing clippings from the book. Even today, the book gets glowing reviews from his fans on Amazon's website.

The Diaries was later picked up by Barricade Press, a small publishing house owned by Lyle Stuart, an American Jewish businessman who liked to call himself "the last publisher in America with any guts." His timing was opportunistic, at best. He brought out the book a year after the bombing but before McVeigh stood trial. Stuart liked to test the boundaries of good taste and, answering criticism, said he was publishing it because "people should know what the enemy is thinking." (8). He offered to make a $1 donation for every copy he sold to a gun control charity run by Sarah Brady, the wife of the late Jim Brady. She refused to accept the money. Brady, the former press secretary to President Ronald Reagan, was shot in the head during the 1981 attempted assassination attempt of Reagan. He died 33 years later.

Soon after the Diaries came out, Barricade filed for bankruptcy after losing a libel case against Las Vegas casino owner Steve Wynn. Barricade had alleged that Wynn was fronting for organized crime and was ordered to pay him $3 million in damages. The award was overturned on appeal in 2001 and sent back for a new trial but Stuart did not pursue the matter further. Meanwhile, rights to the Diaries reverted to Dad.

The Diaries earned Dad a place in the pantheon of Nazi nasties, which thrilled him no end. The book "was successful beyond my wildest dreams" and "sold like hotdogs at a ballgame," he bragged. It was translated into German, French, Swedish and Polish, he noted.

But he later engaged in all kinds of verbal gymnastics to try to distance himself from McVeigh without actually disavowing the beliefs they both shared, fearful of legal repercussions. When the CBS news show "60 Minutes" interviewed him in 1996, Dad evaded journalist Mike Wallace's questions when asked whether he endorsed McVeigh's actions. Eventually, he said his biggest problem was not what McVeigh had done, but the fact that he did it too soon, because the revolutionary infrastructure was not in place to allow the White Race to capitalize on his actions by rising up to crush their enemies.

A year or so later, Dad was asked him again if he thought McVeigh was morally justified in what he did. His answer was, basically, yes. "If one is waging war against the government, civilians are going to be killed," he said. "Under circumstances like that, if it were part of a war, then a bombing of the Oklahoma City sort is justified." The white race was engaged in a war for its survival, he said. "In a war, people jump the gun, it's not unusual." (9)

If his book did inspire McVeigh, "the only thing that would concern me would be the legal aspects of it," he said. In the future, he said, he would be careful to include a disclaimer on anything he wrote to the effect that it was fiction, not advocacy. "I'd have a lawyer craft something and print it in very small type on the back of the title page."

Dad liked to refer to McVeigh as "Tim" and said he would have liked to have met him. He even helped McVeigh's lawyers prepare his defense. He said he was excited when he heard about the bombing and wondered if there were more to come. He maintained that the news media was lying when it linked McVeigh's actions to the Diaries, saying the bomb he described in his book was made from ammonium nitrate fertilizer and fuel oil, while McVeigh used ammonium nitrate fertilizer and nitromethane, a liquid explosive used for rocket and racing fuel.

Dad was a good debater in high school and turned out to be a fine, early practitioner of what is known today as "what about-ism" whenever he was challenged on uncomfortable issues. The Alliance itself promoted the Diaries as McVeigh's manual, but later, when interviewers reminded him that McVeigh cited the Diaries as his inspiration, Dad would wriggle and pivot to the 1993 massacre at the Branch Davidian cult compound in Waco, Tex. He claimed revenge for the 51-day siege was what really motivated McVeigh. He would then attack one of his favorite targets, President Bill Clinton, saying Clinton and his Attorney General, Janet Reno, bore the blame for the fiery fiasco that ended when cult leader David Koresh and 79 of his followers set the compound ablaze. It was all a conspiracy by Clinton, Reno and the Bureau of Alcohol, Tobacco and Firearms to kill Koresh, instead of just arresting him, he said.

It emerged at the trial that McVeigh had called a National Alliance hotline in Arizona five or six times over a two-day period before the Oklahoma atrocity. There were reports, too, that he called Dad's unlisted number two weeks before the bombing and spoke to him for 45 minutes. Dad dismissed that as a rumor started by his enemies at the Southern Poverty Law Center. Morris Dees, then-SPLC leader, had already asked major retail chains not to sell The Turner Diaries, saying Dad was responsible for one of the worst horror attacks in American history. Dad, for his part, admired McVeigh, saying he had much in common with Mathews, in that he never tried to wriggle out of responsibility for what he had done and behaved throughout like a soldier.

Timothy McVeigh was 33 when he was executed by lethal injection on June 11, 2001 at a U.S prison in Terre Haute, Ind. I do sometimes wonder what he would have thought had he lived to read my father's quote about The Turner Diaries some years later. Dad described those who read it as less than intelligent, and he clearly held the book's fans in low esteem.

"Many of the lower class white people who are affected by the book are not the kinds of people I am trying to recruit because they are not particularly useful people. They don't have good character and they aren't really strong and capable people," he opined. (10).

Dad claimed that the Diaries had sold 160,000 copies by 1993. Since then the book has been sold through Amazon and Barnes and Noble, with sales estimated at 500,000 by 2000. Dad was so pleased with the trouble he had stirred that in 1983 — the same year he deserted his family — he began work on Hunter. He published it in 1989 and considered it to be far superior to the Diaries. Terry Nichols, McVeigh's accomplice in the Oklahoma bombing, was obviously a fan — the FBI found a copy of the book when they searched Nichols' home.

The Anti-Defamation League and the Southern Poverty Law Center, two respected rights groups that battle bigotry and extremism, have cited multiple murders and other violent crimes that were inspired by my father's dark fantasies.

One of the latest victims of the Diaries was Jo Cox, a member of Parliament and mother of two young children who was brutally murdered on a British street in 2016 by Thomas Mair, a 56-year-old neo-Nazi now serving a life term without the possibility of parole. He was a longtime supporter of the National Alliance and spent more than $400 on NA publications, including copies of Dad's "Revolutionary Notes" series on how to make explosives and guns (11). Mair shouted "Britain First" and "death to traitors" when he stabbed Cox with a military-style dagger 15 times and shot her three times with a sawn-off rifle (12)

According to the ADL, other cases include those of:

- Eric Hanson, an Alliance member, who was fatally shot in June, 2001 after resisting arrest by the Illinois State Police on weapons charges. He had been previously arrested in 1999 for physically threatening an interracial couple and possessing illegal weapons in two separate cases, seriously wounding one of the arresting officers.

- Steve McFadden, an Alliance member, arrested in October 2000 after a police search of his apartment discovered swords, revolvers, pistols and shotguns. About six months earlier, police arrested another man in the same New York neighborhood for violating his parole. A cache of weapons and an Alliance handbook were found in the home of Michael Sagginario. He had been previously arrested in the early 1990s on an explosives possession charge.

- David Copeland, a British neo-Nazi, who killed three people, including a pregnant woman, and injured another 140 people, four of whom lost limbs, in a series of bombings in London in April, 1999. The bombs each contained 1,500 four-inch-long nails and were left in holdalls in public areas. Copeland, 22 at the time, was a neo-Nazi militant and a former member of the British National Party and the National Socialist Movement. He was convicted of murder the following year and given six concurrent life sentences. When he was 21, he had read The Turner Diaries, and learned to make bombs after downloading a "terrorist's handbook" from the Internet.

- Todd Vanbiber, an Alliance member, who was arrested by the FBI in Florida after a pipe bomb he was building exploded in his face. Other Alliance associates testified that Vanbiber's gang had robbed three banks and donated some of the proceeds to my father. He pled guilty to illegally constructing and possessing explosives in 1997 and was sentenced to six and a half years. Agents searching the storage unit where he assembled the bomb found 14 explosive devices, weapons and ammunition, bomb-making manuals, and National Alliance and Nazi memorabilia. He admitted that he and his gang planned to plant the bombs on major highways in the Orlando area to create distractions while they robbed two banks. The federal complaint said that on their way back from a robbery in Connecticut, Vanbiber and an accomplice stopped at my father's compound in West Virginia, where they donated $2,000 and bought $700 worth of literature.

- Larry Wayne Shoemake opened fire on a black neighborhood April, 1996, in Jackson, Miss., killing one person and wounding seven others, a week before the first anniversary of the Oklahoma City bombing. Shoemake stashed a pile of weapons in an abandoned restaurant and started shooting into the street, preventing medical workers from helping the dying victim before he took his own life.

In a search of his home, authorities found a Nazi flag draped over his bed, a copy of Mein Kampf and National Alliance publications. Shoemake is said to have borrowed The Turner Diaries from a friend and from then on became a National Alliance subscriber. "It was like an eye-opener for him," his ex-wife wife said.

- Dennis McGiffen, who plotted to bomb state capitols, post offices and to add cyanide to public water supplies as part of a March, 1998 conspiracy to possess and make machine guns as part of a group called The New Order. McGiffen, an Aryan Nations leader, together with two others were charged with conspiracy to possess and make machine guns. All were convicted. An FBI agent testified that the men planned to bomb the headquarters of the Anti-Defamation League in New York and the Southern Poverty Law Center in Alabama, as well as the Simon Wiesenthal Center in Los Angeles. McGiffen's beliefs were reportedly heavily influenced by The Turner Diaries. James Burmeister and Malcolm Wright were given life for the December, 1995 murder of a black couple in North Carolina. They were members of the 82nd Airborne Division at Fort Bragg, and committed the double murder close to the base — Dad used to concentrate recruitment efforts on military bases because of the easy access to weapons. Both Burmeister and Wright read National Alliance propaganda.

- John William King was convicted in the 1999 killing of James Byrd, Jr., a black man. He and two other white supremacists chained Byrd by his ankle to a pickup truck and dragged him for three miles. Byrd survived for a mile and a half until his body hit a culvert, severing his right arm and head. They drove on for another 1.5 miles before dumping his body in front of a black cemetery. King reportedly told police, "We're starting The Turner Diaries early." One of the men has been executed, the second was released, and King was executed by lethal injection on April 24, 2019.

- Peter Langan, a leader of the Aryan Republican Army, committed 22 bank robberies and bombings across the Midwest between 1992 and 1996, according to authorities. Langan was convicted in two federal trials and four other members of the group pleaded guilty to robbery charges. The FBI found a video in which Langan praised

Mathews and advised people to "learn from Bob." The Diaries was required reading in the Aryan Republican Army, authorities said.

CHAPTER 19

STANDING UP TO DAD
AT LAST

After Mom took away Dad's power to beat us at will, he changed. Slowly, bit by bit, he withdrew from us and poured his venom into a book he was writing. It was The Turner Diaries but, of course, we didn't know that then. As the book progressed, he grew more and more distant. It was a welcome change for us. And yet, I missed him.

Nothing changed for Mom, though. She kept working and taking care of us the best she could. She worried endlessly about losing her job and not being able to make ends meet, and always feared some dire danger would befall us. When Dad left for his office in Arlington, she would remind him every day to signal her. He was supposed to call, let the phone ring twice, and then hang up, so she would know he'd arrived safely. Often he didn't call, and then she'd fret that something had happened to him. Sometimes, I secretly hoped that she was right. She would fuss for an hour, then call him to make sure all was well. It was a pattern repeated for years. I don't know if he truly forgot to call her, or just didn't bother, although he'd always remember to signal when he was on his way home, so she would have a hot meal waiting for him. Even if the call came long after she'd gone to bed, she would get up, put on her robe, and make him dinner.

While Dad didn't engage with us much anymore, he kept up his experiments at home. I remember when I was 15, he told me he needed my help in the basement. I followed him reluctantly. It was always so cool and damp down there, and I had plenty of bad memories of the place. He had set up a workbench in the back, with a large cardboard tube laying horizontally in a set of brackets at each end of the bench. The tube was from a roll of carpet he had scavenged from someone's trash. He had cut it down to about 6 feet in length and next to it he had placed a huge spool of a thin copper wire. The copper was shiny, obviously brand new.

He told me to slowly roll the tube as he guided the wire onto it. It took us a while to sync up our efforts but soon we were working very intently and after a couple of hours we had several inches of the tube neatly covered in copper wire. We worked in absolute silence except for me asking what he was making. He paused for a few seconds, and then said, "A Tesla coil." I had no idea what that was. We worked, on and off, rolling copper wire on to that tube for months.

We could work together, a couple of hours at a time, without speaking a word. I didn't mind, I was happy to be spending time close to Dad without him hitting me.

Then, one evening, there was a loud zapping, crackling sound coming from the basement and I went down to investigate. There was a strange, sickly-sweet smell, then the sound again, really loud this time. I was about to run back upstairs when I saw Dad, leaning over his work bench. The coil now had a thick wire coming out of each end and arcing up and toward the center of the tube. At the end of each of the two wires he had attached a metal ball about the size of a marble, roughly six inches apart. There were also wires running to a square object next to the coil that seemed to be made from glass plates, with thin sheets of metal between each plate.

Dad saw me and grinned from ear to ear. He looked happy. When I asked what the smell was, he said it was ozone and then added casually that it was "a poisonous gas." I was scared but he assured me that there wasn't enough in the room to be harmful. I paused, then asked where the ozone was coming from. He smiled. "I'm making it with my Tesla coil," he said. "Here, watch this." He pushed a button and, without warning, I saw and heard a huge arcing spark flow between the two balls above the copper coil. It was incredibly loud and very neat, like something out of a "Frankenstein" movie. The spark and sound lasted several seconds until he stopped pushing the button. It was one of the coolest things I had ever seen.

"I thought you'd like it," Dad said. He explained that the spark was very hot and was creating a chemical reaction with the air in the room, producing the ozone. I asked him to do it again. He pushed the button and the spark flowed again and was just as fascinating as before.

Then, he handed me a screwdriver, telling me to stick the metal end of it into the spark. I remembered he had nearly shocked the life out of me with a car spark coil years before and emphatically refused. He laughed and promised it wouldn't hurt me. He pushed the button again and I cautiously reached toward the spark with the tip of the screwdriver. Suddenly the spark seemed to split in half and jump toward the screwdriver. I felt a mild tingling in my arm and my right foot started involuntarily jumping up and down in rapid fire motion off the concrete floor.

I pulled my hand back quickly and gave him a wide-eyed look. He was laughing so hard that tears were running down his face. "I didn't realize you were barefoot, and the floor is wet," he said, between fits of laughter. "It didn't hurt you, did it?" I smiled and said I'd just been kind of scared. He was still laughing and invited me to do it again, but I declined. I watched him play around with the thing for another few minutes and then went back upstairs. I felt really good about making him laugh and having had some really interesting fun with him.

But there was one time at this house that made me wonder if Dad was really trying to kill me; or was he just doing his best absent-minded professor imitation? He had rented a U-Haul moving van to pick up a piano that a friend had offered him for free. The whole family went to pick up the piano. It was extremely heavy and we had a very difficult time getting it into the truck. The four of us finally wrestled the piano up a long metal loading ramp and into the back of the van. It was an upright and had four small metal wheels. Despite the wheels, the thing was almost impossible to move around without all of us pushing at the same time. We slowly backed it into the far corner of the truck, up against the back and side wall. "Okay, Midgets, you can ride in the back with the piano and hold onto it in case it starts moving," Dad said. Erik and I stood in the truck in wide-eyed silence as Dad closed the rear door. It suddenly became very dark, so dark that I couldn't see anything at all, not even Erik. Then the truck started up and we slowly moved down the driveway. I felt uneasy on my feet and I leaned onto the piano to steady myself.

Coming out of the driveway, Dad accelerated out into the traffic and suddenly the piano started moving. I tried to hold onto it but it was way too heavy for me. I couldn't see it but it seemed to be moving quite fast for such a heavy piece of furniture. Seconds later, it smashed into one of the walls of the van with a loud crashing sound as the plywood wall splintered on impact. Erik started screaming at me that we had to get out now, but we didn't know where the damned thing was.

Then it started moving again as Dad went round a curve and I felt a breeze as 400 pounds or so of piano flashed by me and smashed into the other side of the van with another loud sound. By now, we were scared to death and yelling as loudly as we could, pounding on the back of the truck with our fists. But it kept going, rounding another curve. I tried to gauge the piano's position by the sound of its wheels so I could try to dodge it. There was another crashing sound and I had visions of dying in the back of that rental truck. It seemed like a slow-motion nightmare with Dad playing a dangerous game of Russian roulette with a speeding piano. After several more near-misses with the missile in the dark, Dad stopped at a traffic light. We thought our deliverance was at hand, but then the truck lurched forward again. We pounded and pounded on that wall and then, by some miracle, Dad and Mom finally heard us and the truck stopped.

Dad opened up the back of the truck. I squinted in the bright light when Dad finally opened the truck door. He stared in disbelief at the inside of the van, smashed to pieces in many places. By now, Erik and I were almost hysterical. Dad just shook his head. "I told you to hold onto the piano," he said with disgust, shaking his head as he jumped up into the back of the van. He grabbed some straps and within a couple minutes had strapped both handles at the back of the piano to the metal hold-down rings on the side of the van. Erik and I had jumped out of the van and were regaling Mom with our horror story. Before we could finish Dad hopped out of the van and told us to get back in. "It should be OK now," he said. We looked desperately at Mom and she came to our rescue. "Bill, I know it's crowded in the cab but I insist that the boys ride up front with us. What if the straps don't hold? They both could have been killed!" He muttered a reluctant agreement and all four of us climbed into the cab of the truck for the rest of the trip home. I never did hear how Dad explained to the rental company how the damage occurred, but I'll never forget the experience.

By now I was at James Monroe High School in Fredericksburg. And because I still yearned for Dad to be proud of me, I made one of the most embarrassing mistakes of my freshman life — I asked him for help with a project for my history class, hoping to attract his attention. Knowing how he felt about Adolf Hitler, I decided to do my paper on the virtues of the genocidal maniac.

I wish I could go back in time and tell my freshman self how dumb that would be.

He immediately started extolling Hitler's virtues — how he was a smart man, an artist and a First World War hero, and how he was only trying to regain territory wrongly taken from Germany after World War I when he invaded Poland, incidentally setting off the Second World War. And, Dad said, he was completely justified in purging the Jews because they were such a scourge on Germany, and so on. He gave me books to read and encouraged me to do my own research.

Like an idiot, I believed everything he told me and was quite excited about turning in my paper. I felt like I was in on a secret that most people didn't know and would be respected by my teacher for having such knowledge. It turned out that my history teacher was a WWII veteran and held somewhat different views. In fact, he was so surprised at my ideas that he asked me to present my paper to the whole class. I desperately did not want to do that because I was terrified of public speaking, but he pretty much insisted. I am amazed to this day that he just stood there during my presentation with a look of pure pity on his face. I can only imagine what was going through his mind as I spouted my nonsense in front of the class.

Probably to no-one's great surprise, I was still being bullied by the older kids. I very badly wanted to join the football team so I might be popular, but Dad forbade it. "I will not have you taking showers with niggers!" he declared. All I could do was look on in envy when the football players wore their game jerseys to school. I went to all the games and tried to imagine myself on the field, representing my school and scoring points.

One of the guys on the JV team was in my freshman class. He was as big as any of the seniors on the team and was generally feared as he strode through the hallways like some kind of king. I was afraid of him, but for some reason he took a liking to me. He never picked on me and would occasionally ask when I was going to join the team because they needed me. It made me feel really good but how do you explain that you can't sign up because your father won't let you mix with "niggers"?

That summer, I made a life-changing decision: I decided it was time to stand up to Dad. Telling no-one, I joined the football team and started attending practice. Mom figured it out almost right away and silently supported me. It wasn't long before Dad guessed, too. I had just come back from practice, drenched in sweat, when Dad confronted me. "Midget, are you doing what I think you are doing?" he asked. "I am playing football, if that's what you're asking," I replied. He grabbed my arm just below the shoulder, as he had done so many times before, made a fist and pulled his arm back as if he was going to slug me.

"You need to quit the team right now, you know I told you not to join," he said. I turned and gave him a look that I had never given him before. It was obvious what my look meant and he stared at me for several long seconds. I braced for his blow, but it never came. He just shook his head and walked away.

After that, I joined the track team, and threw the discus too, and very much enjoyed that as well. It was a new beginning for me. I slowly started coming out of my shell and feeling better about myself. Before every game or track meet I would look around to see if maybe Dad had come to watch me play, but he never did for the three years that I played. Mom, however, was always there, even in the pouring rain, she would be in the stands to support me.

My first year of football was a real growth experience for me. Before I joined the team, I was terribly self-conscious and did everything to just fade into the background. That changed in a big way on the first day of practice.

I even managed to survive our JV football coach. He was a first-class jerk and for some reason picked on me almost daily throughout the season. At one of the first practices, he told us to pair up and get down on our hands and knees, facing each other. We were to leap forward at each blow of his whistle and ram our shoulder pads against each other.

He blew the whistle and everyone dropped to the ground except me. I hesitated; I wasn't sure what he wanted us to do. Everyone else knew because they'd played before, but I hadn't. I was left standing, odd man out.

"Pierce! Why the hell are you just standing there?" he screamed. "Get down on the ground and you can use the goal posts as your partner. Do it now!" So I lined myself up opposite the main goal post support pole and when he blew the whistle I rammed my shoulder into the post as hard as I could. After doing this a few times, he noticed that the goal post was wobbling and started laughing. "Wow Pierce, look at that! The goal posts are shaking like crazy! You're an animal!" By now the whole team was in stitches. He kept screaming at me for the rest of the practice about how impressed he was that I could move the goal post. I hated him.

I was big for my age and athletic enough that I quickly made the starting lineup. I was so proud to wear my game jersey to school on the day of our first game. But as I walked down the hall, my head held high for once, I heard an incredibly loud voice from way off, screaming at me. "Animal! Look at you! You animal!" I was horrified, my face turning beet red. Everyone in the hall turned to look at me as the coach kept screaming "Animal" at the top of his voice. He yelled like that whenever he saw me for the rest of the season.

I hated him, but I loved being on the team. Finally, I felt like I belonged somewhere and was actually earning some respect from my peers. The older kids who used to bully me now left me alone and started treating me like I was an equal because I was on the team. For the first time in my life, I made friends with my classmates and no longer felt alone or worthless.

The next year I learned to drive and my confidence grew when I bought my first car. It was a 1969 Z-28 Camaro with a 302 engine and I was proud beyond words that it was mine. I was soon out on Friday and Saturday nights, drag racing against other muscle cars. We would race for $25 or so, and I'd spend every penny I won souping up my car to make it go even faster. My favorite place to race was on Route 3, out near the civil war battlefields. One of my football buddies was a car enthusiast, too, and we became best friends as we spent hours working on our cars together. Soon I was buying and selling other cars, looking for that perfect machine. My favorite was a 1970 Barracuda. I never lost a race in that car. It was loud and fast, and pretty soon I had a lot of new friends. Guys at school loved the way it looked and sounded and I would find myself in the school parking lot, popping the hood and listening to their "Wows!" of admiration as I made the engine roar. Some even talked as if they owned it themselves, calling it "one bad ass 340!" that could beat any other car around.

I knew several of them from football and soon I found myself making friends with blacks for the first time in my life. I was afraid of some of them and still thought of them as "niggers," but I was beginning to question those instincts for the first time in my life.

By now I was no longer getting into trouble with Dad, simply because he ignored me 99% of the time. It was that last 1%, when he tried again to assert his authority that he failed miserably after Mom screamed and I kicked him in the face.

With Dad no longer a physical presence in my life, I felt I could do whatever I wanted. Mom tried to be a responsible parent but I just ignored her most of the time. When I got home from racing one evening, she came out of the kitchen and asked me what I'd been up to. "Nothing," I said. I didn't even bother to look at her as I started toward the stairs.

Then, Dad came around the corner from the kitchen. "Answer your mother!" he demanded. I ignored him and started up the stairs. Suddenly, he reached out, grabbed my ankle, and yanked so hard that I fell face down on the stairs. I glared at him and then, with a quick motion, reached back with my other foot and kicked him firmly right in the side of his face, screaming, "Fuck off!" I ran up the stairs as fast as I could, went into my room and locked the door as Dad followed in hot pursuit. He was boiling mad and screaming at me, "Get back here, you son of a bitch!" I then heard Mom yell. "Bill, don't you dare! Leave him alone!"

To my surprise, he stopped, and I didn't come out of my room until he left to go back to Arlington later that evening. I had been lifting weights at school for some time now and was getting pretty strong. I was no longer afraid of Dad and wouldn't have hesitated to go toe-to-toe with him. Mom told me later that she really thought he was going to kill me. It was the maddest she had ever seen him.

Mom was distraught that I had shut her out of my life and one evening she broke down, sobbing and pleading with me to let her back in. I told her that as long as she kept telling me what to do, I would ignore her. I'd developed a pretty strong aversion to authority by now and was extremely resentful at both Mom and Dad for how I was raised. I was in full rebellion mode and didn't give a damn what either one of them thought about me at this point.

But Mom kept hammering away at the wall I'd put up and I hated to see her so hurt. I finally decided to just tell her everything and see how she liked it. She didn't. I told her about my drag racing and it scared her half to death, but she never tried to stop me. I guess she thought she'd take what she could get of me. After that, she stopped trying to control me and our relationship changed dramatically. We became very close and I made it a habit to talk to her about everything that was going on in my life. She soon became the only person in my life that I could talk to about anything that was going on with me. Our relationship continued like that until the day she passed away in 2015.

CHAPTER 20

A WALKING BAG OF HATE

By the time I left for college, I was a mobile advertisement for my father's moral code. I'd absorbed many of Dad's beliefs and knew beyond doubt that blacks were lazy, aggressive complainers and Jews were just out for themselves. Then I started to meet some of them and began to realize that a person isn't defined by his race or skin color, but by who he is inside and what he does. But it took a while.

I was an angry young man, tortured by my thoughts, terribly shy and unable to look anyone in the eye or hold their gaze, terrified that they would see right through me and know how worthless I was. Looking back, the sad thing was that I had no idea how messed up I was; I was not consciously aware that my father was an abuser or of the anger within me. I just thought everything I had been through was normal, and that how I felt was normal too.

Nothing much changed for me my freshman year. I'd look at my classmates and play a mental game, picking out the Jews, saying to myself, "Yep, Jew." I had learned from Dad what their most distinctive physical features were, what the most prominent Jewish names were and how they sounded. It was like being trained to spot enemy aircraft during a war.

I wasn't enjoying my first year of freedom from my father in the least, perhaps because I was in the wrong college. Through entirely my own fault, I had ended up in Bridgewater College, a small, private,

Christian college in Virginia where most of the students were white. There were a few blacks sprinkled here and there, but not much in between.

At the start of my senior year in high school, Mom had scheduled me to take the SAT but I refused to go. I told her I had no intention of going to college and planned to work construction after finishing school. She begged, I refused, and so it went. She approached me one last time in November that year, saying it was my last chance to take the test, practically sobbing. I gave in and sat for the stupid exam, but did no preparation for it whatsoever. I hadn't even given a thought to the colleges I wanted the results sent to, but remembered at the last moment that a track buddy who had graduated the year before had put down Bridgewater, so I wrote that down.

I got the results back and they were terrible, a mediocre 990, and so I shelved the whole college idea. Weeks later, I got a call from someone at Bridgewater, saying they'd like to offer me a place in next year's freshman class. I was stunned, but the voice on the end of the phone assured me that it was no mistake. I asked if they offered a computer science major and the voice said, "Sure do!" He said he'd mail me an application. I didn't give it much thought after that, but evidently the application came and, without me knowing, went out again. Mom had filled it out.

In the spring, Mom handed me the Bridgewater acceptance letter and pleaded with me to give college a try. The summer went by quickly and then it was time to leave home for the first time in my life. I was excited, but mostly scared. When the day finally came for Mom to drive me to Bridgewater, Dad was gone. He hadn't even bothered to say goodbye to me when he left a few days earlier. I thought he'd come home for the weekend, as usual, but this time he didn't. So, Mom and I loaded up the car together, and off we went.

I settled in quickly at Bridgewater but was disappointed to discover that, contrary to their assurances, they sure didn't offer a major in computer science, only a couple of classes. I had no idea what to major in, so I took mostly humanities courses while I tried to decide. The classes were interesting and pretty easy, so I made mostly A's. I also joined the track team and threw discus and javelin. I asked Mom to come to my first home track meet and she said they'd both be there. I was shocked because Dad had never attended any of my high school events and I was excited to think that he would actually come.

When the meet started, I scanned the spectators, but there was no Mom and no Dad. I did my three discus throws and won a second place medal. I was about to walk back to my dorm when they showed up. Dad had been two hours late getting home and Mom was really upset. But I was still happy to see them and showed them my medal. "I got second in the discus," I declared with pride. "Oh yeah, who beat you?" Dad asked. I pointed to the guy who won first place. He was a big black guy, a senior at Bridgewater. "That's Sam. He got first place," I said. Dad stopped smiling and stared at me in silence. Then all the old feelings of failure flooded back and I looked away. "I guess we'll head on back then," Dad said and turned to go back to the car. On the verge of tears, Mom hadn't said a word the whole time. I looked at her and said, "It's OK Mom, I love you." Then the dam burst and she blubbered back to me, "I love you, too."

Dad never tried to visit me again in college, and I found out later that the real reason he had agreed to come to the track meet that day was because he was going to see a printer a few miles from the campus who was printing "The Turner Diaries" for him. I didn't know at the time that he had finished the book. I found out only when it started making a hate-headline splash.

When Mom came back a few weeks later to pick me up for fall break, she asked me to drive while she read to me from a bunch of college catalogs. When she got to the wind tunnels at Virginia Tech that were part of the Aerospace and Ocean Engineering major, I knew that was for me. Somehow, with Mom's help I suspect, I got into the Virginia Tech College of Engineering as a transfer student. I couldn't wait to finish my freshman year at Bridgewater. Without doubt, I wanted to be an Aerospace Engineer.

That year I hadn't given much thought to the beliefs Dad instilled in me. I paid little heed to politics or race relations, except to react against blacks at an instinctive gut level. It wasn't a real thought process, just an automatic reaction based on years of conditioning. When I came across blacks, I mentally labeled them as "nigger" and then dismissed them. As non-whites, I knew they were inferior to me and I even felt annoyed that they blamed us for their social woes. I clutched tightly to that belief, like a crutch, and felt a surge of energy pulse through me whenever I focused my hate on someone from another group. It made me feel superior to be part of the white race but yet, deep, deep down, something didn't quite feel right about it, either.

Strangely, I never picked up Dad's loathing of Jews. They didn't spark fear inside me, though I'm not sure why, given Dad's all-consuming hatred of them. Perhaps it was because I'd had no personal interaction with Jewish people up to this point. While I was certainly brimming with hate, I chose to focus it on blacks, gays, and any type of authority figure who tried to exercise control over me. I despised police officers, calling them all "pigs." I would comply with an order, but seethe inside. I simply couldn't see both sides of a situation and had no idea what love for others felt like. Most of my thinking was based on fear, but I did a good job of hiding it from the world, except perhaps, from my mother.

I was not a religious person and had not been allowed to attend church growing up. But in my junior year of high school, a friend invited me to join a church league basketball team and it was after one of those games that I met my first girlfriend. She was the pastor's daughter and I started attending services and bible classes just to spend time with her. I even agreed to be baptized by her father and at one point I declared myself to be "Christian," but that pretty much got shelved the moment I left for college. To Dad, Christianity was verboten. He declared it "like other Semitic religions, irredeemably primitive" and was furious at my apparent conversion.

But he needn't have worried. I soon decided that perhaps there wasn't a God after all and started to dismiss all religions as phony. I decided that the answers must lie in science, so I put all my mental energy into that in hopes of figuring out the riddle of life.

I began to change when I enrolled at VA Tech in the fall of 1979. Suddenly I was being exposed to people from all over the world, every color and creed, every race and religion. One of my first roommates was a South American man and he was nothing like what I thought a nonwhite would be. After living with him, seeing how he reacted to what was happening politically and socially in our country, I began to question what Dad had taught me. This man was not white, yet he was thoughtful, caring and very intelligent. I enjoyed his company and learned a lot from him about our world. Dad had taught me that non-whites were beneath us and not worthy of what we aspired to because they were not capable of our levels of intelligence and accomplishments. For the first time, I was beginning to see life at a different level.

Instead of identifying and labeling people by the physical features that my eyes were relaying to my brain, I was becoming more curious. Maybe Dad was wrong and being different didn't necessarily mean something negative? Instead of fearing and hating differences, perhaps we could embrace them instead? Just, maybe, it wasn't race that determined if a human was worthy but how they behaved. Perhaps people seemed different because of something else, like the culture they were raised in, and not deficiencies in their gene pool?

A defining moment was when Ronald Reagan was elected President. My roommate was devastated by the election results. He adored Jimmy Carter and the caring virtues he stood for. Back then, I would have more closely identified with conservatives than liberals. Conservatives tend to be more racially minded and don't embrace social welfare or aid for the less fortunate, and that was how I was raised to think. But my roommate believed all people were equal and that everyone deserved to be fully included within our society. I still can see the front-page picture of Ronald Reagan in the newspaper the day after the election. My roommate was so upset that he drew a dagger on Reagan's forehead, with drops of blood dripping down his face, then threw the paper on the floor in disgust. That was the first time I began paying attention to politics. Why was my roommate so angry and what was really happening in the world outside of me? I really had no idea. For the moment, I stuck with my familiar prejudices because they were more comfortable than questioning my own beliefs.

But I did start watching the evening news on TV, although I wondered at the back of my mind if it was real, because Dad had taught me that all media was controlled by Jews who had a sinister agenda behind everything America was told.

I was sure Dad finally would be proud of me when I got into VA Tech. Here I was, about to study the sciences, just as he did, and I knew he had an avid interest in aviation. He was at home, reading in his chair when I told him my big news. He didn't even look up from his paper.

"That's nice, Midget," he said. And that was it. I stood there a few seconds longer, hoping for more, but nothing came, so I walked away. He just couldn't acknowledge me and let me know that I was OK, he was not capable of showing me such a simple kindness.

I tried to pretend that I didn't give care anymore. I no longer felt that burning hatred for him I had from years ago. Instead, I became absolutely convinced that he was suffering from mental illness and that was what lay behind the years of hatred, abuse and neglect. I told no-one about him, or what he did. I knew by now that he was greatly admired by his followers and universally hated by his detractors. I did my best to not think about him because it was just too painful a process for me. I was also afraid that people would associate me with him. I didn't consciously think about how messed up I was, or how damaged I might be below the surface.

For the four years I was at VA Tech, I almost never saw him. When I was home in Fredericksburg during the summer break, I worked as an engineering aide at Naval Facilities Engineering Command at the Washington Navy Yard, and was gone every day from 5:00 in the morning until about 6:00 pm. That first summer I was at home alone for a couple of weeks because Mom was in California, visiting her family and Dad didn't come home, since there was no-one to cook meals for him.

One night I was awoken by a phone call about 2:30 am. I picked up the phone, still in the deep fog of sleep. The voice at the other end of the phone said, "This is Jason from the FBI. Who is this?" As my head began to clear, I replied "Kelvin." It hadn't sunk in that the caller had identified himself as being from the FBI when he spoke again, "Do you know where your father is?" Again I thought for a moment, and then realized that Dad hadn't been home for at least a week. "No," I replied finally. "Are you sure you don't know where he is? We haven't been able to determine his whereabouts recently and we need to know where he is and what he is up to." I told him that Dad hadn't been home for a while, and then the caller hung up.

I pondered for a few minutes what had just happened, and then I got angry. I had nothing to do with Dad or his business and yet I was being harassed in the middle of the night. Then I began to wonder if something had happened to him or what he had done now to attract this extra scrutiny. Then I forgot all about it and didn't even mention it to him when I saw him next.

CHAPTER 21

DAD'S TAKES HIS LEAVE — "I JUST DID WHAT I HAD TO DO"

My father was an extraordinary man — but not in a good way. When he deserted us, it was not for love of another woman, but for the love of himself, his ego and his political beliefs. I know of no-one else who would have dared to make such a statement about himself, but he did, and he did so with not a twinge of regret or a sigh of shame. He even put it in writing.

Mom was devastated when he announced he was leaving. She had not seen it coming, despite his long-term cruelty toward her. But one good thing came of it all. Mom went on to find someone who loved her. Though tragically she wasn't to have him in her life for long, she was happy for that time. He was a kind man; someone I like to think would have been a good father. He was an anchor when to me I needed it most and taught me a lot about life...and plumbing.

I'd known for a long time that my parents' marriage was on shaky ground but I didn't know just how close it was to total collapse because I was away at VA Tech. The edifice finally crumbled when Dad tried once more to convince Mom to quit her teaching job and join his cause full-time.

"Now that the boys are gone most of the time, I would like you to seriously consider giving up teaching and joining me full time," Mom said he told her. "We can get some place away from all of this congestion, where I can write and you can take care of the books and typing and manage things here. What do you think?" he asked.

Mom once again turned him away.

"You know how I feel about that, Bill. I know exactly what that would look like and I don't want that. We would be in the poor house and have nothing, and we'd be surrounded by the weirdos that you associate with. What kind of life would that be?" she replied.

But he persisted. She should reconsider now that Erik and I were taken care of, he said. "I would really like for you to join me. I feel very strongly that our government is going to collapse very soon and I want to be ready for that, and I need your help. We could make a go of it together. I think we would make a good team."

Mom declined again. "I'm sorry, Bill, but you know I can't live that kind of life. I like having a nice home with comfortable furniture and I like my status as a professor. If I gave all of that up I'd end up with nothing. You would be absorbed in your work all of the time and I know you well enough to know that I would essentially be broke and alone. I'd be crazy to do that."

That was it. Dad walked away and not long after that started an affair with a woman he had met at his office in Arlington. In February, 1983, he came home for the last time and informed Mom that he was filing for a divorce.

I was in my senior year at VA Tech when she called, crying as she told me the news. I was stunned and really felt bad for her but I was also surprised by her reaction. I couldn't understand why she was so upset. It wasn't like they had anything close to a good marriage. Dad had always been a terrible husband to her and yet here she was, sobbing and saying her life was over.

When she got off the phone, I sat there thinking about what had happened and after a few minutes I started to cry too. The more I thought about it, the harder I cried. I felt betrayed. Even though he was a complete disaster as a husband and father, I still loved him in some way and always secretly hoped that one day, he would change.

He never even called me to say goodbye, or to tell me what he was doing, or why. He just left, and that was it. The next time I saw him was when he came to my graduation at VA Tech in the spring of 1983. I was surprised to see him. He came by my apartment, gave me a hydraulic car jack as a graduation present, and then left again. He didn't say he was proud of me or anything remotely resembling that. By now I was so used to his selfish ways that I didn't give it any more thought, beyond my initial surprise at seeing him at all, if only for a few minutes.

Later, Dad did explain his actions, although he wrote to his own mother about the breakup many months before he bothered to contact my Mom again, or his sons.

I came across copies of his correspondence in a box of old letters among his effects. One from his own mother chastised him for leaving, questioning both his thinking and morals. I was surprised at her tone, given her dislike of my mother that she never bothered to disguise. I was also surprised that he made copies of his own missives. Perhaps he thought they would help redeem his reputation somehow, or justify his actions. But they didn't, at least not for me. Dad told his mother that he had left Mom in a matter-of-fact letter notifying her of his new address and phone number in Arlington, Va.

"Patty and I have had some severe marital problems for the last five years, with the roots going back much further, but until recently I tried to ignore them by working hard and spending as little time as possible at home," he wrote (1). "In the last two months, however, I established a relationship with a woman who works with me in the Alliance, and it became necessary to make a decision. Leaving Patty was by far the most difficult thing I have ever had to do, but it was necessary in order for me to have the peace of mind I need to do most effectively what I must do with my life.

"The break, unfortunately, has been very hard on Patty, although I hope that she will adjust favorably to it with the passage of time. The new relationship was only the final, precipitating factor in the break, not its fundamental cause, but it has been difficult for Patty to understand this. She has, I'm afraid, managed to turn both Kelvin and Erik quite strongly against me but I expected that. Time may or may not heal that problem."

Fortunately, he added hypocritically, Patty was not financially dependent on him "so there should be no legal difficulties." And then he enclosed the latest issue of his magazine.

Grandma Maggie was appalled by Dad's decision. She replied the same day she received his letter, misspelling Mom's name, as usual. "I wish you would not move out," but would "give things time to jell," she said, noting the old proverb about acting in haste and repenting at leisure. "None of us is perfect. Not you, not me, not Patti. No one is perfect. You've had to put up with Patti and Patti has had to put up with you. I've had to put up with both of you and you all have had to put up with me. (Right now, I am having to put up with this typewriter ribbon). You have two fine sons, of whom I am very fond and proud, and they are not perfect. But they and Patti and I all love you — imperfections and all."

"Patti and I were both very upset when you gave up your work in Connecticut and went into your present work, but we didn't turn our backs on you," she continued. "You all have had quite a struggle. Not many women would have stuck it out. Many men between 45 and 50 years or so go off the deep end. I have always believed that you were too smart and too cognizant of your responsibilities to leave your family, as some men do. I hope and pray that I am not wrong in that belief," she wrote.

She was wrong, but kindly continued to help support us when she could.

"I am very upset about the separation, which I hope will be only temporary," she wrote to Mom in February, 1983, enclosing a $700 check to help cover some of my expenses. She also urged Mom to persuade Erik to postpone his plan to leave home. "You need him, his moral and financial support," she wrote. The fact that Mom would be teaching summer school that year would also be a blessing — it would help her financially and she would be "hopefully, too busy to grieve. Work is really the best cure, along with time," she said.

Dad waited 10 months, until December 1983, before he wrote to explain to Mom why he left. In typical cold-blooded fashion, he said he wanted to wait until he could do it objectively, instead of merely trying to "justify his actions," which, of course, is just what he was doing. He said he'd tried to tell her why at the time, but "all you seemed to be hearing was that I 'was leaving you for a younger woman'—or, at least, that seemed to be the message Erik and Kelvin were receiving." His relationship with the woman in his office was not the underlying cause, "only the thing which made it impossible for me to postpone me leaving any longer."

He and Mom now had "different values, different interests, different attitudes, and different priorities" and gradually had less and less in common, he said. "I had come to be concerned about my work, to the exclusion of nearly everything else. I did not care about what kind of furniture we had. You, by way of contrast, had very little interest in what I was doing, except as it affected the family or our living conditions. For example, you seldom read any of the things I published—not even my own writing," he noted, his ego clearly wounded.

He said he didn't "blame" her for the differences in their interests and priorities, and if it were anyone's fault, it was his. "When we were in Pasadena and in Boulder, we talked about our plans for the future — plans which suited you and which I thought suited me also. And it was I, not you, that abandoned those plans later," he admitted.

"I did not mislead or deceive you about my intentions, either at first or later. I just did what I had to do. You were an excellent wife, who went much further than most women would have in adjusting yourself to me, in giving up things that you wanted, and in doing things that you didn't want to do—first to please me, and later to keep the family together," he wrote.

"I certainly didn't make it easy for you. I know you regarded me as selfish and inflexible, always doing what I wanted to do and not caring what you wanted. Despite this, you stayed with me and continued to try to accommodate my needs. I am aware of how much you gave up, and I am very grateful to you for your patience and your love."

That awareness "always made me feel guilty," he confessed. He never knew when he asked her to give up something how many more sacrifices he would ask for in the future. "One thing just led to another. If I could have foreseen where we were heading—and if I had been sufficiently mature to face the issue squarely—then I would have gone my separate way without asking you to come along several years ago, perhaps as early as 1965, when I decided to quit teaching. That, at least, would have given you a much better opportunity to make a new start for yourself. The fact that I didn't do this, consequently caused you so much unhappiness, and finally left you alone after so long will always be a great burden on my conscience."

Then came the great hypocrisy, and how badly she had made him feel with her complaints.

"But it is better for you that I have left now than it would be if I had postponed a separation even longer," he wrote. "And it is better for me, despite my conscience. I am sure that you are aware that our growing differences were imposing a strain on me, if only because of our lack of intimacy for the last five years we were together. I never explained the reason for the latter, at first because I did not fully understand it myself, and later because I knew it wouldn't solve the problem."

After all that, he had the nerve to complain about her worries about money. "All of those arguments about money, all of those recriminations about my not doing my share to support the family, all of the complaints about my selfishness had a cumulative toll on me," he said. "On top of that was my own feeling of inadequacy, both because I wasn't the chief breadwinner and because I felt that I had lost my authority in the family as a consequence."

"I knew some time ago that I would eventually have to leave, but I didn't want to face it because I didn't want to hurt you. Some things finally made it easier for me—for example, your defensiveness where Erik and Kelvin were concerned. I do not begrudge Kelvin a $12,000 car or you a Hawaiian vacation, but things of that sort made it more difficult for me to feel guilty about not earning more money. And they put in a different light your refusal to give up your teaching position and work for the Alliance for the smaller salary I could afford to pay myself. Finally, I met Liz, and the break became inevitable."

Those were manufactured memories to make him look better — I bought that car with the money I earned from my first job as an aerospace engineer and with the help of a car loan after I graduated in June 1983, none of the money came from Mom and certainly not from him. And, yes, Mom did go on a vacation with her sister to Hawaii but that was long after their divorce, so his feigned guilt about not earning money didn't enter in to it. I'm not sure what he was thinking when he used those examples to justify leaving, except how it would look to some future biographer, which is probably why he kept a copy of the letter in the first place.

And then, came the final insult: he offered to send her copies of his magazine so she would understand things better.

"One question I am sure is in your mind, but which I cannot answer adequately in this letter, is why didn't I leave the Alliance and find work paying more money, if I felt guilty about not supporting the family," he continued.

"You asked that question often enough, and I tried a hundred times to answer it. You never understood and always assumed I was acting solely from selfishness. All I can do here is repeat myself: I have done what I had to do, to the extent I knew what that was. I have written about that in our magazine, and I have published what another member has written along the same line. I'll send you the magazines if you really want to try to understand, but I don't think they will help," he said.

"Perhaps it will help you to know that I have resolved to devote all of the time I have left entirely to my work and to make fewer compromises than I did before. This will inevitably lead to hardships that you would have found intolerable if we were still together," he concluded. "And I shall always think of you only with affection and regret." He signed it, "Love, Bill."

His letter was not only self-serving, but smacked of martyrdom — he considered leaving us in 1965, when Erik and I were only five years old? Wow, what a Dad!

I had not known about all of the arguments he alluded to, but I have no doubt they occurred. I can see Mom expressing her dismay and frustrations with him listening, but not bothering to respond and instead just walking away. At the same time, each recrimination from Mom probably deeply wounded him, each building on the other to become a lasting, festering sore. I can easily see him responding to her with his own requests that she quit her job and join him full time working for the Alliance, to live a life of poverty for the cause

His hand-wringing about not being "the chief breadwinner" is more than hypocritical, given an article he wrote in his National Vanguard in 1978. It burns me when I read it, even now. It was a shabby attempt to buff his image as a superhero who gave up everything to save the white race.

According to him, he doubled his salary when he left Oregon State to join Pratt & Whitney in Connecticut and, fortuitously, gained staff privileges at Yale University Library that would allow him to research a book he planned to write on how to save the white gene pool.

Then, to his dismay, he discovered dozens of books on the very same subject, tomes that lay gathering dust on library shelves. So, he donned his martyr-in-chief mantle and quoted Jesus, which was odd, since he despised Christianity and had forbidden us to worship a Jew. "Jesus said it a long time ago, and he was absolutely correct: 'It is easier for a camel to pass through the eye of a needle than it is for a rich man to enter into the Kingdom of Heaven,'" he wrote.

"There was little danger of my becoming rich by following the course I had chosen, but my experiences with wealthy conservatives convinced me that I should take no chance that I might, at some future date, be influenced by concern for material possessions. I divested myself of the property I had left — including my automobile and my bank account — and took a vow of poverty. From then on, I would never own more than he clothes of my back, the few essentials of my trade, and pocket money."

I knew Dad to be an extremely selfish, inflexible man, just as Mom said he was, but this was Saint Bill at his best. He never did anything for the family that he didn't want to do. He never wanted to work for anyone else, so he simply quit his job, even with a wife and two five-year-old boys to take care of, and never earned a penny after that.

The thought of being a father and husband was just too much for him to bear, but he couldn't admit the truth, so he cloaked himself in some kind of righteousness.

The responsible thing for him to have done was to take care of his family. Instead, he developed half-assed theories about racial purity and then built his life around trying to convince others he was right. He was a con-man at best, but mostly mentally ill. The worst thing was that he fed the rage and hate of others who were equally sick but didn't have his capacity to reason.

But perhaps what shocked me most in this whole sorry saga was a letter Mom left behind when she died a few years ago. It was dated less than two years before their divorce and describes a continued faith in her husband that's almost beyond belief.

"To say that I was head-over-heels in love with my husband on my wedding day is putting it mildly," she wrote. "However, I can truthfully say that no one at that small Thanksgiving Day wedding expected it to last more than six months, except possibly the bride and groom." They had known each other only eight months. She was 29 and he was 23, and they were polar opposites. She was a college dropout, he was a first-year grad student. She was warm and affectionate, while he was reserved and withdrawn, except when they were alone. She was "the nose-to-the-grindstone type," while he was the opposite— he loved to travel and do "crazy things." She wanted a family and "he, very adamantly, did not." In addition, both their families disapproved. "My parents said that they were not gaining a son, only losing a daughter."

Nevertheless, their first two-and-a-half years of marriage were "scary, but beautiful!" They climbed mountains, flew in his two-seater plane over the Rockies, brushing the tree tops because the plane was not designed to go that high, and rode cross country on a motor scooter.

"One night we were having dinner with my parents. My father, innocently enough, asked my husband when he was going to be a grandfather. My husband was furious. He replied unequivocally, 'Never!' He stormed out of the house. I said 'Goodnight' to my parents and followed him. Although I was heartbroken, we never discussed it. I resigned myself to a childless marriage, rationalizing that I was too old to start a family anyway."

She wrote that she "doubled" her birth control measures, but obviously something went wrong because three months later, the day before their third wedding anniversary, they were sitting in a doctor's office, listening to him say she was pregnant, but that there wasn't a "tinker's-damn-in-hell (pardon the expression) chance that you can carry this baby."

After traveling home in silence, Dad asked her why she wasn't in bed, resting. "It was then that I knew that I had married the right man, and that, come what may, we would be together for the rest of our lives." Seven months later, on a hot, muggy June evening, she gave birth to us. "Now, with our silver wedding anniversary just a few months away, I am still head-over-heels in love with my husband, and, even if I had the chance, I wouldn't change a thing!" she said.

That last paragraph blew me away. I was there. I witnessed what their marriage was like. Dad was a terrible husband, period. How could she say she wouldn't change a thing? I can understand loving someone and trying to make it work, but to not want to change a thing? I saw how she worried and fretted over him every day. She slaved over him and took care of his every need, except one — she refused to join him in his crusade of poverty and white supremacy.

When Dad left, she went into a deep mourning and the only thing that saved her was a very kind and gentle man called Joe Holmes, a fellow professor at Mary Washington College. Mom had buried herself in her work and he noticed that she seemed sadder and more depressed than usual. Joe approached her one day and asked what was going on. Unusually, Mom decided to confide in him. Joe felt bad for her and invited her to join him and his wife for drinks that evening. Soon the three of them became fast friends. Then Joe's wife died of lung cancer. Mom and Joe continued their friendship and over time, fell in love. They were married in May, 1987.

Mom and Joe continued to teach at Mary Washington College until they retired a year later. Joe wanted to move to Las Vegas after that, but Mom desperately wanted to stay in Virginia, where Erik and I lived. She told me that one of her biggest and most painful regrets was moving to the East Coast with Dad and only seeing her parents once a year after that. Now she was about to do the same thing to her sons. She struggled with her decision but eventually agreed to go with him.

Joe was a good man and treated her like the love of his life. Mom told me that every night before falling asleep, he would hold her in his arms and tell her how special she was and how much he loved her. Dad had finally set her free and, for the first time in a very long time, Mom experienced a truly happy, loving marriage.

Joe died in January, 2001 from complications from diabetes. Mom was in a terrible state and I went out straight away to be with her and help her settle Joe's affairs. We were sorting through his things the next day when the doorbell rang. A few moments later, I heard Mom let out a very loud wail that scared me half to death. I ran to the front door and she was standing there, sobbing, holding a vase of flowers. She handed me the note that came with the flowers. It was from Joe: "To Pat, the love of my life. I am so sorry I had to leave you so early. Please know that I love you and will always be looking over you until we are together again. Love, Your Joe."

He had made a huge difference in Mom's life and in mine. He was instrumental in helping my wife and I set up our construction business. He helped us incorporate, open our first business bank account, and finance the start up. He also taught me much of what I know about construction, especially plumbing. He was a very good plumber and generously shared everything he knew about the trade. He even encouraged me to put a new bathroom in my first house. I was scared to take on such a big project but he guided me every step of the way. It was what eventually gave me the confidence to start our own business, which is still going strong today, 33 years later.

I am so grateful that I knew him, and that Mom found joy before she passed away. As for Dad, he married his Alliance co-worker shortly after his divorce but she fled when she found out that he expected her to live on the remote compound he planned to build in West Virginia. So, he started out all alone again, with only his hate to keep him warm.

He admitted years later that he had subordinated his own family to the needs of the Alliance and had made it his priority in his life, sleeping on a couch in the office from Monday to Friday, hanging on financially "by his fingernails," unable to pay his bills. He felt he would be a failure if he didn't make it work. He said Mom's colleagues at the university questioned his sanity when they saw his name in the paper but he didn't want to have to hold back on his views because of her. (2).

CHAPTER 22

HEW A COMPOUND, SAVE A GENE POOL

Not long after he cut us out of his life, Dad became convinced that a race war was imminent — or, at a minimum, that the government was about to collapse and society would fail on a massive scale. It was simply inevitable, he said, given the pervasive corruption of the day and the influence of the Jews. So he started on a new quest — he would build a safe haven, a place where he and those like him could seed a new, white race out of the rubble of what used to be.

"What must be saved is the gene pool of our race. If we are able to do that, everything else will eventually be achieved. If we fail to do that, everything will ultimately be lost," he wrote.

He worked tirelessly on his grand design and, after months of searching, found the perfect place for his new society: 360 acres on a windswept West Virginia hillside. It was almost inaccessible by road and so would be easy to defend with the weapons he had stockpiled, and with hard work it could be cultivated to make them self-sufficient one day. For some strange reason, he thought wild and remote West Virginia would attract a host of followers to him, but it didn't.

He bought the West Virginia land in October, 1984, for $95,000. I don't know for sure where the money came from, but I'm inclined to believe the account of Tom Martinez, a former associate of Robert Mathews and who became an FBI informant. Martinez maintained in a book he wrote that $50,000 of the proceeds from The Order's robberies was given to Dad. He bought the land the same month he is said to have received the Mathews' donation; other right wing groups were also given money, according to testimony at a trial of Mathews' associates. Dad always denied receiving money from The Order, and insisted that his closest disciples had set up a building fund to pay for the purchase.

A few years earlier, Dad had come up with his own religion that he called Cosmotheism. He proclaimed that mankind is one with a great being, whom he called the Creator. The Creator made everything on the earth, in the universe, and beyond, and that a mysterious consciousness bound all living and inorganic things together. "Evolutionary development, particularly racial differences, is the basic idea behind Cosmotheism," he wrote. Man was a part of the Creator and if he became one with nature and was racially pure, he would evolve into a self-aware species with a higher consciousness, and would himself be almost godlike, he believed.

Dad would point to great men whom he said had a similar vision. Irish playwright George Bernard Shaw, in his play Man and Superman, called the Creator the "Life Force," while German philosopher Friedrich Nietzsche's novel, Thus Spoke Zarathustra, described man's purpose as preparing the way for a more conscious, nearly godlike Superman, the Ubermensch.

By buying those desolate acres, Dad hoped to play Superman and use eugenics to create a community of the best and the brightest that would secure the future of the white race. He likened his new religion to an old Norse belief in a mythical ash tree called Yggdrasil, which was said to link nine Norse worlds and was central to their pre-Christian idea of the cosmos. Dad claimed it was easier to believe that than in Christianity's notions of racial equality and a singleperson God who died nailed to a piece of wood.

Cosmotheism is much like an old pagan belief, Panentheism, which holds that a divine spirit penetrates every part of the universe and beyond time and space. God is seen as the soul of the universe, not as a person, and transcends all things. Many white supremacists have adopted Cosmotheism as their neopagan religion to bolster their white identity and hatred of immigrants but I sometimes wonder how they, and Dad, would react if they knew that some of the oldest religions in the world, among them the mystical Jewish tradition of Kabbalah, subscribe to a similar doctrine.

Anyway, Dad started moving forward with his plan for what he eventually called a Cosmotheist Community in 1974 by splitting people who attended his Sunday talks into two groups. Those who wanted to know about his strategy to deal with Jews and blacks were asked to attend National Alliance meetings. But the special ones, those who shared his fundamental beliefs, were invited to further discussions about society's spiritual woes, which Dad said included the breaking of the bond between the people and the land, the spread of democracy, and Christianity's failure to build a community of blood as well as faith (1).

The special ones also included the people who shared his views about raising kids away from TV and outside a school system where they would come into contact with "the corrupted kids," I suppose like Erik and I meeting blacks at the swimming pool. One of the most important functions would be the education of the Community's children, Dad told his followers. Classroom training would cover not only traditional subjects — languages, sciences, math, geography, history, literature and the arts — but also focus on giving children a strong sense of identity. Lessons in ethics and religion would be "designed to develop in each child a Cosmotheist way of thinking," he said. "Training outside the classroom to build consciousness, character and self-discipline in each child will be at least as important as his formal instruction and will determine the nature of most of his waking activity each day, in both play and work." He even wrote a hymn, "Race of Beauty," to the tune of "Rock of Ages," for his new church.

Some of his writings remind me an awful lot of the Nazi Lebensborn Program. Dreamed up by Hitler's SS enforcer, Heinrich Himmler, the strategy was aimed at raising the rate of "Aryan" children born to people who were classified by the SS as "racially pure." The SS, the police, and even the Army in the end, were ordered to father as many children as possible with Aryan women. Most were born out of wedlock, then taken away and placed in special centers to be raised as true Aryans to help create a "super-race" and replace Germany's war losses.

Dad's discussion group formally organized as the "Cosmotheist Community" in February, 1977. They adopted as their symbol the Life

Rune from the Norse runic alphabet — it looks a bit like a deformed cross — and represents creation, rebirth and renewal. Each Community member wore a Life Rune pin on their lapel or blouse, and a 12-foot tall version of the Rune was attached to their main building when I attended Dad's memorial service in 2002.

"Church" was added to the name a little later, and Dad began calling himself a "minister" whenever he contacted government agencies. It was a transparent attempt to qualify for a federal and state tax exemption for the church, but was only partially successful.

He had previously claimed an exemption for the National Youth Alliance as an "educational group" but IRS put a stop to his antics. Dad sued and lost, with a U.S. Appeals Court in 1983 upholding the IRS decision. The ADL, NAACP and the American Jewish Congress all filed amicus briefs, citing his calls for violence against their members. In the end, he was allowed a state tax exemption but on 60 acres only, plus the buildings used for religious purposes. He had been counting on full tax relief to help his finances — he told donors in 1985 that the Community would be "self-supporting through tax-exempt donations and through the mail-order sale of books and other materials to the public."

Of course, being a "minister" did have other advantages: he was able to conduct his own marriage ceremonies — which he did three times, marrying Eastern European women.

Dad moved into the settlement permanently in 1985. "My wife decided not to come with me and a divorce ensued," he said in a newsletter to followers. The woman he referred to was not my mother, but rather her first replacement, Liz Prostel, who worked at the Alliance. A year later, the wife of another member pulled out with her daughter, and there was another divorce. "For one dark and lonely year, there was just Don (one of his followers) and I. At least there was plenty of work to keep us from thinking too much about our lack of women and children," he told supporters.

When they first arrived at the compound, they labored day and night with only trees and rocks for company. There was a 100-year-old farmhouse on the site, a few older ruins, and water from natural springs. The land was rugged, 2,500 to 3,600 feet up, and about 80% covered with forest, mainly maple, hickory, walnut and oak. They killed and froze for food an assortment of deer, wild turkey and rabbits. The climate was brutal, with winter temperatures dropping to -30 Fahrenheit at times, while summer days would hit, perhaps, 85. The nearest inhabited area was Hillsboro, a small village about three miles away. To reach the compound required a mile-long drive up the mountain from the nearest paved road, so rough it was like a rocky stream bed, though in dry weather a skillful driver might be able to negotiate it in an ordinary vehicle. During the first two years, they drilled three wells, dug three septic systems, and added a bathroom and plumbing, including a hot water heater, to the farmhouse. They bought two mobile homes, hauling them up the mountain with the aid of a donated diesel tractor, then started on the church building, digging ditches for water and sewer lines, and improving the internal road so they could move up heavy equipment. And they planned for the long term. There would be no overhead wires or power poles but rather communications and alarm cables underground to ensure that they would be safe from attack, though I'm not sure from whom.

By January, 1988, there were seven members in all, including three family units, and that was no more than the number he had started with three years earlier. One family backed out when they realized "the primitive living conditions and the grueling work schedule that would be their lot," he wrote. "Finding stable Community members has not been easy." He blamed the 1960s, the boom years for alternative communities, and the 1980s, which were a bust for such activities. The 1990s would be better. In prosperous times, everyone wanted to play it safe and keep their economic security blanket. But "there are very definite signs that security blankets everywhere will be coming unraveled during the next few years," he said.

The nuclear family would be the "basic building unit." He was looking for couples and a "sexually balanced mix of single men and women." He needed four or five couples per year, with an ultimate limit of 50 families for a total 200-300 people, including children, he said. "Hard work and a relatively demanding schedule are things which members should consider permanent features of their lives in the Community," he wrote.

The customary work week was six 11-hour days, with one day a week reserved for family activity, household maintenance, and religious activities. Women were to look after their husbands and children, "although at least some community work will be expected from every able-bodied female." Members should expect isolation and austerity, necessary to protect the Community from outside influences, and they shouldn't look for outside recreation: a trip into town every 10 to 14 days is reasonable, but three times a week is not (2).

And members would need more than an adventurous nature. They had to have a stronger affinity with the trees and rocks and mountain sky than the restaurants and shopping malls, but given the amount of work expected, I think they'd need a touch of martyrdom, too. There would be a monthly allowance of $200 per adult and another $100 per child for food and household expenses. There would be no room for luxuries and all liquor and addictive substances were banned. He admitted that it would be Dad to "coax people to join" his little group.

"One cannot be too civilized, too accustomed to the convenience and softness of American life." Members must learn to do things for themselves, from cutting their own hair to vehicle repairs, plumbing and food production and must see such things "a stimulating challenge not an aggravation," he said. "Manual labor is an activity which should benefit every member, and discomfort in moderation is not necessarily to be shunned."

I will concede that they made an extraordinary amount of progress in three years.

By 1988, there was a 7,000-volume library and the compound had a video cinema and a shop where they could do machining, woodworking and electrical projects. Electricity came via cable from the valley below to power the water pump at the bottom of the well they had built, and run the compressor in the heat pump that circulated hot and cool air. They still depended on fuel from the valley to keep trucks running and to heat their church building, but were able to use wood-burning stoves for warmth everywhere else. There was enough fallen wood on the ground, without the need to cut down trees, to keep 50 families warm, he said.

For food, they harvested fruit from pear and apple trees, and gathered black walnuts and hickory nuts. They raised chickens for eggs and rabbits for meat and fur, and a vegetable garden was planted. Dad hoped they could halve their dependency on food from the valley within two years and, in an emergency, that they would be able to do without outside food entirely. Within a year, they would put in gasoline and diesel fuel tanks, and that fuel should last a decade if they only used it to power chain saws, he believed. Even then, he said, they were more self-sufficient than people in the valley. While there were power cuts at least weekly, but they had battery backup power that kept their computers, communications, lighting and alarm networks running, while extended power loss led to "widespread misery in the valley."

They failed in one task, however. According to FBI files, Dad and his friends made "several unsuccessful efforts" to purchase a storefront building in Hillsboro from which they could operate a bookstore as a way to establish public contact and raise funds from the sale of their published materials. They had offered up to $19,000, but found no takers (3).

And not everything at the compound was rosy.

Their relationship with neighbors was good, except that "Jews have done their best to stir up trouble with wildly alarmist news stories about us in the controlled media," he wrote in his newsletter. "There have been rumors at various times that we were building a terrorist training camp here, were growing marijuana and processing other drugs, and had missile silos and large caches of weapons on the land." But there was an upside: the rumors scared away unwanted visitors. A preacher had written to the local paper saying that West Virginia didn't want people like them and "asking the authorities to run us out," but he fell silent when Dad wrote back, suggesting most people were more open-minded, and telling him to keep his bigotry to himself.

The local sheriff wasn't so easy to brush off, however. He took "a hostile stand," which Dad branded as "grandstanding for the Jewish media." Local stores and gas stations were "uniformly cordial" to the Community and, he claimed, people considered the sheriff "a liar and a busybody." The locals were very conservative and the Community took pains not to give the impression that they were there to make trouble or change their way of life. "The Jews have failed to persuade most of them that that is the case and they are willing to leave us alone as long as we don't bother them, even if they believe some of the rumors about us …except for the professional Christians, the locals don't like Jews anyway."

The local economy was farm-based and "a chronic recession" had the advantage of keeping transients and newcomers away. The population of the county was about 9,000 at the time, and "there are no known Jews or other Asiatics in the county, and only about five black families." Poor whites living in tar-paper shacks were a small minority and he expected no problems, except that the Community might have to resort to courts from time to time "to force politicians to keep their noses out of our business."

Their own economy relied on donations from supporters and mail order sales. He thought they might try selling honey, eggs and nuts at some stage. Their operating expenses were quite low but they were short of capital. A purchase of steel for a vehicle maintenance, equipment storage and food processing facility wiped out what was left of their funds.

Luckily, he wrote, supporters had donated power tools, and they were also able to take advantage of the government's "extraordinarily wasteful surplus disposal program." They got office equipment, furniture and household appliances from the program at a fraction of the market price — they paid just $35 for a near-new Sears fridge that the government had paid $521 for, and $7,000 worth of high-quality drapes for just $5, plus a $1,300 studio quality VCR for $50. The problem was, they couldn't count on getting stuff they needed — like an arc welder — from the government when they needed it.

To house a new family, they would need $15,000, and that was assuming that the family did most of the construction themselves. They needed another $30,000 to build a house for guest workers, with four to six bedrooms, a kitchen area and bathroom. Dad had thought initially that some people who joined would bring in new capital, but the younger ones had not worked long enough to accumulate money, which meant continuing to rely on donations.

He blamed the Anti-Defamation League, "the Jewish secret police agency," for much of his trouble with the IRS. It was hard to make the government understand what they were doing on the mountainside, and even people who were friendly to them failed to grasp their purpose. He recalled making a speech the year before to a group whose leader had visited their settlement. That leader told his members that they were developing "an all-white vacation resort, where white racists can bring their families for a few days of white socializing each year."

I'd love to have seen his reaction when he heard that.

CHAPTER 23

THE FBI'S SURVEILLANCE LOT IS NOT A HAPPY ONE

While Dad claimed his Cosmotheists were a religious group entitled to tax exempt treatment by IRS, the FBI regarded them as a front for more sinister activities. Agents had watched Dad for years, but in February 1985 they got approval for a pen register that allowed them to log, but not record, all calls made from and received by a specific phone number — my father's.

With the trove of numbers they collected, agents fanned out to look into the lives of scores of people who had been in contact with the Alliance. Some couldn't be traced but others were watched and questioned, their vehicle descriptions and license plate numbers noted, and their records scoured for any trace of criminal or suspicious activity. Enquiries expanded to Seattle, Birmingham, Charlotte, Dallas, Denver, Detroit, Little Rock, Philadelphia, San Diego and San Francisco and Tulsa and scores of other cities and, at one point, agents from several field offices attended a meeting in Denver to set their investigative targets, priorities and goals.

The covert operation was dubbed "Cosmocom" and was classified as "a full domestic security/terrorism investigation," based at the Pittsburgh field office (1). Agents believed that the Alliance was engaged in a whole raft of illegal activities — including violation of laws governing rebellion and insurrection, seditious conspiracy, advocating the overthrow of the government, civil disorders, and riots. In 1987 they were given a special exemption to deposit appropriated funds into banks or other institutions as part of a probe into "crimes against the United States."

But they had a huge problem in monitoring activities at the Cosmotheist site.

"The National Alliance is located in a remote and mountainous rural area...and access is only available through one unimproved gravel road, which is located in its entirety within the confines of the 346 acres...Surveillance opportunities are limited and infrequent due to the remote setting," agents reported. "Ground surveillance ...is exceedingly difficult. Anyone from outside the area can be readily identified as a stranger by the local residents. Furthermore, the mere presence of strangers is information which is disseminated quickly throughout the area." The property also had an electrified fence around its buildings, they noted.

The Pittsburgh agents even looked into buying a nearby site for a surveillance base and took aerial photographs of the compound. They also tried to set up an intelligence operation down in the valley among residents who could alert them of "possible future acts of violence ...All individuals in this investigation should be considered extremely dangerous with unlimited ammunition and weapons," they reported.

But they did get a small break when Dad got sloppy with security. That surprised me, given that, when I was a kid, I was made to burn all his private papers once a week.

When he left for West Virginia, the FBI turned to utility companies for help to find him, while the U.S. Postal Service gave agents access to an overflowing P.O. box that hadn't been cleared for days. It was rented by the National Vanguard, the Alliance's publishing arm. In it were letters from across the U.S and overseas, some from military personnel. There followed a flurry of cables between U.S. bases and consular offices in Canada, Germany and South America.

One soldier at a German base said he had been approached by another, an Alliance member, and invited to join them in organizing to "protect the white people of the world against blacks and Jews." He was told the Alliance had training camps in the U.S. and Canada, and was shown a .44 Magnum pistol that was said to be part of a cache stashed in an apartment off base, ready to be used against blacks. A raid on the apartment turned up half a kilo of marijuana, but no guns. Alliance members also had been provoking black troops in the barracks and there were several verbal confrontations, after which some of the Alliance members were sent back to the U.S.

The FBI got lucky when local police keeping an eye on the compound spotted a vehicle belonging to a Community member delivering trash to a county landfill. They got a search warrant for the landfill and hauled away loads of information, including financial records, personal correspondence and computerized mailing lists for every region in the U.S., plus 14 countries — South Africa, West Germany, England, Canada, Mexico, Norway, France, Sweden, Switzerland, Italy, Australia, Belgium, Portugal, and South America and the Middle East.

The presence of law enforcement agents in the area, however, did not deter an attack on a local TV station, WOWK, which had run trailers for a five-part documentary it planned to air on neo-Nazi groups in the state. Five minutes before "West Virginia: A Haven for Hate" was due to be broadcast, the network was knocked off the air when its cables were cut. The FBI assigned two agents to the case. A station VP linked the vandalism to the series because they had received calls threatening lawsuits if it aired. Somebody who "knew what they were doing" had "sawed or hacked" a large cable leading to the satellite dish, taking the network off air, the VP said. Another cable had been cut to prevent local broadcasting also. No charges were ever filed.

Agents also wanted to learn about Dad's involvement in "terrorist activities" after a local resident wrote to the Department of Justice. The writer, whose name is redacted from the letter, said some farmland was used being used as a commune. Hitler swastikas were painted "all over the public highways," and the landowner supported the Ku Klux Klan and "hates Jews."

In the past, the farmland had been used for "machine-gun practice, mortors (sic), hand grenades, and such, by many people from many other states," the letter said. The landowner is not liked locally, and is not welcome. "He does not work, and has plenty of money. He is said to travel a lot, and does a lot of writing." He not only distributes subversive literature but "is a strong admirer" of Adolf, Libya's

Khadaffi, and Ferdinand Marcos of the Philippines, and thinks they "should rule our world." The matter must be investigated further "for fear we have here a terrorist training camp in our very midst."

An assistant Attorney General at the Department of Justice said he had asked the FBI "to look into this matter." The DOJ was "vitally concerned with the activities of terrorist groups" and if there was sufficient evidence, appropriate prosecutive action would be taken. The reply was from Bill Weld, who became a governor of Massachusetts and a would-be challenger to Trump for the Republican presidential nomination in 2020.

I don't know that anything happened as a result of the FBI's inquiries.

But up on the mountain, Dad spent some time in fear that he would be indicted for his involvement with associates of Robert Jay Mathews and The Order. Fifteen white nationalists had been indicted in Arkansas and Colorado on charges that ranged from armed robbery to the murder of liberal Jewish talk-show host Alan Berg in Denver, who was machine-gunned in the street in front of his home. Other charges included counterfeiting, the attempted murders of an FBI agent and a U.S. district court judge, a plot to pollute water supplies and establish guerilla training camps, and a conspiracy to overthrow the U.S. government.

What worried him most was the sedition trial in Fort Smith, Ark., he confided to Grandma Maggie in a letter shortly before the trial started in 1988. His name had repeatedly come up in news accounts, primarily because he had written The Turner Diaries, he told her. "The secret police and the controlled media like to maintain that the book is a 'blueprint' for the overthrow of the government. As the author of the blueprint, I clearly must be involved in the seditious activity of the people they are putting on trial, but they haven't yet figured out how to make a plausible case for that. So they just wave their arms and make general charges," he wrote.

"I read one secret police affidavit, used in obtaining a court order, for a telephone tap on one of the defendants, in which the claim is made that the 'Order' is an ongoing revolutionary enterprise and I am one of the leaders of it. This is pure baloney and I suspect that even the secret police know it, but it makes sensational headlines, so they keep using it," he said.

He was right, at least on one point.

The FBI regarded Mathews as a terrorist and "a close friend of Dr. Pierce." They were keen to bring charges against Dad but had been forced to write off the idea. Dad was "one of eight primary subjects in a major investigation of the right-wing" being run by the Little Rock field office, according to one FBI memorandum. But Arkansas agents acknowledged that "their case on Pierce is the weakest." The FBI's Pittsburgh office also noted that even if he were "indicted and subsequently convicted...a successor will continue [his] activities at the compound. If [he] is not indicted, he will return to the compound and continue with his right-wing revolution activities."

Dad couldn't help getting himself into trouble, even as he skated on the Mathews affair.

In the 1980s, he courted Ben Klassen, the founder of a racist, anti-Semitic, anti-Christian group called the Church of the Creator (COTC). He wrote to Klassen's publication, praising his work and expressing sympathy with Klassen over problems he was having with other supremacists. His letter was suitably servile, saying Klassen's work had helped him move "a substantial portion of the White resistance movement away from Christianity." Later, Klassen promoted the sale of Dad's hate-books, The Turner Diaries and Hunter in his publications.

Then, in 1992, Klassen found himself in deep trouble. His organization was held liable in a civil lawsuit for the murder of an African American sailor by a COTC member. Klassen put his 21-acre compound in Macon, N.C., up for sale in what was thought to be an attempt to avoid paying damages to the family. Conveniently for Klassen, Dad came up with $100,000 to buy the property, a price considered to be some way under market value. Almost immediately, Dad put the site on the market again, at an asking price nearly three times what he paid for it. The eventual buyer paid $185,000. The Southern Poverty Law Center eventually sued Dad on behalf of the sailor's family, contending that the original sale had been a fraudulent pretext by Klassen to avoid paying damages. In 1996, a federal jury ruled against Dad and ordered him to give the sailor's family the $85,000 profit he made on the sale. (2)

The FBI ultimately failed to bring terrorism charges against Dad. Regulations on the amount of time that could be devoted on domestic security and terrorism investigations worked against the Pittsburgh agents. They had not produced allegations of actual criminal activity in furtherance of the Alliance's social or political goals, "primary criteria" for such operations, and FBI HQ refused their request to extend their investigation for another 180 days.

Other investigations continued, however.

The National Alliance was always riddled with FBI informants and I suspect Dad was well aware that there were members in regular contact with agents. His neighbors also informed on him. But given how frequently he railed to his followers about the "secret police," I was shocked to find that he more than twice walked into an FBI office to talk to agents himself. And neither was he above asking for the FBI's protection when he thought his own life was in danger, despite all his sneering condemnations of them in public.

In 2000, he received emails at Alliance HQ threatening, among other things, to put a .38 caliber revolver down his throat, pull the trigger, and watch his blood spatter. For good measure, the sender said he would rip off Dad's skin and watch it burn, but the FBI's Pittsburgh office, which covered West Virginia, couldn't identify the sender.

The FBI kept files on Dad for years, quietly interviewing his former employers and neighbors, sketching out the layout of his office and the weapons he kept there, watching his movements and receiving detailed reports on the meetings he held. They had eight different informants when we were living in the house in Triangle, Va., the scene of many of my misadventures and Dad's experiments with explosives and chemicals.

One year, they watched as preparations were made to mark Hitler's birthday. There were 10 cars altogether, Dad's included, "loaded with various weapons and ammunition," agents said. The convoy drove to a farm in Orange Co., Va., where several shots were heard. The agents concluded that they were engaged in target practice. It's strange to read that all these years later because Dad took me and my brother with him on that outing. I was about 10. He handed me an M1-carbine to fire, and chose a shotgun for himself. He referred to his shotgun as a riot gun and he fired it countless times.

At first he was having difficulty hitting the target where he intended and complained to the fellow standing next to him. "You would think I could easily blow the head off that target with this damned gun" Dad complained. "Wait a minute Dr. Pierce, I have an idea," the man replied with a sly grin. He sprinted to the target and drew a huge Afro haircut on the top of the heads of several of the targets and returned. "Now imagine you are taking out a bunch of uppity niggers!" Dad burst out laughing and suddenly his aim got much better. Pow! "One dead jigaboo!" Pow! "Two dead jigaboos!" Pow! "Three dead jigaboos!" Dad snorted as he steadily blasted away at the human figure-shaped targets about 50 yards away.

Dad didn't give me any instructions on how to fire the M1 carbine but his friend, Robert, did. "Here son, hold the weapon with the butt tight against your shoulder and put your face here gently against the stock. Line up the point of the front sight into the center of the hole of the rear sight. Put that directly on your target and gently squeeze the trigger," he told me. We spent a couple of hours in the hot sun blasting away at the imaginary villains. The next day I remember seeing Dad's right shoulder and it was a nasty mess of black and blue from the recoil of the riot gun he had fired so many times the day before. He wore those bruises as a true badge of honor. That was the only time he ever took me shooting but I remember seeing those same exact guns in his trailer the day of his memorial service.

Informers had so thoroughly infiltrated Dad's operations that agents even had a full report on a dinner Dad held at a Holiday Inn in Alexandria, Va., to honor a cop accused of using unnecessary force to arrest a black kid and where he handed out "White Power" buttons to his guests. His neighbors informed on him, too, though perhaps not intentionally. FBI files note that a moving truck driver stopped to ask directions to our house one day, and a woman neighbor joked with the driver that if he couldn't find it, he could deliver the furniture that she assumed was in the truck to her house instead. The driver declared that she'd probably not want his cargo, since he was delivering weapons, handguns and tear gas canisters.

Perhaps Dad got wind of the neighbor's conversation. A month later, he voluntarily walked into the FBI's Alexandria office and sought to reassure them that the National Alliance wasn't a threat, and National Socialist Arms Co., was no longer in business.

CHAPTER 24

A BOX OF BULLETS FROM DAD

While Dad carved out his compound, rock by rock, I was repairing my life. It was a long, painful process, as much as his must have been, but somehow I got through it. I had left home convinced that I was nothing like my Dad. Yet whenever I felt mistreated or disparaged by anyone, my anger would be huge, far, far out of proportion. An accumulated rage roiled inside me that had been building for years, despite my attempts to suppress it my whole life. It turned out that I was actually just like Dad on the inside. These behaviors caused many struggles for me in my professional career and in my personal relationships. Even now, I am still working to heal the psychological wounds he inflicted on me. At times, I still feel shy, inadequate and unworthy of love — but I am making progress, and I have hope for the future.

I met my future wife at the Washington Navy Yard, where we were both working at the Naval Facilities Engineering Command during summer break. She was at VA Tech, too, studying architecture. I was taken by her beauty but far too shy to say anything. I told Erik about her one evening and he said I should ask her out, but just the thought threw me into a panic. He laughed when I said she was way, way out of my league. "You'll never know unless you ask her," he said. I tried to put her out of my mind, but a few days later she appeared at my desk, a large conference-room table in the back of the office. She said her name was Susan. She had some large drawings for a project that she needed to spread out and asked if she could share my space. I swallowed hard but did a good job of casually consenting to the idea, or so I thought. We would chat while working in the same space but I was too shy to ask her out, though I desperately wanted to. Then one day, she took the matter into her own hands. "You know, if you were to ask me out, I would say 'yes,'" she said. Even then, it took me a couple of hours to muster the courage to do so. I remember that night. We went to see a movie, "An Officer and a Gentleman," I was keenly interested in that movie because I was scheduled to go to the Pensacola Naval Station immediately I graduated from VA Tech to become a naval flight officer.

We continued to date for the rest of the summer and after returning to VA Tech that fall for my senior year. I asked her to marry me in the spring of my senior year, 1983. Much to my surprise she said yes, and we agreed that we would not get married until after she graduated in the summer of 1986. We both knew I was soon to head off to join the Navy and had no idea what lay ahead of us or how we were going to make it all work out.

My stellar career in the U.S. Navy lasted all of three days. One of the first hurdles of my new career was a flight physical on Day One. I was put into a mockup of a navy jet pilot's seat to be measured for reach and such to make sure I could reach all of the flight controls. I didn't give it a second thought and casually sat on the plywood seat as the corpsman measured just about every part of my anatomy. During the process I saw him take a rubber stamp and stamp a big red box on my physical form that said "Outside the Norm." I was immediately concerned and asked him what that meant. "It's nothing, don't worry about it,'" he said, without even looking at me. For the next four or five hours I was poked and probed in just about every way possible and was greatly relieved when it was finally over and we all marched off for chow. I had completely forgotten about that red stamp by then.

On returning to my room after a delicious dinner of fried rabbit, I was told to report to an office on base. I was escorted there and ordered to sit down. A few moments later an officer entered the room and sat at the desk in front of me. "Officer Candidate Pierce, I am sorry to inform you that you have failed the flight physical and have been disqualified from your OCS class. You are going to be immediately placed in X-Company and as soon as we can process your discharge papers we will be sending you home." I was stunned, unable to say a word as I processed all of the feelings of disappointment and disbelief.

Finally I spoke up, "But why? There isn't anything wrong with me!" I retorted. The officer picked up a paper on his desk and showed me the page with the "Outside the Norm" stamp on it. "You see this here?" he asked, pointing to red marks on the page. "This says the length of your legs from your buttocks to your kneecap is two tenths of an inch too long to fit in the T-2 trainer jet. All potential Naval Flight Officers are required to train in the T-2 jet. If you had to eject from that jet you would lose your kneecaps and the Navy isn't willing to take that risk. I'm sorry, but your Navy flying career is officially over."

The next two days were a blur of sadness and recrimination. I had to stay by myself on base as all of my fellow officer candidates started their OCS training. After the third day I was driven to the airport and put on a commercial flight back to Virginia.

I immediately began trying to find a job. Fortunately, I quickly got one at the Naval Air Test Center as an Aerospace Engineer. I was pretty happy to have found it and resigned myself to at least working on and around Navy jets, versus flying in them. In hindsight it was probably a good thing that I failed that physical because knowing now what I was like back then I would most likely have not survived OCS anyway. I was so averse to authority and thin-skinned as a young adult that I would have been eaten alive by the Marine drill sergeants during OCS. I shudder to think how that scenario would have played out as I reflect back on what an emotionally immature mess I was after enduring those years of abuse by Dad.

I was happy with Susan in my life but still felt a void where Dad should have been. One day, I decided to stop by unannounced at his Arlington, Va., office to introduce him to Susan. To my surprise, he seemed pleased and invited us in. Looking around, it was obvious that he was both living and working there. The first thing I saw were hundreds of books lining the walls in just about every place where you could squeeze in a bookcase or shelf. And then there was Herman, his blue point Siamese. He was friendly and Dad was clearly pleased when Susan sat down on the floor to play with him. Herman still had claws and didn't spare her hands, but she played pluckily on, much to Dad's admiration and approval.

After a while I looked Dad in the eye and asked bluntly why he'd given up his academic career and all but abandoned us for his alt-white cause. He turned away for a minute, then looked directly at me. "It was the only responsible thing I could do." I waited for him to elaborate but he didn't. I had many more questions but he obviously wasn't going to say anything more. There was an awkward silence, then we both deflected by turning to watch Susan and Herman. Dad told me he approved of Susan and after another long pause, we said our goodbyes and left. I felt proud that I'd at least had the courage to ask him one question, but I can't forget what he said and how he said it, and I regret to this day not pressing him further. I think he just wasn't capable or willing to consider what he had given up in order to do his "responsible thing."

The next time I saw Dad was at my wedding in August, 1986. I debated whether I should invite him or not to spare Mom any pain, but Grandma Maggie said her son would be there whether I invited him or not because she'd damned well make sure of it. So, I invited him. He came but I didn't have much chance to talk to him because he kept his distance at the reception, talking all the time to Grandma and Uncle Sandy. But he did produce a wedding present. It was a small, heavy box and came with a note saying, "To keep the wolves away from your door!" It was a box of 9 mm ammunition. Totally useless, as I didn't own a weapon but, as they say, it's the thought that counts.

Sometime later, to my shame, issues from my childhood that I had buried so deeply started to creep to the surface, causing those around me a lot of anguish. I was so afraid of being found lacking that I became depressed and took every challenge as a rejection. Before, I had been answerable only to myself. But once I was living with Susan, the problems became obvious. I was immature and behaved that way, not only with her but also in my professional career, even when I was running my own business. When confronted by an unhappy client, I would be thrown right back to the misery of days with Dad and my utter unworthiness.

I remember one morning in particular. It was 6:30 and I was still asleep. I was working as an aerospace engineer for the Navy and we ran a business on the side, designing and building decks. I had used some personal leave days to build a deck that Susan had designed for a neighbor. I had worked 'til dark the night before and was hoping to finish it the next day. Susan came in, jumped on top of me, shaking me awake. "Hey, you," she said, smiling. "I'm leaving for work and you need to get up and get to work yourself." I scowled. I wasn't ready to get up, and she said it wasn't fair that she had to work whilst I slept. I thought all day about what she said and it bothered me more and more. I felt she was trying to control me, and I resented it. I gave her the silent treatment that night, my immature way of punishing her for rejecting me. She, of course, had completely forgotten the incident from that morning but I held onto it and built it up in my mind as some huge deal. Childishly, I shut down and shut her out. It was behavior I'd learned as a child and it had always worked with Mom, so I did it over and over again as an adult. Except that all it did was create an unhealthy dynamic between the two of us.

I remember I went to great lengths to avoid attracting attention from anyone. If Susan insisted we go to a party, I'd hide in a corner, leaning against a wall, waiting for her to say we could leave. I was just trying to survive the evening, but some people thought I was a snob and disliked me for it. Only if I was around people I knew and had things in common with was I more comfortable, but as I didn't have many friends, I rarely enjoyed Susan's social events. I did my best to conceal my depression and it mostly worked until I'd face a crisis in my relationship with my wife or with a client. That would happen fairly regularly, each incident lasting for a few hours or days until I could let the rejection go and move on. Usually the crisis sprung from some silly, everyday-thing, like Susan complaining about something I was doing or not doing, or a client upset about our service. I took everything as a personal rejection, even when the criticism was small and well-meant. I'd play the victim and withdraw into myself, hoping for sympathy and acceptance, and it nearly destroyed my marriage.

Susan used to say that I was a mystery to her because I never talked about my innermost feelings and was emotionally unavailable to her. She didn't know that there were so many things I wanted to share with her over the years but was too afraid to do so. I was scared that if she really knew who I was, she would leave me. For relief, I had started smoking pot in college and fast became a chronic user. At times I resorted to alcohol and isolation, too, but nothing worked long term. Sometimes, I even thought about ending it all because when I tried to look into the future, I saw nothing but more of the same. Despite all this emotional baggage in my life, somehow our business took off.

We spent most of our time either working or hang gliding. She had given me a hang gliding lesson as a present for my 30th birthday. We took the lesson together and were hooked. That led to years of flying from the mountains in Virginia and nearby states. And, suddenly, I was making friends and having fun and it was then that I began to open up about Dad. Actually, to my great shame in retrospect, I kind of started to brag about him. By now, he was well known, both for his beliefs and The Turner Diaries and, in a way that suddenly made me somebody, too. While I shared none of his views, it felt good to see how my friends reacted when they heard that he was my father. I wasn't afraid of being linked to him anymore because it was obvious to those who knew me that I wasn't like him at all. Most of them had heard about the book and after their initial shock, they'd ask me lots of questions about what it was like to have him as a father, and I'd get a lot of sympathy from them as a result.

Thanks to the isolation of my childhood, I still was never comfortable among a lot of people, which created another strain with my wife. She grew up in a large and loving family that got together often. She was used to visiting grandparents, aunts and uncles and cousins almost every weekend. It was a way of life for her and she loved it. But growing up, I saw my grandmother only a handful of times. It was the same with other family members — we socialized with them only once every few years. Even in our own family, we rarely went anywhere, not even on vacation — Dad never wanted to take time away from his work to spend quality time with us. Even though I love my brother Erik, we rarely spoke or visited each other after we married and had our own lives. It wasn't that we didn't want to spend time together, we just didn't know any better. Susan expected me to feel the same way she did about spending time with family but I resisted. I didn't know most of her extended family well and felt awkward around them. When she wanted to see them, I would stay home. When she wanted to go to parties, I'd fight that, too. She got so upset that she insisted we go to marriage counseling. Of course, I refused to go.

When she finally dragged me to a church-based counselor, he gave us personality tests. He declared that I was extremely introverted and she was mildly extroverted. No surprise there, then, and it didn't solve the problem. In the end, we worked out a deal. We would go out and socialize but we wouldn't stay as long as she might otherwise have done. It kind of worked for a while, but didn't address my feelings of inadequacy.

We were mostly happy together but after a while we began to ask if there should be more to our lives other than just work and play. We were watching the news one night — it was Mother's Day, 1995 — and saw a segment about a couple who had just arrived at Washington National Airport with twin baby girls they had adopted from Russia. I casually mentioned something about us doing the same thing, but we didn't discuss it further that evening. The next day, there was an article in the newspaper about the same couple. Susan read it very carefully, and then asked if I was alright with her looking into the idea of adoption for us, too. I jumped at the idea and so began the greatest chapter in our lives.

CHAPTER 25

DAD AND HIS WOMEN

While we delved into the intricacies of adopting a child, Dad was scouring magazines, looking for a new mountain mate. He could not live without a woman for long. She didn't need to love him, and he certainly didn't need to love her. His requirements were simple: sexual services, cook, clean and do whatever he needed to keep his writing flowing and the Alliance operation moving forward.

My mother had filled that role for him for 25 years. In addition to working as a math professor at Mary Washington College, she kept house for him, cared for Erik and myself and all that that entailed, and spent any time left typing up his handwritten notes for his articles.

Deserting us paid off for Dad in numerous ways, thanks to Grandma Maggie, who not only helped keep him in funds but also paid for some of the work at his compound. Accepting yet another check from her, he told her in late 1985 that his financial situation had improved, "primarily because living expenditures are now so low, consisting almost entirely of the cost of groceries and the electric bill." He sent her pictures of the work at the compound and said she could stay in a guest trailer if she came to visit. And, of course, enclosed the most recent issue of his National Alliance bulletin.

Dad shared everything with Grandma, his progress at the compound, his strange theories, and his plans to cause trouble. In one letter, he told her he had bought shares in AT&T and would present an anti-affirmative action resolution at the next shareholders' meeting to try to stop the company from hiring black people whom, he believed, were intellectually inferior to whites. "That should be interesting," he noted. AT&T execs condemned the motion repeatedly but he continued to present it for the next three years. After that, he submitted proposals calling on AT&T to stop doing business with Israel. AT&T managed to block his motion, a move later upheld by the U.S. Securities and Exchange Commission.

Dad also told Grandma his woes about his love life, or lack thereof. On Christmas Eve, 1985, he thanked her for "the Yule box" she sent (he preferred the pagan term for Christmas) containing warm clothes for the winter weather, then described how he had been dumped by Liz Prostel, the woman he married after leaving Mom. A divorce the next year "seemed quite likely," he said. There had been no other man or woman involved and he and Liz still had a great deal of affection for each other.

The problem was, they just could not live together. One of their difficulties was Liz's belief in reincarnation and spiritual matters. When they married, Dad had assumed that it was just a casual interest but soon found that it was "an obsession," one he couldn't share because he believed there was no reality to the things that were of the greatest importance to her. "My disbelief in these things has caused Liz as much anguish as her belief in them has caused me," he said.

There had been other issues, too, such as Dad's belief in the "proper roles of men and women in society," and in the end Liz asked him to move out of her apartment in February that year.

They had put aside their differences at the last moment, but the problems were not solved. "Liz is a strong-minded and strong-willed woman who insists on going her own way, and I am a strong-minded and strong-willed man who insists on going his way," he told Grandma.

When he decided to move to the compound in August that year, Liz refused to go with him. She wanted to retain the freedom she had living in her Alexandria, Va., apartment, which she feared she would lose it in the wilds of West Virginia "where she would not have the same degree of control over her life," Dad wrote. "As for me, I need a woman, and I told Liz that I am looking for one I can live with."

Frankly, Dad's views on marriage and the roles of men and women would put off many people. Of course, Liz might also have balked at

Dad's request because she didn't relish the idea of living in a used trailer with no running water, eating freeze-dried rabbits, and helping to dig ditches, but I could be wrong there.

Dad believed that "a woman's battlefield is the maternity ward" and her "greatest 'diploma' is to give birth to the 'superman' or superwoman.'" A woman's role was to bear and raise children and care for her mate, and she shouldn't even be allowed to vote, he said. A man's role is to provide for the family and discipline the children. Creating the next generation is the "highest personal responsibility with which each man and woman of our race is charged" and "the greatest possible care" should be taken to choose a sexual partner based not so much on compatibility, but "on genetic quality."

Eugenics should be a national policy, Dad believed. The best and the brightest could be encouraged to breed more than average Americans by altering the way taxes are collected and by getting rid of the welfare system, which "encourages the least fit to propagate." He liked to point to the ancient Greeks who killed newborns that they believed were defective to ensure the survival of their race. (1) A man and woman are morally obliged to use contraception if they have any "genetic shortcomings." Sex with a Jew or a Negro was "the same as sexual intercourse with an animal" and "will, or is likely to create, a deformed, ugly, diseased or otherwise deficient child of our own race," he said. The "primary sin...is to defile the most precious treasure in the universe — our genetic pool, the genetic heritage of our race. A related sin, a sin of omission, is to willfully fail to enhance that heritage." (2) He hated feminists, too, of course. They were "a threat to our race" and should be dispatched, in the same rail cars, with Jews, homosexuals, and other race-traitors.

Probably not surprising, then, that he had trouble finding, let alone keeping a mate. After Liz kicked him out, he placed an ad in the personal columns of the Washingtonian magazine and chose a woman called Kathy from what he claimed was a "flood of responses" he received from businesswomen, lawyers, and the like. Kathy was of Anglo-Saxon stock, had a doctorate from Princeton University and had been a professor of French literature at Yale. She had been married to a math professor at Columbia but the marriage didn't work out and she found herself alone and unemployed in New York City. She eventually got a law degree and went to Washington, D.C., to work for the U.S. Securities and Exchange Commission.

According to Dad, she was attractive and "a little bit randy, so we hit it off just fine as far as the physical side of it went." But she drank a lot, smoked two or three packs of cigarettes a day, and saw a physiotherapist and hypnotist regularly because she suffered from migraines. Dad couldn't resist offering his opinion on her life. He told her that "no woman ought to be a lawyer" because it was a man's occupation and that she was living by herself in Washington, D.C., "a dog-eat-dog city." Not surprisingly, Kathy got mad. "She was infected with all the feminist crap. As soon as I started talking ideas with her our relationship was soiled," he said (3). After his third failure with an American woman — if you count my Mom — he turned to Eastern European women for comfort. He found them to be more feminine than American women, and they didn't see it as demeaning to assume the role of a homemaker. "They don't look down at the idea of trying to please a man," and were "warmer and less neurotic."

Pretty soon he found a young Hungarian immigrant willing to join him. Of course, she had no idea how extremely selfish and preoccupied Dad would be. Once they married, she found herself alone on the mountainside in West Virginia for at least 15 hours a day as Dad holed up in his office, scribbling his screeds. Her name was Olga Skerlecz. Dad called her Oli, and they married in early June, 1987, after Grandma paid for her rail fare down from Connecticut. She had been a piano teacher and fashion model before marrying a biophysics professor at the University of Stockholm, Dad wrote to his mother a week after the ceremony. After divorcing her husband, she had arrived in the U.S. sometime around late 1984 and had been staying with relatives. "Her English is still a bit awkward, but we are making good progress," Dad said. "Oli is an excellent cook and I have gained about 15 pounds during the six weeks she has been here. I look and feel a lot better than I did last August."

As usual, Grandma sent him more money to help out. Dad used part of one check she sent at Easter 1989 to buy Olga a baby African Grey parrot to keep her company. They called him Herkimer, perhaps after the American Revolutionary War militia leader Gen. Nicholas Herkimer, but they didn't always get on well. Herk gave them "a few painful bites,"

Dad complained, but he praised the eugenic heritage of the bird. "The parrots of his species are the most intelligent of all birds and we're looking forward to the time when he begins to talk." Olga also had done artwork for one of his newsletters that, of course, he enclosed with his reply to Grandma.

I met Olga for the first time a year after our own wedding. I had written to Dad in another bid to establish some form of communication with him. He was living on his compound in West Virginia by then and I hadn't heard from him since my wedding and had no idea that he had split with his second wife, Liz Prostel. About a month later he wrote back, saying he and his third wife, Olga, would be in town for a conference and asked if he could stop by for a quick visit. A few weeks later he and Olga appeared at our door. Olga was young and had bleached-blonde hair and a very thick eastern European accent. She was pleasant and Dad appeared to be happy and friendly. They had dinner with us and we talked about his compound and our new business, remodeling people's houses. Before I knew it, they were up and on their way and I never got to ask him any serious questions.

Dad had invited us to visit him at his compound when he came to dinner with us, and Susan and I made the drive down there in the summer of 1992 after he sent me a hand-drawn map and directions. He seemed extremely pleased to see us and proudly gave us the grand tour, which included hiking all over his compound for at least two hours. We finally ended up back at the main building, which served as his church, his bookstore and offices. We sat around talking about how he and a few supporters had built the place with their own hands. Then, around 5:00 pm, the phone rang. It was Olga, wanting to know when we would be at his trailer for dinner. He said we'd be there in 30 or 40 minutes, but then decided he had to show us his make-shift theater, and his favorite movie. I assumed it was a short film because of his promise to Olga, who by then had rung to say dinner was now ready. He assured her we were on our way, and then proceeded to show us the movie — it was "A Clockwork Orange" and ran at least two hours. The phone rang four or five times more during the movie but Dad just ignored it. I found the film profoundly disturbing and didn't enjoy it in the least.

Finally, about 8:30 pm, we made our way up to Dad's trailer, a 10-minute walk from the main building. Olga was visibly upset and didn't say a word to any of us. Dad ignored her glares, cheerfully declaring how hungry he was. "What's for dinner, Sweetie?" he asked. Olga took a pan off the stove, slammed it on the table, and sat down in silence. Dad took the lid off, looked over the food inside, and said, "Yum, I love your rice dishes!"

He served himself a huge helping and handed the pan to me. The first thing I noticed was the smell. The rice was burned so badly that it smelled like fireplace ashes. I took a small serving and handed the pan to Susan. I took a bite and it was all I could do to swallow it. Now I knew what charcoal must be like. But Dad chowed down without a hint of dissatisfaction and actually appeared to enjoy it. It was the worst thing I had ever tasted and I marveled that he could eat an entire plate of it. He finished quickly, thanked Olga for a wonderful meal and invited us to spend the night. We hadn't planned on that but it was pretty late and the drive home would take five or six hours, so we agreed. We slept on the floor of his spare room in the trailer. It was so uncomfortable that I barely slept, and was very happy to see the sun rise and say goodbye to Dad and Olga.

Dad's pleasure with his new wife was soon tempered with problems with the Immigration and Naturalization Service, which he said was trying to deport Oli back to Hungary.

"This is a real nightmare for us. I thought that once we were married, Oli was safe. But the Congress passed a new law in November 1986 which allows the government to deport even the spouse of a citizen," he wrote to Grandma in January, 1988. He had hired an immigration lawyer who "formerly worked for the other side" and a hearing on her application for asylum was due in May. If they lose, he said, they'd have to appeal and use legal maneuvers that "could drain us financially." He had to find an expert witness who could testify and convince the court that Oli "will be persecuted by the secret police in Hungary as a political dissenter if she is deported."

I don't know what happened after that, but I never saw Olga again. The marriage had lasted just under three years when she fled into the arms of a wealthy Californian, a retired antiques dealer. Dad filed for divorce in March 1990, at her request. He wrote to Grandma, saying he hadn't wanted to tell her about the break-up, or even think about it, while Oli remained at the compound. She left in November that year.

"Oli has wanted to leave for a long time. She has always thought that I spend too much time working, that she doesn't have enough opportunity for shopping and doing other things, and that

I didn't give her enough money," he told Grandma. "It is true that I work long hours and that I am somewhat frugal; that's the only way I could have survived in my chosen line of work. Oli, of course, could have spent more time with me if she had some interest in my work, but her interests always have been different."

He'd hoped that a succession of visitors from Hungary, including a lady called Marta, would compensate Oli for the time he spent at work. "But in Marta's case, there was jealousy, because Marta was a very good helper who spent more time with me at the office than Oli did." In the meantime, Oli had been corresponding with "a number of men" and finally decided on the antiques dealer who "is much more likely to give her what she wants than I." She had visited him three times and, with an insurance settlement for an injury to her hand, she would have a degree of financial security, even if she did not remarry, Dad said.

I don't know what happened to Herkimer, if he stayed or left with Olga, or if died on the mountainside, a meal for one of Dad's Siamese cats.

After Olga left, Dad set out to find yet another companion.

"I cannot live here very long without a woman, however, or depression will become a problem. Besides, I need help with the house and the office. So I have been corresponding with a few women in Hungary and Romania and it is likely that I will have one of them over here very early next year," he wrote to his mother, after telling her of Olga's departure.

The woman he chose was called Zsuzsa, or Susan. She was a 30-year-old divorced Hungarian woman who was a former mining engineer and at the time was teaching mechanics in a trade school. "She seems very bright, and we have had a good exchange of letters (with Oli's help as a translator)," he added. He married Sue, as he called her, in 1991, after she answered an ad he placed in a Hungarian women's magazine. She left him in 1996 for Florida and remarried. I met her only once and remember her as being attractive and friendly.

The last woman Dad married was from Bulgaria. Her name was Sevdi. She appeared frightened much of the time and carried a gun because she was scared by the death threats Dad received, according to Robert Griffin, who met her when he arrived at the compound in the summer of 1998 to write his book about Dad. She married Dad in 1997, just a month after meeting him, and spoke very little English. She was previously married to an actor for 17 years and was an art teacher, but Dad didn't want her to teach here because it would distract from her homemaker duties. She had wanted a TV, but he wouldn't get her one, saying she'd spend all day watching it and wouldn't attend to the home. She had also wanted to go into town to see a movie, but he wouldn't let her, though he did sometimes let her go with him when he went to collect the mail once a week. She had whispered to Griffin that she was lonely and fretted about her Green Card immigration status.

Dad's preference for Eastern European women would have been something of a heresy in Hitler's Germany. The Nazis believed that Hungarians were inferior to Aryan Germans, classifying them as "tribally alien" but not necessarily "blood alien." Of course, Hungary was strategically positioned for an invasion of the Balkans and so its people were not regarded as totally racially impure, unlike the Slavs, who only became acceptable when Hitler needed more troops.

There was no sign of Sevdi when I went to Dad's memorial service. I do know that she left him, though. While Dad was officially between wives when died, he wasn't without company. While he was married to Sevdi, he had been having an affair with a woman he had secretly installed in a house off the compound. She later complained in an Internet post that she had been having sex with him for quite a while, but never became pregnant. Apparently, he never told her that he had had a vasectomy after Erik and I were born, some 40 years.

"All the women I have been married to have been good women in one way or another, but none have been soul mates in the sense of shaping my decisions or sharing the work I have been doing," he told Griffin at one point. "My work is not really compatible with a family life, and one way or another, it has broken up all my marriages, or at least my first four. I have always felt the need for a woman's company, but there is this problem." Then why did he continue to import those poor, unsuspecting women when he knew it would never work out?

CHAPTER 26

BUILDING A FAMILY, STEP BY AGONIZING STEP

Within a couple of weeks we found an adoption agency close to our home. I remember vividly how I felt when I went to the first meeting. On the lobby wall was a photo of a young girl. I saw a child who wasn't wanted and wasn't loved, I saw myself. I just wanted to hold her and make her feel safe and loved and to tell her that she was perfect and worthy of love. Tears started running down my face as I remembered how I felt at her age. From then on, I worked tirelessly to make our dream a reality. At the end of the meeting, we put down a significant deposit and started the process. First, we would have to complete a home study with an independent agency, which would take about six months and would include personal interviews and lengthy questionnaires, financial statements, references and background checks. Early on, Susan suggested we adopt two kids at the same time as it was all so involved. I was all for that.

Unfortunately, the agent, I'll call her Maria, was not on the up-and-up. After completing the home study, we waited for weeks but heard nothing back from her. I called several times but never reached her, nor received any return calls. We started to worry and, fresh out of ideas on how to reach her, we drove to her office, which was located in her home. It was December, 1995. We rang her doorbell and a minute or two later, she answered. She gave us a blank stare and it was clear that she didn't know who the hell we were. I told her our names again and said we wanted an update on our adoption process. She apologized for her memory lapse, saying she was jet-lagged from travel. We followed her up to her office and immediately starting peppering her with questions. We got no satisfactory answers. As we looked at her in dismay, she got up from her desk and went into the next room, returning with a piece of paper in her hand. She handed it to me. On it were two names with birth dates that were only a few days earlier. She smiled and said, "Those are your two new baby girls."

She said she'd just received the fax and they were ours if we wanted them. I was stunned. The birth dates showed the babies were born in the Republic of Georgia less than a week earlier, three days apart. In that moment, I forgot all my anger and suspicions as I imagined being the father of two baby girls. Never had we thought we would essentially be adopting twins. I looked at Maria in stunned silence for a few moments before I found my voice. "Are you serious? I thought we were going to adopt an older sibling group from the Ukraine, as we discussed earlier."

Her expression changed, she looked surprised and then offended. "If you don't want them, I'll give them to someone else," she said, a bit huffily. I quickly reassured her that I was a bit confused, that was all. She relaxed a little. There had been corruption problems with adoptions in Ukraine and the government had closed the country to foreign adoptions, so she had set up a new program in Georgia where she could get infants.

"I want you to be the first ones to adopt from Georgia," she said. I looked at Susan and, after a minute, replied that adopting infants would be absolutely awesome. Then all the other questions came rushing out. How did they become orphans? Were they healthy? How long will it take to adopt them? Is the paperwork the same as for Ukraine? What are our next steps? I was worried we would have complete all the paperwork again. We did, and we had to make another trip to Richmond to get new state seals on everything. Maria said we should be able to complete the adoption in a couple of months and she would schedule a travel meeting with us for some time in January. We went back home visualizing the best Christmas present we had ever received in our lives.

Our next meeting with Maria was in late January and we were supposed to plan out trip to Georgia to pick up our babies. We were so excited that we could barely stand it. We arrived at Maria's office and were surprised to see another couple in the waiting room. Maria didn't greet us as she normally did so after several minutes my wife started a conversation with the other couple. We learned that they were there for the same reason as us.

Suddenly, I was worried. Maria had never mentioned another couple adopting two babies from Georgia. Maria finally came out of her office and invited all four of us in. Maria looked at us for several seconds, as if she was pondering her next move.

Finally, she spoke. "I've called you all here today to discuss your adoptions," she said. "Since you are both adopting babies, instead of older children, I need to collect more fees." She said her program in Georgia was brand new and her costs greater than expected. She wanted another $10,000 from each of us.

Then there was silence for several minutes while we wondered what she was up to. Had she waited until she could dangle our babies before us and then demanded more money? Then, the other parents spoke. They said they'd write another check straight away. I looked at Maria. It was an unpleasant surprise, I said, but we obviously had very little choice but to write her a check, too. When would we travel to get our babies, I asked. Then she dropped her bombshell. While she admitted promising us two babies, she'd made the same pledge to the other couple, too. She then picked up a piece of paper and I could see it was the same piece that had the names of the two babies she had promised to us earlier. She held the paper up and appeared to be deep in thought. Finally, she said she could give one of us the two babies, or split them up and give us one each, then try to find two others that she could split between us. I was burning with silent rage. It was clear from her face that Maria was relishing every second as the four of us sat on the edge of our seats, holding our breath.

Then, she handed me the paper. "I think I will give the Pierces these baby girls because the other couple have said they want at least one boy. I am sure when I go to Georgia next week I will be able to find two more babies and I will make sure that one of them is a boy." I remember feeling a tremendous surge of relief and gratitude. The other couple readily agreed and so it was settled. We spent the rest of the meeting discussing travel plans and what we needed to do to get finished so that we were prepared to complete our adoptions once we all arrived in Georgia.

We settled on a travel date for about three weeks hence and went home and made our travel arrangements in conjunction with the other couple. By now I'd developed a deep distrust of Maria but I mostly put those doubts aside because completing the adoption and bringing my babies home was the most important thing in my life. I could not think of anything else. I joined an Internet chat group about foreign adoptions that had hundreds of subscribers. Most of them were discussing the difficulties of navigating the foreign adoption process. Most of the conversations centered on Russia and a few other Eastern European countries, but no one mentioned anything about adopting from Georgia and I found that troubling.

Then I remembered that Maria had said hers was a new program and no one else was licensed to adopt from there so dismissed my concerns from my mind. Then, the night before we were to leave for Georgia, I received a fax message from Maria. She said there had been fraud in Georgia and she needed time to work out the details so we needed to cancel our trip. She promised to get in touch when she was ready for us to come. I called the other couple and they confirmed that Maria had sent them the same message from Maria. We were devastated. This woman had $40,000 of our money and was continuing to play games with us. I couldn't stop thinking about it and I remember sitting in my rocking chair late into the night, going over everything in my mind again and again.

Then, it struck me. I had the ticket to Georgia for the next day, so why not just go and see what the hell was going on. I could find out what Maria was really up to, and if the babies actually existed." I suddenly got really excited and rushed upstairs and woke up my wife and told her my idea. I called the other couple and asked them what they thought. They loved the plan and said they'd pay half of my expenses if I looked into their babies, too, and gather as much information as I could. I called Maria's office and told them to tell Maria that I was coming as planned. They told me not to go but I refused to listen to them and demanded that they let Maria know that I was coming, regardless of what she thought about it.

CHAPTER 27

THE ROAD TO TBILISI

The next day, I left for Georgia for what became one of the most memorable experiences of my life. The flight over was a grueling 30 hours. I had no experience with international travel at the time, so it was all new to me. The final leg of the journey into Tbilisi was aboard an antique Russian passenger jet in extremely poor condition. I was the only American on the plane and the moment the plane took off from Frankfurt, passengers got up out of their seats and started roaming around the plane, smoking cigarettes and talking with their friends in Georgian. I wondered why they were ignoring all the rules. It was just about the longest five hours of my life.

It was 4 a.m. when we landed, pitch black outside, and not a building in sight. I thought something had gone wrong, but after 20 minutes a cabin attendant opened the door and there was a mad rush for the exit. The air was frigid as I carefully walked down a steep steel stairway to the tarmac. There were dozens of Georgians milling about, chatting to each other. I shivered in the dark until a bus pulled up and everyone piled onto it. A few minutes later we arrived at a darkened building where uniformed men holding rifles stood by a single door. When the bus stopped, there was another huge surge toward the door and I squeezed in among the pack. I found myself in a large room with no furnishings and two small light fixtures on the wall, so dim that there was barely enough light to make out the size of the room. It was as cold inside as outside.

After about 20 minutes, a door on the far wall opened and people quickly moved forward. I tried to establish myself in the line but it was nearly impossible in the chaos around me. I was bumped and jostled from all sides and my first inclination was to give ground. But then an old lady about half my height grabbed me by my arm and pulled me out of the way so she could get in front of me. I was stunned but decided that I needed to behave like a Georgian, too. I shoved the old lady aside and repeated the process until I found myself at the door. I was horrified by my behavior but no-one else seemed worried. I felt I actually gained some respect from them. After another hour, I had worked my way through customs and finally saw Maria waiting for me. I can't tell you how relieved I was to see her. I was completely exhausted and suffering from an extreme case of culture shock and a familiar face was exactly what I needed to calm down. When I finally reached her, she told me she was going to take me to a hotel to get some rest.

What I remember the most about my ride from the airport was how dark Tbilisi was. There were practically no lights anywhere. I asked David, our driver, why it was so dark. He explained that conditions are so bad in Georgia that most people have electricity for a few hours a day only, and that's if they're lucky. The roads were in poor shape too, and many times we had to slow down to only a few miles an hour and perform extreme, evasive maneuvers to get around potholes that could swallow a car. We eventually made our way to a Sheraton Hotel. David said it was the only hotel in Georgia with electricity around the clock because it had onsite generators. Maria promised to pick me up about 3:00 p.m to take me to the hospital to see my babies. I collapsed into bed and slept like a log for eight hours straight.

At 3:00 p.m., I went down to the lobby and sat down to wait for Maria. I gazed around the hotel. It had a huge and beautiful lobby that was open all the way up to the roof. The building was about 13 floors high and all of the guest rooms were situated along the perimeter walls with open walkways to access the rooms that looked down onto the lobby floor. It was a very modern building, in stark contrast to the rest of Tbilisi, which was ancient, dark and dirty. Maria finally showed up, 45 minutes later, greeting me warmly. We got into David's car and picked our way again through streets pockmarked with potholes, some so huge that there were actually wrecked and abandoned hulks of cars nestled within them.

After about an hour we arrived at the Republican Children's Hospital on the city outskirts. It was about five stories high and made out of concrete and windows. It was quite nondescript, with dozens of cars in the parking lot. It was getting dark as we made our way into the building. The first thing that struck me was the smell, like a construction site portable toilet that hadn't been cleaned out in forever. I gagged as climbed the stairs to the fourth floor. It was about 40 degrees outside but actually felt colder in the building.

Maria led us into an office in the middle of the building where we were met by a Dr. Nino. She was the chief of pediatrics and the woman Maria was working with on adoptions. She was about 40, tall and very beautiful. She ushered us into her office with a friendly smile. David acted as our translator and I remember being able to see our breath as we were talked to each other. A nurse walked in and exchanged a few words with Dr. Nino, then gave me a long stare. She seemed surprised. She said something to Dr. Nino, and they all smiled. David told me that the nurse was amazed that I was there — in Georgia, he said, a man would never be the one to go to the hospital to see their children. She also said I looked a lot like one of the babies. Then it suddenly sunk in: I was about to meet my babies!

A few minutes later, she returned with another nurse, each with balled-up blankets in their arms. They laid them on a table, slowly unwrapping them. Two beautiful babies materialized in front of me and when my eyes met theirs, I felt a strange and profound transformation. I can only describe it as a moment of grace that I have never felt before. I felt miraculously part of them at a cellular level and my only mission in life now was to be their daddy. I was done. There was no way that I was not going to adopt these two girls and not be their protector for life or raise them as my own. I suspect that this is how biological parents must feel when they see their own kids being born. That these babies were not biologically related to me made no difference, I was instantly bonded to them. I just stood there, tears flowing down my face. Even though they were both malnourished and covered from head to toe in scabies with their heads like two giant scabs because of cradle cap, I saw them only as beautiful and perfect. I held both of them for a few minutes and then took pictures of them before the nurses insisted of wrapping them back up because they were getting cold. Before I could object, the nurses hustled my girls out of the room and suddenly I felt very alone.

Then the nurses brought in two more babies, smaller than mine. These were going to be the other couple's babies. One was about a month old, the other was only two weeks old. They were both girls. I turned to Maria and said I thought at least one of them was supposed to be a boy. Maria just shrugged her shoulders and didn't say a word. The nurses unwrapped the babies and they, too, were beautiful. I took pictures and practically interrogated Dr. Nino about them to ensure they were healthy and would, indeed, be the actual babies that the other couple were going to adopt. Again, in too short a time, the babies were wrapped up and carried off. We spent another 30 minutes or so chatting with Dr. Nino. I really liked her and trusted her and felt a tremendous amount of relief. My babies actually existed and it looked like Maria had told us the truth and our adoption was actually going to happen after all. Then Maria said it was time to leave, but I didn't want to. Dr. Nino promised that I could return tomorrow to see my girls again. I don't remember much about the ride back to the hotel. All I could see in my mind were my babies and their faces as they looked back at me.

To say I was a completely changed man is a ridiculous understatement. I called Susan as soon as I got back to the hotel and told her how beautiful our daughters were — twelves on a scale of one to ten. I also called the other couple to tell them about their daughters. I was worried that they would be upset because they weren't getting a son but that wasn't the case at all. They were as relieved as I was and thanked me profusely for making the trip, seeing their daughters and verifying that they existed and seemed healthy. I was exhausted but barely able to sleep that night. All I could think of was my daughters and that now I was their Dad. I longed for dawn to break so I could go back to see them again.

CHAPTER 28

NEARLY LOST IN TRANSLATION

Maria called the next morning. She told me to put on my best clothes because we were going to an important meeting before we returned to the hospital. I put on my suit and tie and went down to wait for David and Maria. It was another cold day. Soon David delivered us to a large government building in the middle of Tbilisi. Maria said we were going to meet with the Minister of Health. We found ourselves in complete darkness when the door of the building shut behind us, although it was only midday. There were no windows in the lobby and the electricity was off in the entire building. I had a small flashlight in my pocket and we slowly made our way to the Minister's office. Once inside, there was plenty of light coming in through the windows. The office was large with ceilings at least 12 feet tall and the doors, windows and moldings were old and very ornate. The only furniture was a large wooden desk with three small chairs in front of it. Behind the desk sat a man about 60-years-old. He was wearing a large overcoat and a woolen hat and had a heavy scarf wrapped around his neck. There was a small kerosene heater on the floor next to him. The temperature in the room was only 45 degrees or so.

The Minister extended his hand, smiled warmly and motioned for us to sit down. A young woman came in and sat next to us. She introduced herself as our translator and she and Maria began a conversation that was then translated for the Minister. I had no idea what the meeting was about but soon realized that Maria was discussing her ability to perform adoptions in Georgia. After several minutes of discussion, I heard her ask the Minister, "Why can't you just make this happen for me?" He told her that she needed to submit the proper paperwork before Georgia could issue her a license to perform adoptions, and she hadn't done so. Maria was angry. She said she had submitted her paperwork to the Minister of Justice two days ago, and asked why she should have to do it all over again. The Minister calmly told her that she had to submit the proper papers to his office as well, before she could get a license.

Maria was getting more frustrated by the minute and asked why the Minister of Justice couldn't just fax over copies of the papers to the Minister of Health. The Minister looked at her and laughed and spread his arms. He asked her if she could see a fax machine anywhere in his office. And, even if he had one, there was no electricity to make such a machine work. She would just have to submit the proper papers if she wanted a license, he told her.

Maria suddenly stood up, pushed her chair over, and stormed out of the room, slamming the door behind her. I sat in stunned silence and looked at the Minister as he looked back at me, wide-eyed. I couldn't believe what was happening. I could hear the sound of someone crying out in the hallway. It was Maria, standing just outside the door and sobbing loudly.

I had no idea what to do. The Minister smiled uncomfortably and asked me where I was from. "I am from Virginia," I said. "Where in Virginia?" he asked. "Fairfax County," I replied. Then he smiled. He opened his desk drawer and pulled out an old newspaper. It was a copy of the Chantilly Connection newspaper. "I know Fairfax County," he said. "I was there a few years ago and brought this back with me." I smiled broadly back at him and said, "Oh my gosh, I live very near to there!"

Another awkward silence ensued. Finally, Maria's sobs subsided and she opened the door, came into the room and sat back down on her chair, wiping her face with her sleeve and smearing her makeup. She muttered a quiet apology and then asked the Minister for a cigarette. He handed her one from a box on his desk and lit it for her, and then proceeded to scold her. She had no business crying like that, he said.

Then he opened his desk drawer again and pulled out a plastic grocery bag, showing us the two cans of baby formula inside.

He said he'd just bought it on the black market for his grandson and it was very expensive. "I had to do this because my daughter can't afford to buy food for her son because she has no job," he said. "There is practically no work in Georgia and we are all barely surviving. You have everything and here you are crying because you don't want to spend any of your time filling out paperwork!"

Maria took a deep drag on her cigarette and glared back at him. If she wanted a license, she needed to file the proper papers, there was no other way, he said. He motioned for us to leave. I thanked him for his time and followed Maria out in utter disbelief at what had just transpired.

By the time we got back to David's car, I was furious. I asked Maria why she had lied to me about having a license to do adoptions in Georgia. She started crying again and told me that I could just go home and forget my babies if that's how I felt about her. I stared at her for several moments, and then caved. I softened my gaze and apologized. I said I was just very tired and stressed out, and begged her not to give up. I know you can do this, I said, please do it for me. She stopped crying and smiled at me, and said, "That's better". After another very long pause, she said she would do the damned paperwork and everything will be alright. "I just got frustrated with the Minister, it's no big deal," she said. She was a lying little baby, I thought to myself, but I knew I couldn't tell her what I really thought because she'd just throw another tantrum and threaten to take my babies away from me. "Please God, help me to get my babies," I prayed. I sat in silence for the rest of the car ride as we made our way back to the hospital.

I put my concerns about Maria aside when we arrived at the hospital and turned my focus back to my babies. I had a wonderful visit with my girls and got to spend more time holding them and looking into their eyes, imagining being their Daddy. I talked to Dr. Nino for a long time. She told me how bad the conditions really were there at the hospital. Lots of babies were dying for lack of food, medicine and surgical supplies. The biggest problem was the lack of electricity, because made it very difficult to perform emergency surgeries at a moment's notice. I made a silent vow to try to do something to help. I cried again when I said goodbye to my girls, wondering if I'd ever see them again. I was to leave for home early the next morning.

Maria promised when they dropped me off at the hotel that evening that she would complete all the required paperwork the next day and I should be able to come back in about 10 days to pick up my babies. The trip back home was uneventful. The first thing I did after getting a good night's sleep was to go onto the foreign adoption listserv and post a long note telling everybody about my trip. I told them about Georgia and how I was going to be able to adopt infants, which was very rare in Eastern Europe, and how impressed I was with Dr. Nino and the Minister of Health. I said I was feeling good about Georgia and that there didn't seem to be any corruption involved in their adoption process, like many other countries were experiencing.

Little did I know that posting that information was a huge and dreadful mistake. The next thing I did was call Maria's office to check on the status of her paperwork. I was shocked when they told me that she had left Georgia the same day as I did for a vacation in the Caribbean. I was shocked into silence, then managed to find my voice enough to ask that Maria call me when they got a message to her.

She called a few days later, totally oblivious to any concern on my part. I was careful as I spoke to her. I asked if she'd finished the paperwork, as she'd promised, before leaving for vacation. She said she'd be going back to Georgia in 10 days to complete it. Then I totally lost it.

She had said we would return to Georgia in one week to pick up our children.

"How can we do that while you're lying on a beach somewhere? I'm really worried about my babies. They're malnourished, we need to get them home as soon as possible so we can get them the proper food and medicine. They could get sick and die at any time!" Maria resorted to her usual behavior — she started crying. She said she'd worked hard and "deserved this vacation." If I didn't agree with her, I could just find someone else to help us adopt children. "I don't deserve to be treated this way by you!"

I gave in again, obviously. I told her she was right, she did deserve a vacation and I was happy that she was able to take one. I apologized for raising my voice and promised to be patient and asked her to tell us when she was ready for us to travel. "I really do trust you and I know that you'll get your paperwork done soon," I lied. She immediately stopped crying and said she'd be back in touch as soon as she got back to Georgia. I didn't hear back from her for three weeks. In the meantime I lobbied all of my family members and many of my contractor friends for donations so I could buy a generator to take back to Georgia with me for the children's hospital.

The next thing we heard from Maria was another fax from Georgia. "You must come to Georgia at once. There is a big problem and I need you here to help," it said. I immediately called her office but they couldn't or wouldn't tell me anything about what the problem was, but did verify that Maria wanted all of us to travel to Georgia at the very first opportunity. I called the other couple and we quickly made plans to travel to Georgia in two days.

David picked all four of us up at the airport and told us that we were going to be staying with two host families. My wife and I were taken to a woman's apartment in Tbilisi and the other couple were taken to another apartment close by. The woman who we stayed with was a widow because her husband was killed during the recent civil war in Georgia. He had been a former government minister and was assassinated because of his allegiances. She was living in the apartment alone with her 11-year-old daughter. The apartment was very cold because they only had electricity for one to two hours a day. Despite that, she made us comfortable and fed us well. Her daughter was a pianist and played for us a couple of times. It was amazing how good she was. She also spoke English fluently, so she was able to translate for her mother.

Maria picked us up the next morning and I was surprised to see that Dr. Nino was driving. It was the most harrowing car ride I've ever had. Dr. Nino drove like a crazed woman and several times I was convinced we were all going to die. She drove way too fast and if another car happened to get in her way, she would just veer out to oncoming traffic and pass the offending driver. She almost mowed down several pedestrians along the way. The four of us were crammed into the back seat of the small sedan and were white as ghosts by the time we arrived at our destination. I immediately recognized where we were. We were back at the Ministry of Health. I thought the worst: that Maria never got licensed and we were about to be told we couldn't adopt our babies after all. "What's going on?" I asked Maria, but she was just as puzzled. She said Dr. Nino had told her there was a problem and she needed us to come straight away. I felt a sense of dread as we walked into the building. Dr. Nino led us into a big room with a large conference table with several chairs around it. There was no one else in the room when we arrived. Dr. Nino asked us to sit down and she disappeared back out into the hallway.

Dr. Nino came back a few minutes later, followed by the Minister of Health and a young man, who was to be our translator. I noticed that the Minister didn't smile when he looked at me. He appeared to be in a bad mood. After he sat down, he threw a piece of paper onto the table and demanded in a very gruff manner, "What is the meaning of this?" I looked at the piece of paper and could see it was in English. It was a copy of my post to the foreign adoption listserv. "You accuse us of corruption! I have decided to cancel all adoptions. We must write official adoption laws in our country so we don't get accused of corruption. I am sorry but you must go back home now! Goodbye."

He got up to leave. I begged him to stay, saying he had misunderstood and that I was saying exactly the opposite of what he believed I had posted. I picked up the paper and saw that it was an email from another adoption agency that had copied my post and told the Georgians that I was accusing them of corruption in their adoption process. The author demanded to know why her adoption agency was not getting equal access to Georgian babies. I asked Maria what she knew about it. She looked at the paper closely and then said she knew the woman involved, and had worked for her before she left to form her own agency. I pleaded with the translator to explain to the Minister that we were not accusing him of anything. The translator said something to the Minister, who angrily slammed his hand down on the table and repeated that he had closed the country to all foreign adoptions.

"We must wait until our Parliament addresses this issue and makes new laws. No adoptions until we do this. We must not be accused of corruption!" he said. We went back and forth like this for another 30 minutes before I looked at the translator and asked him, "Do you agree that this paper says that we are not accusing Georgia of corruption?" He gave me a puzzled look and replied, "No, I do not. It says corruption right here." And he pointed to the word corruption on the piece of paper.

Then it dawned on me that he really didn't fully understand English. I slumped back into my chair, my mind racing, trying to figure out a way I could make them understand. Then it came to me. I asked the translator if anyone else in the building spoke English. He said he knew of one woman and I begged him to fetch her. The translator and Dr. Nino spoke briefly to the Minister, then left the room. After what seemed an eternity, Dr. Nino returned with a young woman. Dr. Nino spoke to her rapidly and handed her the paper. The woman read it carefully, then spoke directly to the Minister. He listened silently, seemingly in deep thought before speaking again. He acknowledged that, perhaps, I had not accused them of corruption after all. However, they were a new country and had to do things properly and could not tolerate such accusations. "Unfortunately, I have already cancelled all of your paperwork. But since you are already here, I will allow you to redo it, and then you can take your children home," he said. He made it clear, though, that our adoptions were the only ones he would allow to take place — there would be no further foreign adoptions until the Parliament had enacted laws governing the process.

By now, we had been in this conference room for a couple of hours and I was exhausted but extremely relieved. We agreed to the Minister's terms and immediately set about redoing all of our paperwork. We ended up staying in Georgia for another three weeks, working every day to complete the clerical stuff and finalize the adoptions. Most of the matters I had to deal with were things Maria was supposed to have done for us, but if I had waited for her to do her job we may never have completed the adoptions. Every day I was out visiting with various government agencies, submitting reams of paper so we could get the birth certificates and passports and everything else required before we could leave with our children. Susan, meanwhile, was spending time in the hospital with them every day, beginning the bonding process. After about 14 days, the Georgians gave us permission to take our babies out of the hospital so we checked into the Sheraton Hotel, so we could have access to hot water and electricity full time.

One of the most wrenching, memorable moments came when we were all watching CNN Euro one evening at the hotel. They were airing a special report about the state of orphanages in Georgia. There were graphic images of children that were bedridden because of severe malnutrition. They reminded me of the pictures I'd see from the Holocaust. To our horror, the report included an interview with the wife of the then-president of Georgia. She said he was completely opposed to foreign adoptions and that, as far as she was concerned, she would prefer that Georgian orphans die in the orphanage system rather than be adopted by foreigners. It terrified us, and that's not an understatement. All I wanted was to complete the paperwork and get out of Georgia with my babies before they changed their minds.

We still had to visit the American Embassy to file papers there and wait for them to complete their investigations. When we submitted the applications, embassy staff said there was a reasonable chance that the adoptions would fall through, and we were scolded for removing the babies from the hospital. Apparently, the embassy needed to check whether our children were actually orphans, and not stolen from their parents in order to be sold into adoption. We were told of numerous cases where would-be parents thought their adoptions were legitimate, only to have their children taken away when it was determined that they were not orphans after all. The next 10 days were the most nerve-wracking of our lives. We struggled daily with the fear that we might lose our babies. I called the embassy every single day to ask about the status of their investigation. Finally, we were allowed to leave Georgia with our children.

The next step was to fly to Moscow to get a medical evaluation of our children and to apply to the American Embassy there for their U.S. resident alien or 'green' cards. We made our way to the Tbilisi airport to board our flight to Moscow, checked in, and sat in the waiting room for our flight to board, each of us with a baby in our arms. About 15 minutes before boarding, a well-dressed woman wearing an expensive-looking fur coat walked into the waiting room. She immediately scanned the room, looking at all the waiting passengers, then focused on us.

To our horror, she walked briskly toward us, took one look at our babies, and started screaming at us. "Where did you get these babies? Where did you get these babies? What is wrong with these babies? Tell me where you got these babies?!" We stared back at her in stunned silence, then she wheeled around and practically ran out of the room.

We looked at each other in complete panic. We expected her to come back at any second, accompanied by the authorities and take our babies back. Thankfully, within a few minutes we were invited to pre-board. We walked as fast as we could to the plane and practically flew up the steps. Once seated, I plastered my face to the window looking for the woman to come back and board the plane. It took an agonizing 25 minutes for boarding to finish. I can't tell you how relieved we were when the plane took off for Moscow. After three days in Moscow, we had our babies' green cards and were we finally headed for home, made complete with our own new families.

CHAPTER 29

THE LAST TIME I SAW DAD

I tried to keep Dad up to date on my babies' major milestones, but he was never one for writing long letters, unless it was to his mother. I sent him a copy of the adoption notice in April 1996, but he didn't respond. I wondered if perhaps he didn't approve of the adoption, or thought that my girls just weren't white or pure enough. It wasn't until the following year, 1997, that I wrote to him again, telling him about my family and a climbing trip up Mount Baker in Washington. He said it was interesting for him to see how closely "your choice of hobbies has followed mine." He said he had climbed Mount Baker in 1955, while a graduate student at Caltech. "I found the crevasses in the glacier fascinating. Leaning over the edge and looking into those yawning, icy depths and hearing water rushing past hundreds of feet below was an eerie experience," he said.

The rest of the letter was largely devoted to his progress in constructing a storage building at the 3,150-foot level of the mountain, near the house site. It was to be a steel-arched building, quonset-style, 40-feet-wide, 50-feet-long, and 16-feet-high, set on a concrete floor. They only had to put the end walls on, and then he would have a place to keep his tractor, dump truck and other equipment out of the weather, he said. He acknowledged my girls in one short sentence, saying he was glad to hear that they were well. He invited me for another visit to West Virginia, but I never went. The last time I heard from him was two years later, when he told me of Grandma Maggie's death and included an obituary he had written about her.

But Dad and I did have one big thing in common — hang gliding. I discovered his interest in it in 1993 when I wrote to tell him about my new business, a design and building company. Susan does the architectural drawings and I supervise the actual construction. One of his letters included a picture of him and his fourth wife, Sue, learning to hang glide at Kitty Hawk, N.C.

The last time I saw Dad was seven years before he died. It was Labor Day weekend, September of 1995. To my astonishment — and secret delight — he had come to see me hang glide at Spruce Knob, W.Va. It was beyond doubt my fondest memory of being with him. My hang gliding club was having an end-of-summer fly-in at a campground at the base of Seneca Rocks, W. Va. There were several flying sites nearby, one of which was Spruce Knob. On a whim, I had invited Dad to watch us fly but was pretty sure he wouldn't show up. We were in the area flying for the entire three-day weekend and it was Labor Day Monday, our last day of fun before heading back home. I was thinking about him as I crested the top of the mountain in my truck. The drive to the top of Spruce Knob is by way of a very long, winding road and it takes a long time because of all of the switchbacks, so I had plenty of time to ponder. After parking I scanned the area. I didn't see him and mentally kicked myself for ever thinking that I would. I took a breath of the cool, fresh air and refocused on the task at hand. I hopped onto the rear bumper of my truck and started untying the hang glider from the rack.

Just as I started to pull it down, I heard a voice behind me "You need a hand with that?" It was Dad, standing there with a hint of a grin on his face. I was stunned. "You actually came!" I blurted out, "Yes, I did," he said, then turned to a woman standing beside him. "I would like you to meet my wife, Sue." She was beautiful and looked about the same age as me. I was shocked into silence.

"So, do you want a hand with that thing or not?" Dad repeated. The launch area is only accessible through a steep uphill hike of a couple hundred yards from the parking area and it can be quite difficult wrestling an 80-pound glider at the same time. Dad grabbed one end of it and we made quick work of the hike up. The set up area at the top is a beautiful open, grassy area about the size of a football field. There are a dozen or so huge boulders scattered about but they still allow room for 20-30 gliders to set up without crowding each other. I picked a spot and began setting up. Sue jumped in to help, chatting as she did so, while Dad stood to the side. He was quiet but seemed content and at ease.

The top of Spruce Knob is the highest point in West Virginia and can be a difficult site for hang gliding. I had flown from there a half-dozen times before but had never managed to get up and over the mountain itself. My flights had always been what pilots call "sled rides," where you launch and steadily descend down to the landing field below. Since it is so far away, I would usually launch and then head straight for the field, to make sure I didn't get too low and end up in the trees. I was still pretty cautious as hang glider pilots go. I rarely took chances like the more experienced pilots did when searching for lift. Just before I suited up, I thanked Dad for coming and pointed way out into the upper valley to the landing field hidden below. I said I'd love him to get down there after my flight so we could talk a bit, but he was non-committal. I wanted to say much more but I was pretty nervous about getting ready to fly and my mind usually didn't work very well about this time. It took most of my mental energy just to push back the anxiety that was threatening to overwhelm me. I took one more look at Dad and then turned toward my glider. I suited up in my harness, hooked into my glider, and slowly walked my glider to the launch area.

After the glider in front of me took off, I moved into launch position. Looking to my right I could see Dad, with a look of keen interest on his face. I was about to run off the top of a 5,000 foot mountain with nothing but a sea of trees below as far as the eye could see. I think Dad was quite aware of the seriousness of it all. I picked up my glider and after about three seconds the wing balanced out and I yelled, "Clear!" I started running down the steep launch slope. After only four or five steps I was clear of the ground and flying away from the mountain.

I had pretty much decided to just do another sled ride and pointed my glider in the direction of the landing field that was still out of sight. A typical sled ride at Spruce Knob is roughly a 20minute flight. After about 30 seconds I heard my variometer start beeping and I felt the familiar tug of my glider rising rapidly. It felt like a really strong thermal. I toyed with the idea of turning away from the landing field. It was a risky proposition. The field is so far away that you really can't afford to waste much altitude searching for lift on your way toward it. But Dad was watching and I thought, just maybe, I will impress him for the first time in my life. I cranked up a tight turn in the lift and continued to rise rapidly. Within only a few minutes of turning in the strong thermal I was nearly 2,000 feet above the mountain, looking down at the people at the launch site who were just little dark specks.

The view spread below me was idyllic, majestic mountains and valleys as far as I could see. It was mostly trees, but there were about a dozen or so farms and fields that dotted the lower reaches of the mountains and into the valleys. I had never seen such unparalleled beauty. I was taking it all in when my thoughts turned back to Dad. I wondered why he had shown up. Did he actually want to see me, or was it because he thought hang gliding was cool and wanted to see that, instead? I was soaring thousands of feet over the mountain and all I could think of was whether he'd be proud of me. After about an hour of flying, I decided to head to the landing field, which I could easily see now because I was so high.

After another 30 minutes I glided down to an easy landing in a huge flat field next to the road. I walked my glider over to the break down area next to the farmer's driveway, giddy with joy. There were several other pilots in various stages of breaking down their gliders and we excitedly shared our flying experiences. After about 20 minutes, I set myself the task of breaking down my glider. I had pulled just a few of the battens when I heard an excited voice behind me. "Wow, Kelvin that was absolutely amazing!" I turned to see Dad standing there. "I saw your whole flight and that was incredible!" He had a look of pure pride and awe in his eyes. I almost started tearing up. I had never once done anything that Dad was proud of and here he was, impressed. He said several more times how incredible my flight was, and asked questions about hang gliding. I was 35-years-old and reveling in my father's admiration for the first time in my life. After 30 minutes or so, he and Sue got into their car and he went back to his life of hate at the compound.

I never saw or spoke to Dad again.

CHAPTER 30

GIVING TO GET BACK

We gave our babies Georgian names, Mariame and Marieka, in honor of their birth and heritage and it is through them, and learning how to give back, that I have started to find true healing.

Up to this point, my whole belief system had been about self-protection. I held on tightly to everything I had, especially my fear of failure, resentment and self-loathing. I gave no thought at all to others who were less fortunate than me.

Then, one day in 2004, I was walking to my daughters' elementary school to meet them and walk them home, as I always did when I had time. On my way, a neighbor who had also adopted his child from Eastern Europe, stopped his car and leaned out the driver's window. He gave me an article from the New York Times that he had saved for me, about the situation in Georgia and the orphans there.

I didn't get around to reading it until later that evening. There was a large picture of children huddled around a wood stove at an orphanage in Georgia. Conditions had improved since we adopted our girls, but not by much. As we talked about it over dinner, I asked aloud if there was a way we could give back to these kids as a way of acknowledging the great gift we had been given from Georgia, our girls. I also wanted Mariame and Marieka to have some sort of connection to their birth country, in case they were ever interested in going back one day.

The response from Susan and the girls was overwhelmingly positive so I set myself to the task of figuring out how to help these kids.

Of course, it started with self-doubt, a feeling that I could never make a significant difference in their lives so why even try. After months of aimless apathy, I decided that the only way to proceed was one step at a time. If I could help only one kid, it was better than doing nothing.

I called a friend who was an attorney and he helped me to set up a corporation. He asked me what I wanted to call it, and the name Divine Child Foundation somehow popped up in my mind. I liked it, so stuck with it. I established the foundation, applied for and received tax-exempt status from IRS, formed a board of directors and we began raising funds.

The first step was to fly to Georgia, visit several orphanages and pick one to start helping where we thought we could make the most difference. In January 2007, Susan and I traveled to Georgia, teamed up with a translator and driver, and spent the next two weeks visiting every orphanage we could find. It was exhausting, yet at the same time, extremely rewarding. At the end of the trip, Susan, I and our two helpers held a vote to select the orphanage. It was unanimous. We chose an orphanage in Saguramo, Georgia. It was home to about 45 children, from six to 17 years of age.

The orphanage was an old, three-story, Soviet-era school house in extremely poor condition. There were 92 windows, approximately 90% of which were either missing or broken, allowing the wind to whistle through. There was no heating because all the system components had been stripped after the collapse of the Soviet Union. In the middle of the day, it was actually colder inside than out, because at least then there was some sunshine to help warm you a little on the 20 to 30-degree days that are common there in January. The electrical system was barely functional, with exposed wires hanging down in several places. There were no flush toilets or running water and the smell inside could never be forgotten.

The kids had absolutely nothing except the clothes they were wearing, which were old, torn and dirty The roof leaked in several places and the foundation walls were crumbling and in some areas there were just large holes where the masonry had collapsed and fallen to the ground. Outside, it looked like a junkyard, with trash and waste strewn everywhere, with a few abandoned and rusting old car and truck bodies here and there. The incredible people we met, the experiences we had, and the things that we saw made it an experience we will never forget.

We spent the next few months planning for a trip back to Georgia later in the year to make a start on the process. One of our former clients, Gilbert "Gil" Jullien, decided he wanted to help. He made a significant donation and offered to travel to Georgia with me to start rebuilding the home. We arrived in November with tools and donations of clothes, toys, medical and school supplies, and anything else we could think of. United Airlines was very kind and looked the other way when we arrived at check-in with a dozen huge and very heavy containers.

The trip over was about 25 hours long and Gil and I spent nearly every minute of that getting to know each other. Soon the main topic of conversation became my dismally low self-esteem and that was something Gil decided to make his mission to help me with. I owe him a huge debt of gratitude that I know I will never be able to repay. His constant support and unconditional love over the years has been just as crucial to my healing as my individual counseling and reading and self-examination has been. Whenever I faced a crisis in my life, Gil was there to support and guide me through it and reaffirm that I was going to be OK. The difference he has made in my life and the healing he has given me cannot be understated.

We spent two weeks at Saguramo assessing all of the current building conditions in great detail, mapping and drawing the entire building, meeting with government officials, getting to know the orphanage staff and physically rebuilding the entire electrical system (Gil did most of the electrical work by himself). And we spent a huge amount of time with the children. We returned several times a year and completely rebuilt the home. We replaced the electrical system, repaired the roof and the entire exterior, and added new windows and doors. We put in a new heating system and bathrooms with running water, adding flush toilets over time. We bought them new beds and blankets and pillows, new clothes and toys, school supplies, books and backpacks.

The director at the orphanage, Lali, was absolutely key to much of this success. She maintained a steady, loving influence for the kids throughout all the upheaval and used her extensive network of colleagues and friends to provide donations of goods and labor, in addition to what Gil and I were doing. My family, friends and the Rotary

Club of Vienna, Va., have constantly supported us with donations, year in and year out, so we could keep our work going. Over time, the home was transformed from a broken down shelter into a warm and comfortable house. The harder part was repairing the children.

The orphanage also presented an unexpected, personal challenge for me. I came face to face with sad and resentful children and that brought a lot of stuff flooding back. I would look at a child and smile but they would either look away or frown at me and I thought I was being rejected. Eventually, I realized that it wasn't always about me, and that I shouldn't take it personally, as I had before, if a child didn't smile back. It dawned on me that what these kids really needed was unconditional love, and lots of it. I made it my mission to break through to them, to let them know that I was going to love them, no matter what. I made extra efforts to engage with each and every one of them, looking them in the eyes and giving them a smile that relayed nothing but love.

And you know what? It worked. Some kids were tougher than others to crack but slowly they saw that someone in the world cared for them. We started to see wonderful things happen. That ragtag bunch of kids morphed into a family and they learned to extend love to themselves and to others. Gil and I have known dozens of them now, from the time they were five or six or 10, and have watched them grow into young adults. We still keep in touch with them on Facebook and in person when we travel back to Georgia to check on them and help with whatever they need. I feel blessed to have the opportunity to work with dozens of orphans in Georgia.

Gil, Lali and I are now responsible for five houses over there and we get to experience how good it feels to look each one of the kids in the eyes and let them know, without a doubt, that they are worthy and that we love them, no matter what they look like or where they came from.

There is nothing in the world that feels better than that.

DAD'S LEGACY MAY LEAVE SOMETHING TO BE DESIRED

Dad said his most important legacy would be "the memory the living will have" of the way he conducted his life. While he was "vilified" in his lifetime, he believed that future generations would remember him in a different light and "one day have a positive view of him." But most of all, he wanted to be known for contributing to one thing: the "salvation of the white race." (1).

Whether he achieved that or not depends, I guess, on how you define "salvation." Thanks to "The Turner Diaries," he remains an icon of the radical right and the rag-tag army of white extremists that he inspired then has now metastasized into a menacing presence in the U.S. and Europe, bombing, shooting and maiming those they deem to be different because of the color of their skin, their religion, or gender. Today, they go by various names — neo-Nazis, white nationalists, white supremacists, white separatists, the white power movement, and Identarians, among them. But whatever they're calling themselves, they are a danger to us all.

Despite all his professed knowledge of human behavior, Dad certainly didn't do well when picking the future leaders of his movement.

He had pledged to grow the National Alliance into a "rock-like edifice." He would shut out the gays, bar the "paranoids, kooks, cultists" and other "deviants" from joining and deter those he scornfully called the "hobbyists," who join a half-dozen groups but commit to none. Instead, he promised to only recruit the "right people — intelligent, level-headed, capable, willing to work, idealistic, patient, long-sighted people who did not expect results overnight." But things didn't work out that way. His chosen leaders failed, some quite spectacularly. Dad had always preached that a political movement should have more than one leader because a group built around one man alone would simply fade away when that man died, but he abandoned his long-held belief on his deathbed. Thinking that members were scheming against him, he named as his successor Erich Gliebe.

Gliebe had controlled Alliance units in Ohio, Indiana and parts of Michigan before becoming the brains behind Resistance Records, the white hate music label that became a huge profit maker for the Alliance. Gliebe had business smarts and was big on bombast but lacked leadership skills and political savvy.

In April 2002, shortly before he died, Dad told his last leadership meeting that he had no interest in the Alliance becoming part of the greater white power movement. Gliebe went even further, saying the Alliance now had the chance to "wipe out this make-believe world." The Southern Poverty Law Center obtained a tape of their remarks that day and promptly published them. It was the beginning of the end for the Alliance. By the time Gliebe quit a dozen-plus years later, the Alliance's coffers were greatly depleted and membership decimated.

Word of what was said that day infuriated Skinheads and white power devotees who proceeded to boycott Resistance Records. Sales dropped from a high of $50,000 in March 2002 to less than $7,000 by July that year. Dues revenue started to slide, too. Then Gliebe further alienated Alliance members by refusing to help pay for the defense of a regional coordinator in Georgia, an ex-felon who had been convicted of being in possession of a gun. Disillusioned supporters ended up organizing their own fund-raising campaign, pulling together $75,000 for the man's defense. By the fall of 2003, the Alliance had only 800 or so dues-paying members left, down from around 1,500. Members of state units, the backbone of the Alliance, quit, some to join other groups, others to form new organizations. (2).

Shortly before he died, Dad had appointed a guy called Shaun Walker as Alliance membership coordinator. He was a former Marine sniper with a degree in molecular biology from the University of California and joined the Alliance in 1998 as part of its Internet Response Unit, helping to spread its message of hate through websites and chat rooms. When Dad died and Gliebe became chairman, he promoted Walker to chief operating officer and together they alienated more supporters. Long-time staffers and directors quit and soon members were demanding action.

One former member complained about wasteful spending and demanded an audit of Walker and Gliebe's failed Alliance business ventures. He cited as an example one of Gliebe's more memorable merchandise purchases — $50,000-plus on boots made in China with swastikas imprinted on their soles. Gliebe called them "a great investment." (3). He also commissioned a calendar that was supposed to highlight Aryan female beauty but actually featured strippers from a club he patronized. Alliance members were further scandalized upon learning that he had married a former stripper.

Another of my father's favorites was Kevin Strom, the sound-engineer who recorded Dad's white separatist broadcasts. Strom supervised the building of the compound's sound and video studios and the installation of its phone and alarm system, which was buried underground to keep it safe from government attack. Dad trusted Strom and Strom liked Dad — his own father had hanged himself when Strom was in his 20s. Dad had put Strom in charge of producing the National Vanguard magazine but Gliebe was not among his fans. In 2004, when Strom missed a deadline, Gliebe ordered that his pay be docked by $1,000. The next year, Strom launched a petition drive to demand Gliebe's resignation. Strom was fired, but he was one step ahead of Gliebe — two days prior to his departure, he had legally transferred ownership of the National Vanguard website to a publishing firm owned by his then-second wife, Elisha. (4)

Tired of all the in-fighting, Gliebe quit shortly afterward. Walker, another Dad favorite, took over as chairman but lasted only a year. He had at one time run the Alliance's Salt Lake City unit and his actions there led to his downfall. He was forced to resign from the Alliance after his conviction in 2006 on federal civil rights charges that he organized and took part in attacks on Mexicans and Native Americans in Salt Lake City bars in 2002 and 2003. He was sentenced to 87 months in prison, but was released in 2009 when his sentence was reduced on appeal.

With Walker gone, Gliebe returned and ran the Alliance again for the next eight years. Meanwhile, Strom was firmly in control of the National Vanguard website and persuaded many Alliance members to defect and sign up with his new organization, which he called, unsurprisingly, National Vanguard. Several Alliance state units joined him and he was supported, too, by former Ku Klux Klan leader David Duke and Don Black, operator of the neo-Nazi Stormfront website.

Things started to unravel for Strom when he was arrested in 2007. Police had found images of child porn on his computer, with hundreds of photos of naked girls in "sexually suggestive positions." He was charged with possessing child pornography. Two other charges of enticing a minor to perform sex acts and intimidating a witness were dismissed at trial. The federal judge said Strom had followed and anonymously sent gifts to a 10-year-old girl. While Strom did not try to have sex with her, the judge said that there was "overwhelming evidence he was sexually drawn to this child." Strom's wife had also made numerous legal complaints made against her husband, but the judge decided that they did not amount to intimidation. (5)

Strom pleaded guilty to one count of possessing child porn in return for prosecutors dropping several other possession counts. At his sentencing, he begged the judge not to send him back to prison. He claimed he did not deliberately download the porn, but had been "spammed" by a website he visited. He admitted he "enjoyed erotic — but not pornographic photography depicting beautiful young women" — but only as an art form, he told the court hearing in Charlottesville, Va. The judge didn't buy it. In 2008, Strom was sentenced to 23 months but got credit for a year already spent in prison. He was released four months later, but had to register as a sex offender.

By 2009, with the SPLC writing about allegations of wasted money and in-fighting, Alliance membership had slumped to around 100 dues-payers.

Gliebe's management style was so disastrous that a group of early members of the Alliance sued him, seeking $2 million in damages for alleged financial malfeasance and other irregularities. They called themselves the National Alliance Reform and Restoration Group (NAARG). Among them was my Uncle Sandy, Dad's younger brother. I saw him again a little while ago. Now in his early 80's, he is vague about the whole situation.

I do know that Uncle Sandy helped NAARG raise money, appealing for donations to help pay their huge legal bills. One of his main concerns, he told me, was what would happen to Dad's most prized possession, his library. NAARG had obtained a restraining order barring Gliebe from selling Alliance property before the lawsuit was settled. When they learned that Gliebe had sold some of the books, they asked the court to act. But they were too late. Gliebe had made the sale in March, in return for a "donation," a few days before the restraining order was issued in April. "Sanders Pierce is late for the dance," Gliebe gloated. "He needs to understand that March comes before April. If they're banking on that, they might as well be waiting for the Easter Bunny." (6)

Then, out of the blue, Gliebe resigned in the middle of a court hearing, just as the judge ordered him to produce financial and membership records for NAARG's inspection. Gliebe suddenly announced that he was no longer chairman of the Alliance, having quit in favor of William White Williams, a long-time racist who had led the Alliance's North Carolina unit. It was a shock to everyone, but NAARG pledged to continue the fight.

Williams, another Dad favorite, had waited 12 years for his chance to seize the Alliance. Just as Gliebe was looking for a way out of the NAARG lawsuit, Williams offered to take the group off his hands. By then, there were only two members left on the board. Williams and Gliebe hatched a plan: Two weeks before the court hearing, Williams would be elected to the board, so that he could then vote for himself as chairman when Gliebe resigned. On Oct. 23, 2014, the board met in Williams' motel room, Gliebe resigned, and Williams was elected in his place. The next day, Gliebe took the courtroom by surprise, dramatically declaring he had quit.

Williams bragged that he'd been pretty "slick." Through a bloodless coup, he'd won what was left of the Alliance — the compound, its publishing business, inventory, websites and bank accounts. There is a YouTube video showing him going room to room in the compound, pointing to the stuff he wanted, including Dad's library. He had already privately purchased 12,000 volumes from Gliebe and had to use two semi-trailers to haul the entire 27,000 volumes to his property in rural Mountain City, Tenn., where he was opening a new Alliance HQ.

Gliebe put the West Virginia compound up for sale but Williams paid the back taxes on it and says it is now his. Gliebe kept Resistance Records for a year, then quietly sold it (8). Williams had been patient in pursuit of his quarry. He had made his first try in 2007, laying the groundwork for a legal challenge with a group of ex-Alliance members who called themselves "The Beginning." They went looking for a lawyer but no attorney would touch the case for less than $20,000 upfront, twice the amount they had raised. Williams realized he couldn't take on Gliebe at that time but managed to keep the whole thing secret, he boasted later to a British nationalist magazine.

Over the years Williams has been associated with several supremacist groups, including the Klan, the White Patriot Party and Ben Klassen's Church of the Creator. An ex-Vietnam Special Forces veteran, he helped write and draw the Alliance's comic, "The Saga of White Will," centered on a white teenager's time in an integrated school who targeted blacks and Jews. He was working for Klassen when he met Dad and moved to West Virginia to become an Alliance membership coordinator in 1992. At one point, he claims, he helped sneak Dad into Britain, in defiance of a government exclusion order, to attend meetings of the British National Party. He left the Alliance when Gliebe took over, buying an Internet domain in 2004 to slam Gliebe's "mismanagement" of the Alliance.

"Too many good people had invested too much of themselves into the Alliance to allow it to be destroyed," Williams asserted. He despised Gliebe but would not join NAARG, calling them a "Big Tent" group, open to "any and all 'pro-White' comers of any ideology." Dad would never have approved of NAARG and their "watered-down message," he said.

Williams and Strom went on to join forces and relaunched National Vanguard and the American Dissident Voices Internet radio show, leaning heavily for content on Dad's broadcasts and writings. Williams has claimed that Strom is "the ideological backbone" of the Alliance and that the porn case against him is "bunk." A skilled propagandist for the Alliance, Strom turned his talents to creating a new story about his conviction when he got out of prison. These days, he asserts on neo-Nazi websites that he was the victim of a government set-up involving his exwife. He alleges she was violent and abusive to him, physically attacking him and causing him to flee for his life.

According to the Southern Poverty Law Center, Strom even created a fake mainstream newspaper online, The Charlottesville Times. It was made to look like a small town paper with weather reports and editorials and news articles aimed at defending himself. Other articles attacked his ex-wife. The previously unheard of newspaper emerged shortly after Strom was released from prison and shared the same IP address and proxy hosting service as Strom's other websites. Despite the "almost amateurish transparency," his ruse seems to have persuaded some neo-Nazis that the case against him was false. (9)

Williams has also had trouble with the law.

In December 2015, an Alliance clerk told police that Williams had tried to choke her, according to a criminal complaint filed at the time. Another Alliance employee pried Williams's hands from her neck, she said. That witness backed up her claim. He told police that Williams had argued with the woman when she walked into her office, lunged at her, made a motion with his left hand to smack her, and then started choking her with his right hand. He said he pulled Williams off to prevent injury to the clerk.. In August 2018, Williams was convicted of misdemeanor battery and barred by conditions of his bond from returning to the compound. Williams and the clerk now occasionally snipe at each other on Internet forums.

There was also a situation involving an accountant who called the police claiming Williams had threatened him at gunpoint. Later, the accountant handed over to the Southern Poverty Law Center a thumb drive containing copies of documents that exposed alleged embezzlement, money-laundering and tax fraud involving more than $2 million in taxable income at the Alliance. The accountant, also a radical-right activist, said he had been given access to Alliance records going back to 1985 and made copies of several thousand pages of sales receipts, donation records and ledgers. He said he warned Williams that he saw a pattern of possibly "prosecutable" actions going back 15 years, including off-shore bank wire transfers to a South African bank that he alleged suggested money laundering.

Williams blamed Gliebe for any past problems with the accounts, saying that any possible improprieties with Alliance finances occurred on Gliebe's watch, not his. He called the former accountant "an "extremely unstable employee who stole proprietary financial records when he was fired recently," and implied that the accountant had violated a non-disclosure agreement.

Overall, based on his hopes and desires, I'm not sure that Dad's legacy is worth that much to the nation, but someone, somewhere is sure trying to make a pretty penny off it, at least judging by the Amazon retail website. There are ads offering for sale a collection of his writings, "The Best of Attack! And National Vanguard Tabloid 1970-1982." The prices being asked for used copies range from a low of $2,468 to a whopping $5,001.

Dad would probably have been wryly amused by the amount being sought for a collection of his writings, given that he had had so very little money of his own. In his will, dated just four days before his death and filed with the county eight days later, Dad left all the compound's trucks, tractors and other vehicles to Fred Streed, a long-time Alliance member who was also his executor. He left 290 acres of the compound to the Alliance, meaning the organization then owned a total 357 acres. Other lots were owned by Alliance staffers and 60 acres by the Cosmotheist Church. There were at least eight different businesses but Dad distanced himself legally from them, to protect them from becoming asset seizures. He listed himself as secretary of the Alliance only, and director and treasurer of National Vanguard Books, and a manager of the limited liability companies. He left his stock in all the companies to the Alliance. (12)

CHAPTER 32

SINS OF MY FATHER

There's no shortage of warnings in the Bible about the sins of the fathers being visited upon their sons, even though they may be innocent of any transgression. I even have close relatives who fear that they somehow are tainted by my father's shameful legacy, so much so that they talk about changing their name to escape the stink and stigma of William Luther Pierce III.

I understand how they feel — I considered doing it myself for quite a while. But I've chosen another path. Instead of hiding, I'm going to do what little I can to make amends for my father's hatred that has helped set so many on the road to racism. Even if I make just the tiniest dent, I will have gone some way to putting things right.

Unbidden, a memory of my first boss popped into my head a while back. I was working as an aerospace engineer for the U.S Navy at the time, after graduating from college. His name was Jonah Ottensoser. He was an Orthodox Jew and I grew to love and respect him. I admired his gentle way, his compassion for others, how he doted on his family and how important his faith was to him. He accepted others without judgment and was unfailingly kind and nurturing. He was everything Dad said Jews never could, or would be, and he became more of a father to me than Dad ever was. To this day, and I try to treat people with the same patience, courtesy and kindness that Jonah showed to me.

Thanks to my father, I served my time on therapist couches. I spent eight years struggling to cope with my depression and low self-esteem after he died until one day I finally decided that I was sick and tired of feeling sick and tired. I found a psychiatrist close to my home and made an appointment.

My first visit was spent mainly talking about Dad and my childhood and the next session was pretty much the same. At the end of it, the psychiatrist declared that Dad was a sadist and I was suffering from depression, so nothing new there. He picked up his pen, wrote a prescription for an antidepressant, and told me to give it a try. At the pharmacy, they said the six tablets would cost $58.00. I was about to fish out my credit card when I suddenly had an overwhelming feeling that pharmaceuticals were not the answer. It just didn't feel right. I handed the pills back, apologizing profusely for changing my mind and taking up their time.

I wasn't sure what to do next until one day in late 2004 when a colleague approached me. He said he sensed a deep sadness within me that reminded him of where he had been several years ago. He said he started to find healing with a more Eastern approach to wellness that helped him reevaluate his entire belief system. I was skeptical, to say the least.

But what really hit home was when he said that my children were going to be profoundly affected by my sadness. "If you won't do this for yourself, then do it for them", he said. It had never occurred to me how my attitude to life would affect them and it really hurt when he said that. I decided then and there to give it a try and he kindly gave me the name of his counselor.

My first session with the counselor had an immediate impact on me. She forced me to look inside myself and examine my beliefs, especially about myself. She taught me not to heed that voice that played on a continuous loop inside my head about my lack of worth, and instead to be more loving and compassionate toward myself and others. I also joined a spiritually based ministerial program and read a lot of books by people like the German-born writer Eckhart Tolle, according to the New York Times, one of the most popular spiritual authors in the United States today. Slowly, I started to gain inner peace and insight into how others see the world, and why.

I know now that my hate was an addiction, as insidious as alcohol or drugs, that I would turn to whenever I wanted to feel better. It would work for a while to boost my self-esteem, like a shot of some feel-good substance, and it was surely better than looking at my inner mirror and seeing the true me reflected there. But always I ended up feeling bad. That nagging, negative voice still said I was no good. I was always wrong, I was ugly, I'd never be successful. I would recall something I had said or done and then shrink and curl up inside with embarrassment.

Sometimes I even prayed aloud, "God, please help me, please, please help me!"

Now I know that we are more a product of our environment than the product of our genes. I've learned a lot about myself and I'm grateful beyond words for the help I received. Somehow I managed to raise two beautiful, well-adjusted daughters who are doing well and I hope and pray that I have given them a more positive perspective on life than I inherited.

It has dawned on me that the human race is not at all well. Mental illness is rampant at every level of society, from the homeless on the street to the deluded leaders in their palaces. And, unfortunately, there'll always be enablers, the sycophants who swallow every word that spills from their lips.

Among those feeding and fueling Dad's ego was Kevin Strom, who seemed seemed to regard him as some kind of seer, imbued with powers to tell the future. My father happened to celebrate his last birthday, his 68th, on September 11, 2001, the day terrorists flew planes into the Pentagon and the World Trade Center. "So many things he warned us about came true on that day, or shortly thereafter," Strom wrote in a 2004 essay. He was even more impressed when Dad listed his occupation as a "teacher" on a corporate form. "He was a teacher of facts, of principles, of ideas. A teacher of deep spiritual truths. And he was a teacher by example. His scholarship, his insights, and his character will be lessons for our people for centuries to come," he warbled on in the same vein. (1)

Dear God, what a grand view they all had of themselves.

Sadly, the business of hate is now booming in our country, and much of the blame for that must be laid at the door of President Donald J. Trump. Had he not energized the radical right, the horrific events in Charlottesville, Va., might never have occurred. As the Southern Poverty

Law Center said, Trump should apologize to Heather Heyer's family and to all those who were injured for the hate unleashed that day.

Funnily, not even my father liked Trump. He would have been appalled that America has elected as its leader a man who cannot speak in coherent sentences without a teleprompter, and would rather bully by Tweet than govern by policy. In fact, Dad despised Trump, but for all the wrong reasons — he believed Trump, along with Gov. George W. Bush and Sen. John McCain (R-Ariz.) to be Gentile frontmen for the state of Israel. (2).

But in many ways, Trump has succeeded where Dad failed. He has taken hate and discrimination mainstream. He targets Latinos, saying he's saving the nation from drug-dealers and rapists, and brands Muslims as potential terrorists, all under the guise of protecting national security and has emboldened white supremacists and mass-shooters by his words and deeds.

We can't say we didn't have any warning, but we elected him anyway. The alt-right greeted him as a savior as soon as he announced he was running for President. Rocky Suhayda, chairman of one of the current iterations of the American Nazi Party, told his followers that Trump presented a big chance for white nationalism to go mainstream.

"Now, if Trump does win, okay, it's going to be a real opportunity for people like white nationalists, acting intelligently to build upon that, and to go and start — you know how you have the black political caucus and what not in Congress and everything — to start building on something like that," he declared on his radio program in July, 2016. The movement didn't have to be anti- things but rather "pro-white," he said. "It's kinda hard to go and call us bigots if we don't go around and act like a bigot. That's what the movement should contemplate." (3)

The Ku Klux Klan was equally thrilled by Trump's candidacy, using it as a conversation starter to sign up new recruits — Trump had already electrified its members, said one regional organizer. Then, in February 2016, former KKK leader David Duke called on everyone to vote for him, because "voting against Donald Trump at this point is really treason to your heritage."

Even if he doesn't realize it, Trump follows the white nationalist lead, as ably demonstrated by Andrew Anglin, the controversial founder and publisher of the neo-Nazi Daily Stormer website who published hundreds of articles supporting Trump, officially endorsed him in 2015, and then helped organize the Unite the Right rally in Charlottesville, Va., in 2017.

Anglin controls a so-called "Troll Army" that he uses to harass online those with whom he disagrees. Anglin was among the first to spread the news of what he called a "migrant caravan" moving through Central America to the U.S. border, saying "the hordes are on the move." (It was actually a protest march that had taken place annually since 2010, organized by activist group Pueblo Sin Fronteras). He urged his followers to call the White House every day and demand that the National Guard be deployed at the border. "That is within the power of the President and there is nothing any wetback judge can do to stop it," he said.

Anglin showed how easily Trump can be manipulated when he rallied his trolls to petition Trump to use the word "caravan" when referring to the migrants moving northward. Together with other supremacists, his trolls used the hashtag "#Stop the Caravan" to urge Trump to characterize the caravan as "invaders" and deploy the National Guard. Then Fox News took up the chant and Trump obliged everyone with a tweet saying that "more dangerous 'Caravans' are coming." A few hours later, Vice President Mike Pence used the word several times. When Trump then dispatched the National Guard to the Mexican border to protect the U.S. against what he was by then calling an "invasion," Anglin declared it a great victory for the alt-right "Trump has at least heard us," he bragged. (4)

These days, Anglin is said to be living outside the U.S. to evade a federal judge's order that he pay $4.1 million in libel damages to Muslim-American comedian Dean Obeidallah for falsely claiming Obeidallah was behind the terrorist attack on a 2017 Ariana Grande concert in Manchester, England. Other damage awards are piling up — another $14.72 million so far — but he is still reportedly operating his website on the Dark Web. It's unclear how much money any of his victims will ever see.

Recent mass-shooters have also referenced Trump in the manifestos they left behind. Robert Bowers shot to death 11 Jews at a Pittsburgh synagogue in October 2018, the deadliest anti-semitic attack in the U.S.

to date. Six days before the massacre, he used the term "invaders" in an online post after Trump complained about a migrant "invasion."

Brenton H. Tarrant, a 28-year-old Australian who murdered 50 Muslims at two New Zealand mosques in March 2019, decorated his weapon with Nazi symbols and expressed admiration of Trump "as a symbol of renewed white identity and common purpose."

Even after Tarrant's attack, Trump told reporters that he did not think white nationalists were a growing threat around the world. "I think it's a small group of people that have very, very serious problems," he said at the White House on March 15. "It's certainly a terrible thing."

Since Trump's election in 2016, the U.S. has seen a sharp increase in hate crimes. There was a 37% spike in anti-Jewish offenses and a 23% jump in all anti-religion crimes in 2017, according to FBI hate crime statistics released in 2018. And, according to a recent study by researchers at the University of North Texas, hate crimes jumped 226% in the Texas counties where Trump held public rallies in 2016, compared with those where he did not. (5)

In congressional testimony, FBI director Christopher Wray said in 2018 the U.S had more than 2,000 on-going investigations into potential or suspected terrorists. Of those, 1,000 involved suspected "lone wolf" militants in all 50 states thought to have been radicalized over the Internet, and "that's not even counting" those associated with al-Qaeda or ISIS terrorists.

By July 2019, Wray was telling a congressional panel that the FBI had arrested as many domestic terrorists as foreign terrorists that year, many of them white supremacists. On October 29 this year, he testified again, saying agents had arrested 107 domestic terrorism suspects, compared with 121 international terrorism arrests. "The number hasn't dramatically changed but it's been troublingly consistent," Wray said. "Certainly the most lethality in terms of terrorism attacks in recent years here in the homeland has been on the domestic terrorism side."

White supremacist suspects are now in touch with alt-right groups in Ukraine and elsewhere, in some cases attending military training camps there, Wray noted, and the FBI no longer sees much difference in the tactics used by Islamist extremists and white supremacists. Both groups behave in a similar fashion, linking to global networks of ideology, rather than a structured, operational command. The lack of structure made it harder to infiltrate the groups with undercover operatives, he said. (6)

Frankly, I'm not sure why the FBI and Congress should seem surprised at such a turn of events, since the neo-Nazis, even in Dad's day, had close links to nationalist groups abroad. My father frequently attended neo-Nazi gatherings in Germany and Britain, although he was banned in that country. FBI internal documents describe his efforts to recruit American soldiers at military camps in Europe, because of their easy access to weaponry, and his network of sympathizers included racists in South America, South Africa, Australia and Canada. Federal officials only now are acknowledging that more must be done to counter white supremacist violence, but they are way, way behind where they should be in fighting the rise of hate, and some of the blame for that must lay with a misguided decision by President Barack Obama's administration.

In 2009, the Department of Homeland Security (DHS) issued a report about the rise of white supremacy in the U.S. but it was suppressed by then-Homeland Security Secretary Janet Napolitano because she feared that it would give public credence to white nationalists' views.

In the unclassified study, DHS cautioned that "white supremacist lone wolves pose the most significant domestic terrorist threat because of their low profile and autonomy." Alt-right groups were using economic hardship, illegal immigration, gun control efforts and the election of Obama, America's first African-American president, as recruitment tools. "Rightwing extremists will attempt to recruit and radicalize returning veterans in order to exploit their skills and knowledge derived from military training and combat," said the report, noting that some Iraq and Afghanistan war veterans have already joined extremist groups. (7)

No matter the realities of life, veterans' groups and Republicans in Congress expressed outrage that anyone could even suggest that returning soldiers were anything but true patriots. Napolitano eventually conceded defeat and withdrew the report. The DHS unit that produced disbanded and, for the next 10 years, the U.S. chose to use its financial firepower to counter what it saw as threats from Islamist extremists.

The author of the DHS paper was Daryl Johnson, a former senior analyst who quit the agency after his work was discarded. If the U.S. had acted on his report's recommendations, local police by now would have been trained to watch for white extremist threats, more undercover operations would have been mounted to trap lone-wolf killers, and additional investments would have been made to fight the threat they pose, he said. Instead, under Trump, the DHS office tasked with paying out grants and coordinating with local police departments to prevent threats has shriveled — the budget went from more than $230 million under Obama to less than $3 million under Trump (8).

"Unfortunately, in the last two years, resources have been shifted away from these threats," George Selim, a former DHS and White House National Security Council official testified in September, 2019. "Understanding the threat of domestic terrorism requires us to look at white supremacy. Three of the five deadliest years for murders by domestic extremists in the period between 1970 and 2018 were in the last five years. Of the 50 murders committed by extremists last year, 78% were tied to white supremacy," Selim told a congressional committee. The majority of the 427 people killed by domestic extremists from 2009 to 2018 died at the hands of white supremacists, said Selim, now a senior official with the Anti-Defamation League (9).

Given the blood spilled in the wave of massacres that has swept the U.S. mainland, you might think that the Trump Administration would be doing more to guard against the spread of white supremacy. The DHS was formed to combat terrorism but Trump has used it to enforce his immigration policies and chase down Latin American immigrants "invading" our country. His failure to act has made him as responsible as those who pulled the trigger. There was a dim, if belated, ray of hope recently.

In September, 2019, Kevin K. McAleenan, then-acting DHS secretary, talked about a new strategy document for law enforcement agencies on emerging white nationalist threats and tried to counter criticism that his agency had spent a decade playing down the danger. "I would like to take this opportunity to be direct and unambiguous in addressing a major issue of our time," he said in a speech in El Paso, Tex., after a gunman massacred 22 shoppers at a Wal-Mart store. In his manifesto posted online, the shooter cited an "invasion" of immigrants.

"In our modern age, the continuation of racially based violent extremism, particularly violent white supremacy, is an abhorrent affront to the nation," McAllenan said.

However, the proposals outlined in the new DHS document, "Strategic Framework for Countering Terrorism and Targeted Violence," seem to be little more than the same tactics called for in the original 2009 report. The current plans say DHS offices will work with federal, state and local agencies and members of the community to identify potential extremists before they strike, and will support counter-messaging campaigns by technology companies to guide people away from violent messages online. As one counter-terrorist official recently said, "Terrorism moves at the speed of the Internet." (10).

Who knows if any of that will actually happen — a month after McAleenan's speech, he was pushed out of the agency he had led for only six months and a new acting head was announced.

In Britain some extremist groups are banned and strong hate-speech laws are enforced against those engaging in racist behavior, whether in public or online. One of the most publicized prosecutions involved a fanatical neo-Nazi couple who named their infant son Adolf. Photographs recovered from their house showed Adam Thomas, 22, cradling his newborn son while wearing a Ku Klux Klan white robe; another photo showed his partner, Claudia Patatas, 38, holding the baby while Thomas held up a Nazi flag.

They were members of National Action, the first right-wing group to be proscribed under British anti-terror laws. Thomas was sentenced to six and a half years in prison and Patatas was sent away for five years. Another four members of the group were jailed for similar terms.

But the U.S. cannot take such a tough stand — while international terrorists can be prosecuted under federal laws introduced after the 2001 World Trade Center bombing, there is no similar law as yet covering domestic terrorism or cases related to racially motivated extremism, and freedom of speech remains a cherished principle here. There is also the thorny issue of how to police the Internet, a ready source of radicalization and funding — British far-right activist Tommy Robinson, whose real name is Stephen Yaxley-Lennon, receives funding from U.S. think tanks and a tech billionaire, and political and moral support from non-British groups and individuals across the world. (11)

I have to admit that I was one of those Americans who paid very little attention to Trump before he was elected. He was just some self-aggrandizing, arrogant loudmouth with a reality TV show who got off on being a bully and firing people. I didn't think he had a chance in hell of winning because he clearly had no regard for doing what was right. Naively, I'd always believed that the President of the United States should be one of the best our country has to offer, an intelligent person and a great leader who cares about people and our planet. Trump is the polar opposite and his obvious mental illness makes him unfit to hold public office. He has managed to divide our nation and attack and erode our civil liberties for his personal and political gain, harvesting the latent racism that emerged when Barack Obama was elected to sow fear and hate to win votes.

Someone asked me recently what I would say if I could talk to some of the young white extremists looking to start race wars in our country, but that would take a whole new book.

What I can tell you is that being a hater doesn't make you strong, neither does believing in the "survival of the fittest" theory. Accepting others does not make you weak or a target. It takes real strength and courage to stand up for others. You can control your mind, instead of letting it dictate your thoughts and feelings. Hate is not natural and it is not who you really are.

My healing from hate has been a slow and painful process and is still under way. I still have to remind myself at times that I have a choice in which thoughts I listen to, that I can choose to be happy, not twisted up inside with anger and fear because I feel powerless in today's world. Looking to find the good in someone is better than that temporary charge you get from judging and condemning others because it makes you feel better about yourselves.

Give it a try. You may find that guy down the road with the brown skin or a turban on his head has similar fears about you, and the same anger at the way the world has treated him — there are plenty of people out there just like you on the inside. Apart from the color of his skin, his religion or his strange name, what do you actually know about him? Perhaps he enjoys the same stuff you do — maybe he's a fan of your NFL team, or likes the same music or those fast cars some guys have, or he's a real skateboard pro. Try to make a connection, say 'hi' to him.

And if you do find yourself judging others, ask yourself why you feel that way. Have the courage to look inward and find what's really behind your feelings. If you don't like what you see, do the work required to change. If I can do it, you can too. We all have faults, that comes with being human. But I believe we were all born with innate goodness and the capacity for love, regardless of how we look on the outside, the culture we were raised in, or where we live.

Over time, I have been able to shed the beliefs Dad instilled in me. I know now that different doesn't mean less…or bad…or scary. Now I just see another person, not someone who is white, black, yellow, or foreign in some way. And I remind myself that everyone is doing the best that they can. We all face our own battles, each and every day, and some are harder than others.

You were not born a racist, somewhere, somehow, you were taught to be one. Hate is passed from generation to generation but it doesn't have to be that way. In his last 20 years, I saw Dad only a few times, and then for short periods only. He believed 100% that his mission in life was to save his race. He was a sick man whose fevered fantasies caused pain and suffering to people he would never know but who would be forever affected by his hatred.

But I have to forgive him so that I can finally live my own life, out of his shadow.

INDEX

Chapter 2 Pierce on the Peak

(1), (2), and (3) correspondence between Kelvin Pierce and Erich Gliebe, August, 2002

(4) "New World Order Comix - The Saga of White Will," retrieved from Metapedia, an online data base that focuses on far right, white nationalist and anti-Semitic topics. www.//en.metapedia.org/New_World_Order_Comix-The_Saga_of_White-Will, retrieved 2019.

(5) "Gospels of Hate that slip through the Net" by John Sutherland, The Guardian, April 3, 2000.

(6) CNN: Jewish Group Complains over Sale of Hate Books Online, August 10, 1999; CNN.com; New York Post, https://nypost/1999/08/12/bn-amazon-wont-halt-hitler-book-sales)

(7) "Explosion of Hate: The Growing Danger of the National Alliance," published by the Anti-Defamation League in 2000, archived copy available at www.adl.org, retrieved 2019.

(8) "Neo-Nazi Website The Daily Stormer Generates More Traffic that Many News Outlets Serving Large Cities," The Righting by Howard Polskin, March 21, 2019, www.therighting.com.

(9), (10), (11), (12) ibid ADL "Explosion of Hate"

(13) Arrest of German Neo-Nazi Reveals Growing Internationalization of 'White Power' Music Scene, Southern Poverty Law Center, Intelligence Report, December 6, 2000. March 5, 2002; Southern Poverty Law Center hate-extremist files.

(14) Interview with Hendrik Mobus from his jail cell, april 2001, MourningTheAncient.com

Chapter 3 Before Dad was Dad

(1) The Radicalizing of an American by William L. Pierce, National Vanguard, Issue No. 61.

(2) June 10, 1965 letter from William L. Pierce to Robert Welch of the John Birch Society.

(3) Letter from Robert Welch's personal assistant, Mary F. White, to William L. Pierce, June 18, 1965.

Chapter 5 Moving closer to Mr. Rockwell

(1) Fame of a Dead Man's Deeds by Robert S. Griffin

(2), (3) Correspondence between W.L. Pierce and Procter & Gamble, Purex Corp., Tender Leaf Tea, General Foods Corp., and Stop and Shop Inc., October 1965. Reply from Avram J. Goldberg, Stop and Shop VP, October 29, 1965.

(4) Memo from Matthias Koehl, national secretary of the American Nazi Party April 29, 1965

(5) Memo from Matt Koehl to W.L.Pierce, January 22, 1966.

(6) Intelligence Report, Southern Poverty Law Center, August 29, 2001.

(7) American Nazi Party office memo from Maj. Matthias Koehl to W. L. Pierce, March 21, 1966.

(8) Koehl memo to W.L. Pierce, March 21 1966.

(9) Letter from Matt Koehl, Jan. 23, 1966.

(10) FBI files released under the Freedom of Information Act.

Chapter 6 So, who is this Mr. Rockwell, anyway?

(1) Playboy Interview of George Lincoln Rockwell by Alex Haley, April 1966

(2) American Nazi Party Monograph, FBI, 1965, declassified and released under Freedom of Information Act.

(3) Ibid

(4) Ibid

(5) "American Fuehrer: George Lincoln Rockwell and the American Nazi Party," by Frederick J. Simonelli, published 1999, University of Illinois Press

(6) Ibid

(7) Ibid

(8) American Nazi Party Monograph, FBI

(9) This Time the World by George Lincoln Rockwell, published 1961

(10) FBI Monograph

(11) Ibid

(12) "American Fuehrer: George Lincoln Rockwell and the American Nazi Party," by Frederick J. Simonelli, published 1999, University of Illinois Press

(13) FBI Monograph

(14) Ibid

(15) Ibid

(16) Ibid

(17) Swastikas on Wilson, by Charles S. Clarke, August 12, 2013 (https://arlingtonmagazine.com/author/charlie-clark/)

(18) Ibid

(19) FBI Monograph

Chapter 7 Rockwell and the "defectives"

The Fame of a Dead Man's Deeds, by Robert Griffitn. P.109

American Nazi Party Monograph, FBI, 1965, declassified and made available through the Freedom of Information Act

Playboy Interview of George Lincoln Rockwell by Alex Haley, April 1966

Ibid

American Nazi Party Monograph, FBI, 1965,

"Dr. Pierce Discusses Shabbos Guy Chris Christie", commentary from October 1983 issue of National Alliance Bulletin

American Nazi Party Monograph, FBI, 1965

(8) *National Vanguard*, a web site run by one of William L. Pierce's former staffers. (Sept. 13, 2015 edition)

8. American Nazi Monograph, FBI, 1965

Chapter 9 Dad's Nazi Friends

The Fame of a Dead Man's Deeds, Robert S. Griffin

JET magazine Jan. 21, 1965.

Chapter 10 Rockwell's Last Day

The shadow of an assassinated American Nazi commander hangs over Charlottesville, Washington Post by Michael E. Miller, August 21, 2017.

Playboy Interview of George Lincoln Rockwell by Alex Haley, April 1966

American Nazi Party Monograph, FBI, 1965

"Swastikas on Wilson, by Charles S. Clark Swastikas on Wilson, by Charles S. Clarke, August 12, 2013 (https://arlingtonmagazine.com/author/charlie-clark/).

The Fame of a Dead Man's Deeds, Robert S. Griffin

William H. Schmaltz, "For Race and Nation: George Lincoln Rockwell and the American Nazi Party."

"Swastikas on Wilson, by Charles S. Clark, August 12, 2013 (https://arlingtonmagazine.com/author/charlie-clark/)

John Patler v. A.E. Clayton Jr., Superintendent of the Virginia State Penitentiary, Docket Number 73-1169, 4th. Circuit.

Milner Library, Illinois State University.

"High Times" filing with the U.S. Securities and Exchange Commission

"The Shadow of an Assassinated American Nazi commander hangs over Charlottesville" by Michael E. Miller, August 21, 2017, Washington Post.

"American Fuehrer: George Lincoln Rockwell and the American Nazi Party," by Frederick J. Simonelli, published 1999, University of Illinois Press

Fame of a Dead Man's Deeds, Robert S. Griffin, P. 109

American Nazi Party Monograph, FBI, 1965

Playboy Interview of George Lincoln Rockwell by Alex Haley, April 1966

American Nazi Party Monograph, FBI, 1965

American Nazi Party Monograph, FBI, 1965

American Nazi Party Monograph, FBI, 1965

Chapter 11 Things fall apart, the center cannot hold

The Scranton Tribute, 4/10/70

Federal Bureau of Investigation, Freedom of Information/Privacy Acts Release, Subject: William Luther Pierce

Ads run in National Alliance Bulletin

Nazis Set Up Gun-Selling Operation, Washington Post, undated

The Radicalizing of an American" by Dr. William L. Pierce

Letter from Patti Pierce to Marguerite Pierce, undated

William H. Schmaltz, "For Race and Nation: George Lincoln Rockwell and the American Nazi Party."

National Socialist White People's Party press release, March 31, 1970

National Alliance Bulletin

The Fame of a Dead Man's Deeds by Robert S. Griffin

"American Fuehrer: George Lincoln Rockwell and the American Nazi Party" by Frederick J. Simonelli, published 1999, University of Illinois Press

June 1, 1970 Memo to Matt Koehl from William L. Pierce

August 5, 1970 letters to NSWPP members from William L. Pierce

Email from H. Michael Barrett to Kelvin Pierce, dated July 24, 2007. Barrett's account also appeared on Stormfront, a White Nationalist website.

Los Angeles Free Press, November 3, 1972.

"Legacy of the Commander," by Kate Cough, January 3, 2019, the Ellsworth American (https://www.ellsworthamerican.com/featured/legacy-of-the-commander/); "From the Malinkowski archives: Sarault linked financially to par with mob, Nazi ties", The Providence Journal Jan. 26, 1992, updated August 12, 2016; United States of America, Appellee, v. Brian J. Sarault, Defendant, Appellant 975 F.2d17 (First Circuit, 1992).

Chapter 12 A Farewell to Arms and a New Alliance

Letter to members from W. L. Pierce August 5, 1970

The Fame of a Dead Man's Deeds, by Robert S. Griffin, p. 117

Ibid , p. 119

Blood and Politics, Leonard Zeskind (p. 20)

Ibid (p.22)

The New York Times, 11/1/2015.

Chapter 14 Guerilla Warfare and Things that Go Bang in the Woods

FBI Freedom of Information Act Release, Subject: William Luther Pierce

Chapter 15 The Alliance Stumbles, Dad Takes to Drink, Kills Betsey

The Fame of a Dead Man's Deeds, Robert S. Griffin, P. 132

"From Attack! To National Vanguard," a collection of articles reproduced by the National Vanguard site, March 15, 2015.

The Hatchet, 2/7/72, George Washington University student newspaper

The Hatchet 4/7/72.

"What We Must Do Now," published in the fall of 1971.

Chapter 16 The seeker of truth

Free Speech magazine, July 2001, Volume VII, Number 7.

The Nazi on the Best Seller List by Ward Harkavy, Village Voice, 11/14/2001.

"On Sheep to Slaughter," (www.robertsgriffin.com)

The White Stuff: Professor Robert Griffin...Open-Minded Academic orAryan apologist?" May 8, 2002. (https://m.sevendaysvt.com).

Chapter 18 Lunch: And the recipe for Oklahoma bombing

The Fame of a Dead Man's Deeds, by Robert S. Griffin (p.143)

David Mills, Washington Post, May 16, 1993.

.J.M. Berger is an Associate Fellow with the International Center for Counter-Terrorism in the Hague and a fellow with George Washington University's Program on Extremism, and co- author of *ISIS: The State of Terror* with Jessica Stern and author of *Jihad Joe: Americans Who Go to War in the Name of Islam.*

"What It Will Take," National Vanguard Magazine #103, January-February 1985.

"Alt History" by J.M Berger, The Atlantic, Sept. 16, 2016 www.theatlantic.com/politics/archive/2016/09/how-the-turner-diaries-changed-white-nationalism).

"Don't Think Twice, It's All White," David Mills, May 16, 1993.

The Fame of A Dead Man's Deeds, by Robert S. Griffin, p. 249.

The Guardian 06/28/2006.

The Fame of a Dead Man's Deeds, Robert S. Griffin, p. 172.

The Fame of a Dead Man's Deeds p 161.

Hatewatch, an SPLC publication, June 16, 2016

Financial Times November 23, 2016.

Chapter 21 Dad Takes his Leave

Letter from William L. Pierce to his mother, February 2, 1983

The Fame of a Dead Man's Deeds, Robert S. Griffin, (pps 119, 229.

Chapter 22 Hew a Compound, Save a Gene Pool

Prospectus for the Cosmotheist Community by William L. Pierce, 1985; reprinted by the National Vanguard website Dec. 2, 2017.

Community News, written by William L. Pierce, Issue No. 1, January, 1988.

Memos from FBI Pittsburgh bureau, 1987, regarding investigation into Cosmotheist Community, retrieved through public records.

Chapter 23 The FBI's Surveillance Lot Is Not A Happy One

FBI records from Operation CosmoCom

Explosion of Hate, Anti-Defamation League.

Chapter 25 Dad and Women

The Fame of A Dead Man's Deeds, Robert S. Griffin, P352.

May 1976 National Alliance Bulletin

The Fame of A Dead Man's Deeds, Robert S. Griffin P. 230.

Chapter 31 Dad's Legacy Might Leave Something to be Desired

Fame of a Dead Man's Deeds by Robert S. Griffin, p. 408

Southern Poverty Law Center (SPC), "Neo-Nazi National Alliance Struggles to Survive Under New Chairman Erich Gliebe," September 20, 2002.

"Fall of the Fourth Reich" by Lisa Rab, Cleveland Scene 2/15/2006.

SPLC "National Vanguard's Strom Seeks More Power" 10/14/2005.

SPLC Intelligence Report, Oct. 14, 2005

SPLC Hatewatch 02/11/2015.

Will Williams: Taking the Hard Line, Heritage and Destiny magazine, reprinted by the National Vanguard

SPLC Hatewatch, "Triumph of the Will: Will Williams and the National Alliance," December 17, 2014.

"SPLC Hatewatch: Chaos at The Compound," SPLC May 21, 2015

Ibid

Beyond A Dead Man's Deeds: The National Alliance After William Pierce," by the Chicago-based Center for New Community, August 2002 www.newcomm.org.

Chapter 32 Sins of My Father

"I Remember 9/11" by Kevin Alfred Strom, reprinted September 11, 2016 by *National Vanguard*

A Call for 'Tolerance' by William L. Pierce, American Dissident Voices, Oct. 23, 1999.

"Top Nazi leader: Trump will be a 'real opportunity' for white nationalists," by Peter Holley, Aug. 7, 2016, Washington Post.

"Trump's 'Caravan' is a Made-up Monster Fabricated by the Far Right," by Ian Allen, The Nation, February 8, 2019

The Trump Effect: How 2016 Campaign Rallies Explain Spikes in Hate Submitted by Ayal Feinberg Assistant professor Texas A&M University Commerce ayal.k.feinberg@gmail.com; Regina Branton Professor University of North Texas branton@unt.edu Valerie Martinez-Ebers Professor University of North Texas valmartinez@unt.edu

"FBI Director: Some domestic terrorism suspects travel overseads for training" by Devin Barrett, The Washington Post, Oct. 30, 2019

Rightwing Extremism: Current Economic and Politcal Climate Fueling Resurgence in Radicalization and Recruitment, issued by the Department of Homeland Security, April 7, 2009

"Homeland Security Dept. Affirms Threat of White Supremacy After Years of Prodding," by Zolan Kanno-Youngs, New York Times, Oct. 1, 2019

Testimony on countering domestic terrorism by George Selim before the Senate Homeland Security and Government Affairs Committee, September 25, 2019.

"DHS: Domestic terrorism, particularly white-supremacist violence, as big a threat as ISIS, al-Qaeda," Ellen Nakashima, Washington Post, September 20, 2019.

"Revealed: the hidden global network behind Tommy Robinson" by Josh Halliday, The Guardian December 8, 2018.

Printed in Great Britain
by Amazon

24704779R00172